HTML in a Nutshell

The Bare Bones: Your Web Page Skeleton

```
<HTML>
<HEAD>
<TITLE>Put Your Gnarly Title Here</TITLE>
</HEAD>
<BODY>
Everything else goes here.
</BODY>
</HTML>
```

Lotsa List Tags

Bulleted list:
```
<UL>
<LI>First item
<LI>Second item
etc...
</UL>
```

Numbered list:
```
<OL>
<LI>First bullet
<LI>Second bullet
etc...
</OL>
```

Definition list:
```
<DL>
<DT>First term
<DD>First definition
<DT>Second term
<DD>Second definition
etc...
```

Tags for Paragraphs and Such

New paragraph	<P>
Horizontal rule	<HR>
Line break	
Headings	<H1> (biggest) through
	<H6> (smallest)

Sprucing Things Up with Formatting Tags

Bold	<B>This text will appear in bold</B>
Italics	<I>This text will appear in italics</I>
<u>Underlined</u>	<U>This text will appear—right!—underlined</U>
Monospaced	<TT>This text will look like it was produced by a typewriter</TT>
Preformatted	<PRE>This text will keep all of its spaces and tabs</PRE>

Might As Well Jump: Link Tags

External link	<A HREF="URL">Link text</A>
Anchor	<A NAME="Anchor name">Anchor text</A>
Internal link	<A HREF="#Anchor name">Link text</A>
E-mail	<A HREF="mailto:YourEmailAddress">Link text</A>
FTP (directory)	<A HREF="ftp://host/directory/">Link text</A>
FTP (file)	<A HREF="ftp://host/directory/filename">Link text</A>
Gopher	<A HREF="gopher://host/">Link text</A>
Usenet	<A HREF="news:newsgroup.name">Link text</A>
Telnet	<A HREF="telnet://host">Link text</A>

Picture These Image Tags

Basic image	<IMG SRC="*filename*">
Image aligned with top of text	<IMG SRC="*filename*" ALIGN=TOP>
Image aligned with middle of text	<IMG SRC="*filename*" ALIGN=MIDDLE>
Image aligned with bottom of text	<IMG SRC="*filename*" ALIGN=BOTTOM>
Image with alternative text	<IMG SRC="*filename*" ALT="*Alternative text*">

cut here

que

Cybercarpentry: Table Tags

A Basic Table:
```
<TABLE BORDER>
<CAPTION ALIGN=TOP¦BOTTOM>Caption text goes here.</CAPTION>
<TR>
<TD>First row, first column</TD>
<TD>First row, second column </TD>
<TD>First row, third column </TD>
</TR>
<TR>
<TD>Second row, first column</TD>
<TD>Second row, second column </TD>
<TD>Second row, third column </TD>
</TR>
etc...
</TABLE>
```

Headers:
```
<TR>
<TH>First Column Header</TH>
<TH>Second Column Header</TH>
<TH>And So On, Ad Nauseum</TH>
</TR>
```

Horizontal Alignment:
```
<TD ALIGN=LEFT¦CENTER¦RIGHT>
<TH ALIGN=LEFT¦CENTER¦RIGHT>
```

Vertical Alignment:
```
<TD VALIGN=TOP¦MIDDLE¦BOTTOM>
<TH VALIGN=TOP¦MIDDLE¦BOTTOM>
```

Spanning Columns:
```
<TD COLSPAN=NumberOfCols>
<TH COLSPAN=NumberOfCols>
```

Spanning Rows:
```
<TD ROWSPAN=NumberOfRows>
<TH ROWSPAN=NumberOfRows>
```

Extending HTML: Some Netscape Tags

Font size	`<FONT SIZE=size>Affected text goes here</FONT>`
Basefont size	`<BASEFONT SIZE=size>`
Text color	`<BODY TEXT="#nnnnnn">`
Numbered list style	`<OL TYPE=type>`
Bulleted list style	`<UL TYPE=type>`
Image dimensions	`<IMG SRC="filename" WIDTH=x HEIGHT=y>`
Background color	`<BODY BGCOLOR="#nnnnnn">`
Table border size	`<TABLE BORDER=size>`
Table width	`<TABLE WIDTH=width>`
Table cell width	`<TD WIDTH=width>`
Table cell spacing	`<TABLE CELLSPACING=spacing>`
Table cell padding	`<TABLE CELLPADDING=padding>`
Centering paragaphs	`<CENTER>` Headings, text, and graphics that you want centered go here. `</CENTER>`

The COMPLETE IDIOT'S GUIDE TO

Creating an HTML Web Page

by Paul McFedries

A Division of Macmillan Publishing
201 W.103rd Street, Indianapolis, IN 46290 USA

To Karen, with love and silliness.

©1996 Que® Corporation

International Standard Book Number: 0-7897-0722-5
Library of Congress Catalog Card Number: 95-72606

98 97 96   8 7 6 5 4 3 2

Interpretation of the printing code: the rightmost number of the first series of numbers is the year of the book's printing; the rightmost number of the second series of numbers is the number of the book's printing. For example, a printing code of 96-1 shows that the first printing of the book occurred in 1996.

Screen reproductions in this book were created by means of the program Collage Complete from Inner Media, Inc., Hollis, NH.

Printed in the United States of America

Publisher
Roland Elgey

Vice President and Publisher
Marie Butler-Knight

Editorial Services Director
Elizabeth Keaffaber

Publishing Manager
Barry Pruett

Managing Editor
Michael Cunningham

Development Editor
Lori Cates

Technical Editor
C. Herbert Feltner

Production Editor
Phil Kitchel

Copy Editors
Rebecca Mayfield
Katie Purdum

Cover Designers
Dan Armstrong
Barbara Kordesh

Designer
Kim Scott

Illustrations
Judd Winick

Technical Specialist
Nadeem Muhammed

Indexer
Tom Dinse

Production Team
*Jason Carr, Anne Dickerson, DiMonique Ford, Trey Frank, Damon Jordan,
Glenn Larson, Stephanie Layton, Kaylene Riemen, Julie Quinn, Kelly Warner*

Contents at a Glance

Contents

Part 2: Creating Your First HTML Web Page   41

4 Laying the Foundation: The Basic Structure of a Web Page   43

5 From Buck-Naked to Beautiful: Dressing Up Your Page   53

13 The Elements of Web Page Style   159

14 Some HTML Resources on the Web   175

Introduction

Quick! What do the following things have in common? Dennis Rodman's hair color, the name of Elizabeth Taylor's husband, and Oprah's dress size. Right—they're all things that are constantly changing. But as often as these things change, none of them approaches the endless flux that characterizes the Internet.

Ah yes, the Internet; that amorphous and motley collection of electrons, geeks, slashes, and "dot coms." Trying to keep up with the Net Joneses and their relentless out-with-the-old-and-in-with-the-new culture is a full-time job. (In fact, I know some people for whom it *is* a full-time job!) Here's an example: Only a scant year ago, you were the Coolest of the Cool if you had an Internet e-mail address on your business card. Nowadays, of course, a sizable chunk of the world's Toms, Dicks, and Harriets—nerds and non-nerds alike—have their e-mail monikers plastered all over their cards. Ho hum. No, to be tragically hip these days, your business card must sport the address of—wait for it—your World Wide Web home page!

Which brings me (at long last) to the subject of this book—creating an HTML Web page. You, I'm sure, couldn't care less about what's cool and what's not, or about what's "wired" and what's "tired." All you know is that you want to publish a Web page (or perhaps two or three) and you want to get it done without a lot of hubbub and hullaba-loo.

Believe me, you're not alone. People—and I mean average Joes and Josephines; not just programmers and techno-geeks—are overcoming their digital arachnophobia and are clamoring to spin their own little Web webs. Why? Well, there are probably as many reasons as there are would-be Web weavers. Some folks are tired of being passive Internet consumers (mouse potatoes?) and want to produce their own content rather than merely digesting it. Others have information (essays, stories, jokes, diatribes, shopping lists) that they want to share with the world at large, but they never had the opportunity before. Still, others have had a boss come to them and say "Get our company on the World Wide Web now, before it's too late!", and so they have to get up to speed before it's too late for *them*.

A Book For Smart HTML Idiots

When it comes to producing content for the World Wide Web, a "complete idiot" is someone who, despite having the normal complement of gray matter, wouldn't know HTML from H.G. Wells. This is, of course, perfectly normal and, despite what many so-called Internet gurus may tell you, it does not imply any sort of character defect on your part.

So I may as well get one thing straight right off the bat: the fact that you're reading *The Complete Idiot's Guide To Creating an HTML Web Page* (my, that is a mouthful, isn't it?) does *not* make you an idiot. On the contrary, it shows that

➤ You have discriminating taste and you will settle for nothing less than the best (and it shows you don't mind immodest authors).

➤ You have a gift for self-deprecation (which is just a high-falutin' way of saying that you don't take yourself—or any of this Internet malarkey—too seriously).

➤ You're determined to learn this HTML thing, but you don't want to be bothered with a lot of boring, technical details.

➤ You realize it doesn't make sense to learn absolutely everything about HTML. You just need to know enough to get your Web page up and running.

➤ You're smart enough not to spend your days reading five bazillion pages of arcane (and mostly useless) information. You do, after all, have a life to lead.

This is a book for those of you who aren't (and don't even want to be) Web wizards. This is a book for those of you who have a job or hobby that includes creating Web pages, and you just want to get it done as quickly and painlessly as possible. This is not one of those absurdly pedantic, sober-sided, wipe-that-smile-off-your-face-this-is-serious-business kinds of books. On the contrary, we'll even try to have—gasp!—a little irreverent fun as we go along.

You'll also be happy to know that this book doesn't assume you have any previous experience with Web page production (or even with the World Wide Web, for that matter). This means that you'll begin each topic at the beginning and build your knowledge from there. However, with *The Complete Idiot's Guide to Creating an HTML Web Page*, you get just the facts you need to know, not everything there is to know. All the information is presented in short, easy-to-digest chunks that you can easily skim through to find just the information you want.

How This Book Is Set Up

I'm assuming you have a life away from your computer screen, so *The Complete Idiot's Guide To Creating an HTML Web Page* is set up so you don't have to read it from cover to cover. If you want to know how to add a picture to your Web page, for example, just turn to the chapter that covers working with images. (Although, having said that, beginners will want to read at least Chapter 4 before moving on to more esoteric topics.) To make things easier to find, I've organized the book into four more or less sensible sections:

Part 1: But First, a Few Choice World Wide Web and HTML Tidbits

Instead of diving right into the hurly-burly of HTML, the book lets you dip a toe into the Web publishing waters by starting you off with a few introductory chapters. Chapter 1 is a kind of "Cliff Notes" version of Part 2 that takes you through the entire process of Web page production in 10 easy steps. Chapter 2 takes a bird's-eye view of the World Wide Web (beginners will want to start their reading here, instead of Chapter 1) and then Chapter 3 takes a general look at this HTML stuff.

Part 2: Creating Your First HTML Web Page

Here in Part 2 is where you'll actually start creating proper Web pages. Chapters 4 through 8 build your knowledge of basic HTML slowly and with lots of examples. Chapter 9 shows you how to successfully negotiate the big moment: getting your page on the Web itself for all to admire.

Part 3: A Grab Bag of Web Page Wonders

Part 3 takes you beyond the basics by presenting you with a miscellany of HTML topics, including some cool things that are available with Netscape's Web browser (Chapter 10), how to create tables (Chapter 11), some hints on proper Web page style (Chapter 12), and some Internet resources that will help you create great pages (Chapter 13). This section closes by pulling out the crystal ball to take a look at the future of the Web, just so you're prepared for what's to come (see Chapter 14).

Part 4: Painless Page Production: Easier Ways to Do the HTML Thing

After struggling with all that HTML in Parts 2 and 3, Part 4 shows you a few ways to make all this stuff a bit easier. Specifically, I'll show you how to wield several tools that take some of the drudgery out of putting together a Web page, including HTML editors, Word for Windows templates, and even some Web pages that help you create Web pages!

But Wait, There's More!

Happily, there's more to this book than 20 chapters of me yammering away. To round out your HTML education and make your page publishing adventures a bit easier, I've included a few other goodies:

Tearout Reference Card   This card (it's located at the front of the book, in case you missed it on the way in) spells out all the most essential HTML facts and figures. For a ridiculously handy reference, you can tear it out of the book and keep it by your side while you're building your pages.

Speak Like a Geek: The Complete Archive   You'll find this section near the back of the book. It's a glossary of Internet, World Wide Web, and HTML terms that should help you out if you come across a word or phrase that furrows your brow.

HTML Codes for Cool Characters   This section lists many of the HTML codes you can use to incorporate characters such as £, ©, and ~ in your Web page. (This is all explained in more detail in Chapter 5.)

HTML Disk   The book's major bonus is the disk that's glued onto the back cover. This little plastic frisbee contains tons of HTML-related knickknacks, including all the HTML examples I use in the book, some sample Web pages, an HTML editor, graphics and sounds you can put in your Web page, and lots more.

Also, as you're trudging through the book, look for the following features that point out important info:

By the Way...

These boxes contain notes, tips, warnings, and asides that provide you with interesting and useful (at least theoretically!) nuggets of HTML lore.

Technical Twaddle

This "Techno Talk" icon points out technical information you can use to impress your friends (and then forget five minutes later).

Let Us Know How You're Doing!

Hey, you paid good money for this book, so it's only reasonable that you should be able to get in touch with its author, right? Sure! So, as long as you have something nice to say (complaints will be cheerfully ignored), why not drop me a line and let me know how your Web page is coming along or, heck, just tell me what you thought of the book. If your page is ready to go, send me its Web address and I'll surf over and take a look. My e-mail address is paul@mcfedries.com.

If you'd like to drop by my own home page (be sure to sign the guest book), here's the address:

```
http://www.logophilia.com/Home/homepage.html
```

Also, don't forget to drop by the home page for *The Complete Idiot's Guide to Creating an HTML Web Page* at the following Web locale:

```
http://www.mcp.com/que/new_users/pmindex.html
```

See you in cyberspace!

Acknowledgments (The Giving Credit Where Credit Is Due Department)

The English essayist Joseph Addison once described an editor as someone who "rides in the whirlwind and directs the storm." I don't know if that's true for editors in some of the more sedate publishing nooks (novels and cookbooks and such), but I think it applies perfectly to the rigors of computer book editing. Why? Well, the computer industry (and the World Wide Web in particular) is so fast-paced that any kind of editorial (or authorial) dawdling could mean a book will be obsolete before it even hits the shelves.

The good folks at Que avoid premature book obsolescence by subjecting each manuscript to a barrage of simultaneous edits from a number of specialists (I call it "gang editing"). So a process that normally might take months is knocked down to a few short weeks. This means you get a book that contains timely and relevant information, and a book that has passed muster with some of the sharpest eyes and inner ears in the business. My name may be the only one that appears on the cover, but each of the following people had a big hand in creating what you now hold in your hands:

Martha O'Sullivan—Martha is an Acquisitions Editor at Que, and she's the one who asked me to write this book. (She is, in other words, the one to blame for the whole thing.)

Lori Cates—Lori was the Development Editor for the book. Her job was to make sure the overall structure of the book made sense and to be a sounding board for all my cockamamie ideas.

Herb Feltner—Herb was the book's Technical Editor and it was his job to check my facts and to make sure the procedures I tell you to follow won't lead you astray.

Phil Kitchel—Phil was the Production Editor and it was his job to get the manuscript ready for the production process where the figures are added in, the little icons and pictures are placed just so, and the whole thing is made to look like a true member of the *Complete Idiot's* family.

Rebecca Mayfield and Katie Purdum—A writer, as Oscar Wilde said, "can survive everything but a misprint." As Copy Editors, it was Rebecca and Katie's job to ensure that no misprints occur, and to clean up my slapdash punctuation and rearrange my slipshod sentence structure.

Besides the editorial team, I'd also like to thank the untold numbers of Web denizens and authors who were only too happy to proffer comments, ideas, advice, and laughs.

Part 1

But First, a Few Choice World Wide Web and HTML Tidbits

Any good meal is always preceded by an hors d'oeuvre *or two, perhaps an* apéritif *to wet your whistle, followed by the requisite appetizers. Once you ingest and imbibe these preliminaries, you can happily move on to the main course, safe in the knowledge that your palate is suitably primed.*

I'll take the same epicurean approach in this book (it is, after all, food for thought). Before bellying up to the HTML meat-and-potatoes of Part 2, you'll snack on a few tidbits to get your appetites suitably whetted. Chapter 1 gives you a preview of the rest of the book by taking you through the ten basic steps of Web page creation; Chapter 2 introduces you to the World Wide Web itself; and Chapter 3 clues you in on what this HTML stuff is all about. Bon appétit!

The Top Ten Steps to a Perfect Web Page

One of my goals in this book is to show all you Webophobes out there that putting together HTML pages that are both useful and stylish is a lot easier than you may think. As proof, this chapter covers all the basic information you need to produce an honest-to-goodness Web page, suitable for mass consumption by hordes of Internet surfers. (Not to worry, though: I explain everything in this chapter in more detail elsewhere in the book. I'll point out the relevant chapters as we go along.) So, without further ado, I hereby present my Ten Step Program to a Perfect Web Page:

Step 1: Crank Up a New Text File

If you've seen some World Wide Web pages in your Internet travels, you might think you need some high-end word processor or megabuck page layout software to achieve all those fancy-schmancy effects. No way, José. In fact, any program that enables you to peck out pure text is good enough for creating Web pages that rival anything produced by humungoid corporations or artists with unpronounceable names. That's right: Even the humblest text editor (such as the Notepad accessory that comes with Windows) is all you need to get started in the Web page publishing game.

So, the first order of business in creating a Web page is to fire up your favorite text editor or word processor (such as Word for Windows) and launch a new document. (In most cases, the program will start up a new document for you automatically.) Okay, you're ready for action!

Don't Forget to Save!

As with any computer-related endeavor, you should save your Web work regularly. Browsers always look for files that have names that end with either .HTM or .HTML, so be sure to use one of these extensions (for example, HOMEPAGE.HTM). If you're using a word processor, though, make sure you save the document as a simple text file. HTML pages that were saved in the word processor's native format will give any Web browser a bad case of indigestion.

Step 2: Understand HTML Tags

Web pages are relatively simple affairs. You just type in your text and then you insert markers—called tags—that spell out how you want things to look. For example, if you want a word on your page to appear in bold text, you surround that word with the appropriate tags for boldfacing text.

In general, tags use the following format:

```
<TAG>The text to be affected</TAG>
```

The TAG part is a code (usually one or two letters) that specifies the type of effect you want. For example, the tag for boldfacing text is <B>. So if you wanted the phrase ACME Coyote Supplies to appear in bold, you'd type the following into your document:

```
<B>ACME Coyote Supplies</B>
```

The first <B> says: "Yo! Start showing the text in bold." This continues until the </B> appears. The slash (/) defines this as an *end tag*, which says: "Okay, enough with the boldfacing already!" As you'll see, there are tags for lots of other effects, including italics, paragraphs, headings, page titles, lists, and lots more.

HTML (which stands for HyperText Markup Language) is just the sum total of all these tags. You'll find out more about HTML in Chapter 3, "A Brief HTML Web Page Primer," and I'll serve up some more tag trivia in Chapter 4, "Laying the Foundation: The Basic Structure of a Web Page."

Step 3: Set Up the Basic Structure of the Page

Your HTML files will always lead off with the <HTML> tag, which you type at the top of the file. This tag doesn't do a whole heckuva lot except tell any Web browser that tries to read the file that it's dealing with a file that contains HTML doodads. Similarly, the last line in your document will always be the </HTML> tag, which you can think of as the HTML equivalent for "The End."

So each of your Web pages will start off looking like this:

```
<HTML>
</HTML>
```

The next tags serve to divide the document into two sections: the head and the body. The head section is like an introduction to the page. To define the head, you add a <HEAD> tag and a </HEAD> tag immediately below the <HTML> tag you typed in earlier. So your Web page should now look like this:

```
<HTML>
<HEAD>
</HEAD>
</HTML>
```

The body section is where you enter the text and other fun stuff that will actually appear on the Web page. To define the body, you place a <BODY> tag and a </BODY> tag after the head section (below the </HEAD> tag), as follows:

```
<HTML>
<HEAD>
</HEAD>
<BODY>
</BODY>
</HTML>
```

Yawn. So far, so boring. Unfortunately, these early stages of Web page creation are only marginally more exciting than watching paint peel. It's a necessary evil, however, and it's one I'll discuss in more depth (I'll bet you can't wait for *that*) in Chapter 4, "Laying the Foundation: The Basic Structure of a Web Page."

Down with Drudgery!

To ease the tedium of these early stages of Web page creation, you'll find some help on the disk that comes with this book. I've included a file named SKELETON.HTM that contains all the tags that make up the bare bones (sorry about that) of a Web page.

Step 4: Add a Snappy Title

The page's title is just about what you probably think it is: the overall name of the page (not to be confused with the name of the file you're creating). If someone views the page in a graphical browser (such as Netscape or Mosaic), the title appears in the title bar of the browser's window (I'll show you an example in a sec).

To define a title, you surround the text with the <TITLE> and </TITLE> tags. For example, if you want the title of your page to be My Home Sweet Home Page, you'd enter it as follows:

```
<TITLE>My Home Sweet Home Page</TITLE>
```

Note that you always place the title inside the head section, so your basic HTML document now looks like so:

```
<HTML>
<HEAD>
<TITLE>My Home Sweet Home Page</TITLE>
</HEAD>
<BODY>
</BODY>
</HTML>
```

The following figure shows this document loaded into the Windows 95 version of the Netscape Navigator browser program. Notice how the title appears in the window's title bar.

Most Windows Web browsers display the page title in, of all places, the window's title bar.

The page title

The body text will appear here.

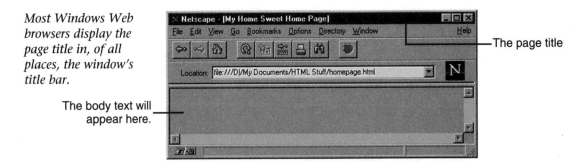

For a few more tidbits about working with Web page titles, head for Chapter 4, "Laying the Foundation: The Basic Structure of a Web Page."

Step 5: Add Text and Paragraphs

With your page title firmly in place, you can now think about the text you want to appear in the body of the page. For the most part, you can simply type the text between the <BODY> and </BODY> tags, like so:

```
<HTML>
<HEAD>
<TITLE>My Home Sweet Home Page</TITLE>
</HEAD>
<BODY>
```

This text appears in the body of the Web page:

```
</BODY>
</HTML>
```

When you want to start a new paragraph, you have to use the <P> tag. For example, consider the following text:

```
<HTML>
<HEAD>
<TITLE>My Home Sweet Home Page</TITLE>
</HEAD>
<BODY>
This text appears in the body of the Web page.
This is the second line (sort of).
<P>
This is the third line.
</BODY>
</HTML>
```

The following figure shows how this looks in the browser. As you can see, the first two lines appear beside each other, despite the fact that they're on separate lines in the original text. However, the third line sits nicely in its own paragraph thanks to the <P> tag that precedes it. I'll talk more about paragraphs and other ways to break up text in Chapter 4, "Laying the Foundation: The Basic Structure of a Web Page."

You need to use the <P> tag to create paragraph breaks in HTML.

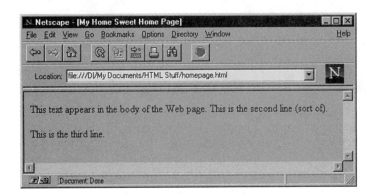

Step 6: Adding Formatting and Headings

Well, you're getting there. So far you've been able to use HTML to convince a Web browser to display a page title and break up plain text into paragraphs. That's a good start, but you won't exactly have Web surfers clamoring to read your page. What you need now is to jazz up the page with some text formatting and a few impressive headings.

HTML has a cartload of tags that will fancify your text. You saw earlier how a word or phrase surrounded by the <B> and </B> tags will appear bold in a browser. You can also display text in italics by bracketing it with the <I> and </I> tags, and you can make your words appear as though you produced them with a typewriter by surrounding them with the <TT> and </TT> tags.

Like chapters in a book, many Web pages divide their contents into several sections. To help separate these sections and so make life easier for the reader, you can use headings. Ideally, these headings act as mini-titles that convey some idea of what each section is all about. To make these titles stand out, HTML has a series of heading tags that display text in a larger, bold font. These are six heading tags in all, ranging from <H1> —which uses the largest font— down to <H6> —which uses the smallest font.

To illustrate these text formatting and heading tags, the next figure shows how Netscape displays the following text:

```
<HTML>
<HEAD>
<TITLE>A Text Formatting and Headings Extravaganza</TITLE>
</HEAD>
<BODY>
Here's some <B>bold text</B>. You can also do the
<I>italic text</I> thing. And, what the heck,
<TT>typewriter-like text</TT> is also available.
```

```
<H1>An H1 Heading</H1>
<H2>An H2 Heading</H2>
<H3>An H3 Heading</H3>
<H4>An H4 Heading</H4>
<H5>An H5 Heading</H5>
<H6>An H6 Heading</H6>

</BODY>
</HTML>
```

Examples of text formatting and heading tags.

To learn more about these tags and a few others to boot, pay a visit to Chapter 5, "From Buck-Naked to Beautiful: Dressing Up Your Page." If you're using the Netscape browser, you have access to a few more text tricks; Chapter 10, "Fooling Around with the Netscape Extensions," fills you in on the details. Finally, if you need to include lists of things in your page, there are HTML tags to handle your every need; Chapter 6, "A Fistful of List Grist for Your Web Page Mill," gives you the complete list lowdown.

Step 7: Toss In a Few Links to Other Pages

If you're a dedicated Web wanderer, then you know the coolest thing about Web pages are the links to other pages. A quick click on a particular link and you're off on a journey to a whole new world.

To give the people reading your Web pages the same kind of thrill, there are HTML tags that you can use to designate a block of text to be a link. Specifically, you use the <A> and </A> tags (the "A" stands for, strangely, "Anchor") to create a link. The <A> tag is a bit more complicated than your garden-variety tag, so let's take a close look at it. Here's the general format to use:

```
<A HREF="Address">Link text</A>
```

Check This Out...

The Duke of URL Addresses of Web pages and other Net locations that use this format are called uniform resource locators, or URLs, for short.

Here, the *Address* part is the Web address of the page to which you want to link. Web addresses are ugly-looking things, but there's just no avoiding them. For example, here's the Web address of my home page:

```
http://www.hookup.net/~paulmcf/logophilia.html
http://www.logophilia.com/Home/homepage.html
```

The Link text part is the word or phrase that your readers will click on to jump to whatever page you specified in the Address part. Here's an example that includes a link you could use to connect to my home page (how flattering!):

```
<HTML>
<HEAD>
<TITLE>Linking to Another Page</TITLE>
</HEAD>
<BODY>
This example includes a link to
<A HREF="http://www.logophilia.com/Home/homepage.html">
some geek author's home page</A>.
</BODY>
</HTML>
```

The next figure shows how the link looks to a Web surfer. To broaden your link education, leap to Chapter 7, "The Jump to Hyperspace: Adding Links."

The <A> tag lets you include in your Web page links to other Web goodies.

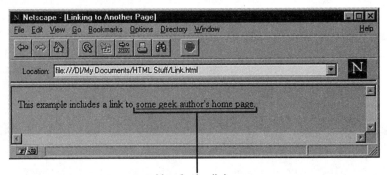

Here's the link.

Step 8: Add Impact with Images

You can really spruce up a dry Web page by adding pictures. Whether it's a corporate logo, one of the kids' drawings, or a picture of yourself, images are a great way to break up the monotony of plain text.

There are a number of issues involved in using images in your Web page (such as what type of format to use, how do you get images on your computer, and so on), but don't worry about them now. (For the nitty-gritty on images, see Chapter 8, "A Picture Is Worth a Thousand Clicks: Working with Images.") For now, I'll just show you how to use the <IMG> tag that tells a Web browser to display a specific image. Here's the general format:

```
<IMG SRC="image">
```

Here, *image* is the name of the graphics file you want to display. For example, if the file is named myface.gif, then you use the following tag to display it:

```
<IMG SRC="myface.gif">
```

Step 9: Use a Browser to See How Your Page Looks

Before you foist your completed page on your fellow Web denizens, you should use a Web browser to make sure everything looks okay. "Wait a minute! How can I use a Web browser to check out a page if the page isn't on the Web yet!" No problem. Lots of browsers have a feature that lets you load a page right from your computer's hard disk. In Netscape, for example, you pull down the **File** menu, select the **Open File** command, and then choose the file from the Open dialog box that appears. In Microsoft's Internet Explorer, you select the File menu's **Open** command, select the **Open File** button in the Open Internet Address dialog box that appears, and then pick out the file you need. I'll talk more about this, as well as give the appropriate instructions for some other browsers, in Chapter 9, "Publishing Your Page on the Web."

Step 10: Publish the Page on the Web

When you're satisfied that your page is suitable for human consumption, you're ready to publish it on the Web for all to see. To get your page online, you need to set up a location on a Web server (A server is a computer that makes documents available to other people on the Internet.) You usually have two choices (see Chapter 9 for details):

➤ Ask your current Internet service provider to set you up.

➤ Contract with a separate company that handles Web pages.

After you establish a Web account, you just send your page to the appropriate location (the provider will tell you where). You'll normally do this using an Internet service called FTP (File Transfer Protocol). I'll describe how this works in Chapter 9.

Chapter 2

It's a Wonderful World Wide Web

In This Chapter

➤ A mercifully brief overview of the Internet and the World Wide Web

➤ Why the Web is so darned popular

➤ A quick Web how-to session using Netscape

➤ A review of a few other popular Web browsers

➤ A semi-comprehensive overview designed to give you the big Web picture

Before you go off half-cocked and start publishing pages willy-nilly on the World Wide Web, it helps to have a bit of background on what the Web is all about. After all, you wouldn't try to set up shop in a new country without first understanding the local geography and customs and learning a few choice phrases such as "I am sorry I insulted your sister" and "You don't buy beer, you rent it!"

This chapter introduces you to the Internet as a whole and to the World Wide Web in particular, takes you through some Web browser basics, and more.

The Internet Nitty-Gritty

Before you can appreciate how the World Wide Web works, you need to step back and look at the big picture: the Internet itself. First off, I'll get the boring definition of the Internet out of the way: the Internet is (yawn) an international collection of networks.

Okay, so what's a network?

Good question. A network is a collection of two or more computers (usually dozens or hundreds) connected via special cables so they can share stuff like files and printers. Large organizations such as universities, research labs, and corporations typically own these networks. The Internet's job, in a nutshell, is to connect these networks together using high-speed phone lines, fiber optic cables, or, occasionally, satellite links.

Hmmm. So could you say that the Internet is a connected collection of collected connections?

Well, you could say that, but you'd just make everyone's head hurt. A network of networks is probably the simplest way to look at it. If an analogy would help, think of the Net as a giant city where the houses are computers. A neighborhood where the houses are connected with side streets is like an individual network connected via cables. In turn, each neighborhood is connected to other neighborhoods via larger roads and avenues or, for longer trips, by highways and expressways. (Insert your own cheesy information-superhighway metaphor here.)

The point is that in any city you can get from your house to any other house by traveling along a particular set of streets, roads, and highways. The Internet works the same way: you can "travel" to other computers on the Net by "following" the various communications lines that make up the Net's infrastructure. (The real good news is that you can do this even if, like me, you have a lousy sense of direction. You just tell your software where you want to go, and it picks out the best route automatically, behind the scenes.)

Sounds good, but what if I don't belong to one of these big-time schools, labs, or corporations that have their networks jacked in to the Internet?

Ah, that's where the service providers come in. These are businesses that set up an Internet connection and then sell access to any Dick or Jane who needs it. You pay a fee (it's often an hourly rate, but you can get monthly or yearly fees that give you a certain number of hours per month), dial in with your modem, and start surfing.

Redefining the Internet

This dull "network of networks" definition is okay for starters, but it really doesn't describe the Internet as it exists today, or capture the diversity, the utility, or the frustration of this most complex of human creations. It also tells us nothing about why the Net holds such fascination for computer pros and amateurs alike. Here, then, is a more realistic definition of the Internet:

The Internet is a means of communication. This is the big one for my purposes in this book. Many Internet types are only interested in perusing the wonders of the World Wide Web, and the Web is (as you'll see) the most attractive way to communicate your ideas to the world at large. I'll talk more about this later in this chapter (and, indeed, throughout the rest of this book).

The Internet is an information resource. To say the least. The Internet has literally millions of computers that are jammed to the hilt with documents, books, pictures, and other information resources. Whether you're researching a thesis or just have an unquenchable thirst for knowledge, the Internet has something for you. (Be forewarned: these resources are so vast and so poorly organized, the patience of a saint is a real asset when looking for things on the Net.)

The Internet is a warehouse. If you scour your own computer, you'll probably find a few hundred or even a few thousand files scattered here and there. Imagine all those files multiplied by the millions of Net computers; this gives you some idea of the massive numbers of documents, graphics, sounds, and programs stored around the Internet. Happily, there are a number of tools (some of which I describe later in this chapter) that you can use to locate and grab these files.

The Internet is a community. Behind everything you see on the Internet—the messages, the documents, the software—stands the person (or persons) who created it. Untold numbers of Net enthusiasts have spent countless hours assembling information, writing software, and answering questions. Amazingly, all this toiling in obscurity somehow managed to create a massive structure that works (most of the time) without the need for any semblance of central authority or governing body. Having said that, however, I don't want to be accused of viewing the Net through rose-colored glasses. Any endeavor that boasts millions of participants is bound to attract its fair share of bozos, buttheads, and bellyachers. Hey, that's life. Overall, though, the Net denizens you'll encounter will be surprisingly helpful and generous and only too willing to engage in random acts of senseless kindness.

An Overview of the Internet Services

Although this book concentrates primarily on the World Wide Web, I'll still need to talk about the other Internet services from time to time. Just to make sure we're always on the same page, let's review some of the available services you can use to interact with the various parts of the Internet:

E-mail   E-mail (or electronic mail) is, by far, the most widely-used Internet service. Every day, untold millions of messages are whisked around the world to digital mailboxes in just about every country on the planet. These days, you're just not "wired" (which, in the modern world, has become a synonym for "hip" or "cool") if your business card doesn't sport an e-mail address. As you'll see in Chapter 7, "Making the Jump to Hyperspace: Adding Links," it's possible to set up your Web pages to include a link that enables people to e-mail you directly from the page.

FTP   FTP (short for File Transfer Protocol) is the most common way to bring files from a particular Net locale onto your computer. You'll almost always use anonymous FTP to log in to the other computer (using the name anonymous and your e-mail address as your password).

Usenet   Usenet is a collection of topics available for discussion. These discussion groups (or newsgroups, as they're normally called) are open to all, and they cover everything from Amazon women to Zima.

Gopher   A Gopher is a system that displays Internet documents and services as menu options. You just select a menu choice, and the Gopher either displays a document or another menu, or transfers you to a different Gopher.

Mailing Lists   This is a system that sends out regular e-mail messages related to a specific topic. For example, if home beer making is your thing, then you'd definitely want to subscribe to the Homebrew mailing list to get things like recipes, how-to articles, beer festival announcements, and more. You usually subscribe by sending an e-mail message to the list's subscription address. You can also post messages to the other members of the mailing list.

Telnet   This is a program that enables you to log in to another computer on the Internet and use its resources as though they existed on your machine. For example, you can often telnet to a library's computer to use the electronic version of its card catalog.

Where to Go for More Info

If you're interested in learning more about some of these Internet services, Que has lots of books that can help. In particular, I highly recommend either *The Complete Idiot's Guide to the Internet* or *The Complete Idiot's Guide to the Internet for Windows 95*, both by Peter Kent.

The Net's Wunderkind: The World Wide Web

The services I mentioned above are important Internet underpinnings, but, with the exception of e-mail, they all take a backseat to the Net's current fave rave: the World Wide Web. (If "World Wide Web" is too much of a mouthful for you, the accepted short form is, simply, "the Web." In writing, you'll also see the Web referred to as W3 or WWW. The latter is still a bit of a tongue-twister, so you'll sometimes hear people pronounce WWW as "triple-dub.")

To demonstrate how popular the Web has become, let me give you a for-instance from the pages of *Wired* magazine, that unofficial arbiter of all that's too-hip-for-words among the digerati. *Wired* has a section called "Net Surf" that lists various interesting Internet sites. I checked an early issue of *Wired* from a couple of years ago, and "Net Surf" had 14 listings: four FTP sites, four Usenet newsgroups, one e-mail address, one mailing list, and four listings related to minor Internet services. However, the "Net Surf" section in the most recent issue of *Wired* had the same number of entries, but every one of them was a World Wide Web site! In other words, even Internet veterans are more or less ignoring the rest of the Net in favor of the Web.

Who (or What) Are the Digerati? The digerati (digital literati) are the beautiful people of the online world; the Internet intelligentsia, if you will.

The Secret of the Web's Success

What accounts for the Web's Elvis-like level of popularity? Well, I can put my fingers on a bunch of reasons, but I think three in particular are worthy of note: handsomeness, hypertext, and HTML (I call this the HHH of the WWW).

Handsomeness? Sure. When some Net brainiacs got together a few years ago to design the systems that would transport Web pages hither and thither, they were smart enough to anticipate the coming multimedia revolution. In particular, they didn't restrict Web pages to mere text. Instead, they made it possible for pages to contain pictures, fancy fonts, clickable buttons, and more. Depending on the browser software you use to access the Web, pages can be a real feast for the eyes and ears.

Hypertext? Sounds like text that's had one cup of coffee too many, but what's it really about? Well, let's look at an example. Throughout this book I'll be telling you about other chapters that are relevant to whatever I'm currently talking about. For example, I might say something like "For more info on the amazing Web watchamacallit, see Chapter 57." Wouldn't it be nice if you could just touch the reference to Chapter 57 and have the book open automatically to the correct page?

That's just what hypertext does. Hypertext is a special word or phrase in a Web page that acts as a link to other Net goodies (such as a different Web page). When you select the link (usually by clicking on it with your mouse), the linked resource automatically appears on your computer. Any word or phrase can be designated a hypertext link. Heck, there's no reason the link even has to be a word or phrase—a picture or button does just as well. There's also no reason why the link should point only to other Web documents. Why not use the link to start a Telnet session, FTP a file, or even access a Usenet newsgroup? As you'll see, the Web can do all this and more.

HTML? This, of course, is what this book is all about. HTML stands for HyperText Markup Language, and it's what you use to design Web pages. It sounds like scary stuff, but it's really just a relatively small set of symbols that determine the look and feel of a Web page. I'll discuss HTML in more detail in the next chapter.

Some Web Words to Surf By

Like all Net services, the Web has its own vernacular and acronyms. To help you out as you work through this chapter and the rest of the book, here's a rundown of some common Web jargon (see "Speak Like a Geek: The Complete Archive," at the back of this book, for a larger list of Internet and Web lingo):

browser   The software you use to display and interact with a Web page. When cobbling together your own pages, you need to bear in mind that there are two kinds of browsers: those that display only text and those that support graphics and other fun elements. I'll talk more about this distinction as you work through Part 2.

form   A Web document used for gathering information from the reader. Most forms have at least one text field where you can enter text data (such as your name or the keywords for a search). More sophisticated forms also include check boxes (for toggling an option on or off), radio buttons (for selecting one of several options), and push buttons (for performing an action such as submitting the form over e-mail).

home page   The first Web document that appears when you follow a link to a Web server (see **Web server**).

hosting provider   A company that, for a (usually) small fee, will publish your pages on the Web.

hyperlink   Another name for a hypertext link.

publish   To make a Web page available to the World Wide Web community at large.

18

surf   To leap giddily from one Web page to another by furiously clicking on any link in sight.

URL (Uniform Resource Locator)   A Web addressing scheme that spells out the exact location of a Net resource. I'll talk more about URLs in Chapter 7, "Making the Jump to Hyperspace: Adding Links."

Web server   A program that responds to requests from Web browsers to retrieve resources. This term is also used to describe the computer that runs the server program.

Browsing Basics, Featuring Netscape Navigator

When Netscape Navigator was first released to the Net community in the fall of 1994, it immediately caused a huge sensation. Here was a new Web browser that came in lots of different flavors (Windows, Macintosh, and Unix), was faster than anything else around (especially with the modem-based Internet connections that many of us use), came with built-in newsgroup access and basic e-mail capabilities, and was as slick as a nude Jell-O wrestler.

Word of this hot new browser spread around the Net like wildfire, and now Netscape is, by far, the number one Web browser. This section uses Netscape to introduce you to some basic Web browsing techniques.

Getting Your Hands on Netscape

To get a copy of Netscape, you need to use the Internet's FTP service. There are two ways you can go about this:

➤ If you have Windows and a SLIP or PPP connection to an Internet service provider, you can use the WS_FTP program that comes on this book's disk. When the program asks you for a profile name, select **Netscape Comm**.

➤ If you're using some other FTP program, go to `ftp.netscape.com` and then head for the `/netscape` directory.

After you're inside Netscape Communications' FTP site, you need to pick the location that corresponds to your computer: mac, unix, or windows. Each directory has a "README" text file that will tell you the file you need, how to decompress the file, and how to install the program.

The Best Things in Life Aren't Always Free

Keep in mind that, unless you're a student, educator, or member of a non-profit institution, Netscape isn't free. You can download and evaluate the product at no charge, but if you plan on using it regularly, you'll need to lay out some cash. (At the time of writing, Netscape cost $44.95.)

A Tour of the Netscape Screen

When you crank up Netscape (SLIP and PPP users should establish the connection to their service provider first), the program heads for the Netscape home page, as shown next (this page changes constantly).

The Netscape home page.

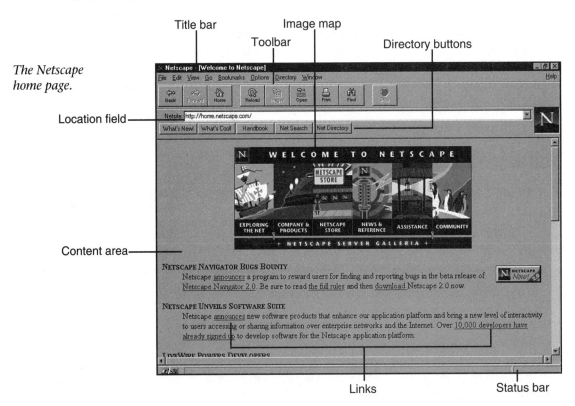

Here's a summary of the main features of this screen:

Title bar   The top line of the screen shows you the title of the current page.

Toolbar   These buttons give you point-and-click access to some of Netscape's main features. If you prefer to hide the toolbar (because, say, you like more screen real estate), pull down the **Options** menu and deactivate the **Show Toolbar** command.

Location field   This area shows you the URL of the current document. If the document is being delivered by a Netsite server (Netsite is the Web server software developed by Netscape), this field is labeled Netsite (as shown in the previous figure). For all other Web servers, the label says Location. If you're entering text into the field (as explained later), the label changes to Go to. You can hide this field (and give yourself more room) by pulling down the **Options** menu and deactivating the **Show Location** command.

Directory buttons   More point-and-click stuff. Here, these buttons give you easier access to the commands on Netscape's Directory menu. (I'll talk about them a little later.) If you want to hide these buttons, deactivate the **Show Directory Buttons** command on the **Options** menu.

Image map   Unlike most Web page graphics which are just for show, these are "clickable" images that take you to a different link, depending on which part of the image you click.

Content area   This area takes up the bulk of the Netscape screen, and it's where the body of the Web document appears. You can use the vertical and horizontal scroll bars to see more of the current document.

Links   Links to other documents (or to other places in the same document) appear underlined in a different color. You select a link by clicking on it.

Status bar   This bar lets you know Netscape's current status, and it tells you the progress of the current Netscape operation.

Okay, now that you're familiar with the lay of the Netscape land, you can start using it to navigate the Net. The next few sections take you through the various ways you can use Netscape to wend your way through the Web.

Navigator Navigating I: Following the Links

As I've said, Netscape displays hypertext links in an underlined font that's a different color from the rest of the text. To select one of these links, just click on it with your mouse. You end up on a different, yet related, Web page. This page will also have links that you can follow. Before you know it, you will have forgotten where you started!

Image maps work the same way: Position the mouse pointer over the portion of the map you want to see and then click.

Navigator Navigating II: Entering a URL

If you want to strike out for a particular Web site, you can specify a URL using either of the following methods:

➤ Click inside the location field, delete the current URL, type in the one you want, and then press **Return**.

➤ Either click on the **Open** button in the toolbar, pull down the **File** menu and select the **Open Location** command, or press **Ctrl+L**. In the Open Location dialog box that appears, type in your URL and then select **Open**.

Navigator Navigating III: Retracing Your Steps

Once you start leaping and jumping through the Web's cyberspace, you'll often want to head back to a previous site, or even to Netscape's home page. Here's a rundown of the various techniques you can use to move to and fro in Netscape:

➤ To go back to the previous document, either click on the **Back** button in the toolbar, select the **Go** menu's **Back** command, or press **Alt+left arrow**.

➤ After you go back to a previous document, you move ahead to the next document you went to by either clicking on the **Forward** button in the toolbar, selecting the Go menu's **Forward** command, or pressing **Alt+right arrow**.

➤ To return to the home page, either click on the **Home** button or select the **Go** menu's **Home** command.

➤ To return to a specific document you've visited, pull down the **Go** menu and select the document's title from the list at the bottom of the menu. (This is a list of the most recent pages you've seen.)

Navigator Navigating IV: Creating Bookmarks

As you navigate the Web, much of what you'll see will be ignorable dreck that's not worth a second surf. However, there are plenty of gems out there waiting to be uncovered—sites that you'll want to visit regularly. Instead of (shudder) memorizing the appropriate URLs or jotting them down on endless sticky notes, you can use Netscape's handy Bookmarks feature to keep track of your choice sites.

Using bookmarks is simplicity itself: when you discover a Web page that you think you'll want to resurf, pull down the **Bookmarks** menu and select the **Add Bookmark** command (or press **Ctrl+A**). That's it; no muss, no fuss. Now, when you want to return to a particular bookmarked page, pull down the **Bookmarks** menu and select the page's title from the list that appears at the bottom of the menu.

Browsers: The Best of the Rest

Netscape, of course, isn't the only browser game in town. With the World Wide Web the Big Deal that it is, you better believe that all kinds of software companies are jumping on the browser bandwagon. So, for the sake of giving equal time (sort of) to these pretenders to the throne, this section looks at the few browsers that you can consider as Netscape's peers.

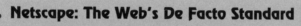

Netscape: The Web's De Facto Standard

Yes, there are lots of other browsers out there, but you'd never know it. I'd say anywhere from a third to a half of all the Web sites I visit say something like `Optimized for Netscape` on their home pages. What does this mean? Well, as you'll learn in Chapter 10, "Fooling Around with the Netscape Extensions," Netscape brings a few fancy features to the HTML table (such as tables and cool background textures). `Optimized for Netscape` means that the page designer has used these so-called Netscape extensions to enhance their site and that you need to be browsing with Netscape Navigator to get the full effect.

Unfortunately, the proverbial space limitations prevent me from giving a detailed treatment of each browser. Instead, I'll only give you a "just the facts" description for each program:

NCSA Mosaic (Windows, Mac, Unix)

Company:	National Center for Superconducting Applications
Where to find it:	FTP—`ftp.ncsa.uiuc.edu`
Directories:	`/Web/Mosaic/Windows/Win3x`
	`/Web/Mosaic/Windows/Win95`
	`/Web/Mosaic/Windows/WinNT`
	`/Web/Mosaic/Mac`
	`/Web/Mosaic/Windows/Unix`

continues

continued

NCSA Mosaic (Windows, Mac, Unix)

Comments: The original Web browser and still a formidable competitor to Netscape (see the next figure). Make sure you read the instructions before installing Mosaic.

The old veteran: NCSA Mosaic.

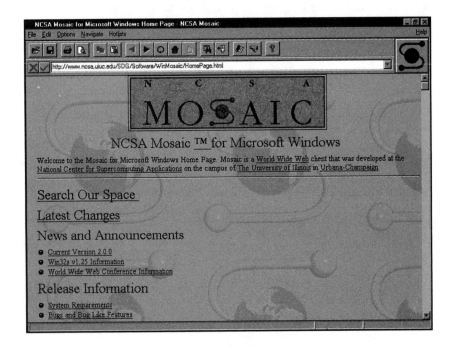

Internet Explorer (Windows 95)

Company: Microsoft

Where to find it: WWW—http://www.microsoft.com/ ie/iexplorer.htm

Comments: A top-notch browser with all the bells and whistles (see the following picture). Perhaps the only browser that really challenges Netscape.

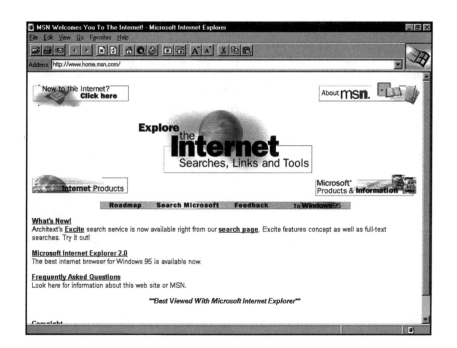

One of the new kids on the Web block: Microsoft's Internet Explorer.

Emissary (Windows 3.1)

Company:	The Wollongong Group
Where to find it:	FTP—`www.twg.com/pub/emissary`
Comments:	The Swiss army knife of browsers. Emissary combines the Web, e-mail, Usenet, FTP, and more into a single package (as shown in the following figure). All this usefulness will cost you: the Wollongongians charge $99.95 for Emissary.

SPRY Mosaic (Windows 3.1)

Company:	CompuServe/Spry
Where to find it (I):	CompuServe—**Go: Internet**
Where to find it (II):	FTP—`ftp.spry.com/AirMosaicDemo`
Comments:	Spry licensed Mosaic from the NCSA and put out their own version of the browser. Then CompuServe bought Spry and introduced NetLauncher, their Internet dialer and browser package (the next figure shows the CompuServe version of SPRY Mosaic). It's a decent program, but it's not in Netscape's league.

25

One stop Net surfing: Emissary.

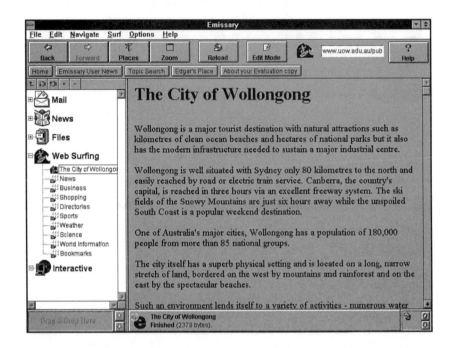

CompuServe's entry in the Web browser sweepstakes.

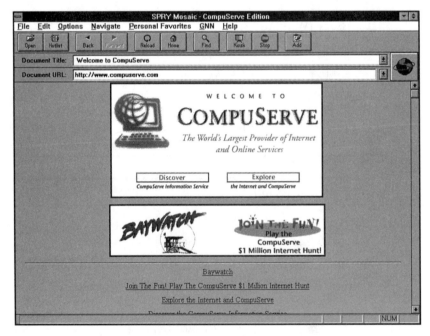

America Online (Windows 3.1, Mac)

Company:	America Online
Where to find it:	Keyword: **World Wide Web**
Comments:	Not to be outdone by CompuServe, America Online (AOL) recently added a Web browser to their Internet offerings (see the next figure). It's a competent program, at best, and its nicest feature is its integration into the AOL interface.

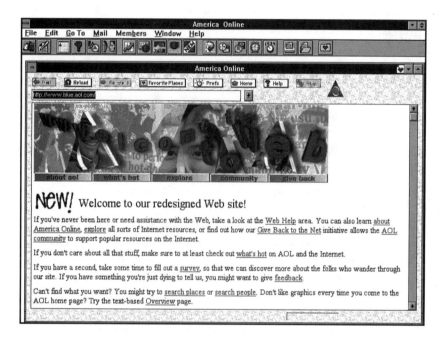

The America Online Web browser.

PRODIGY (Windows 3.1)

Company:	PRODIGY
Where to find it:	Jump: **Web Browser**
Comments:	Everybody else is doing it, so why can't we? PRODIGY's browser has all the standard features (see the following figure), but not a lot of pizzazz (sort of like PRODIGY as a whole).

PRODIGY's (yawn)
Web browser.

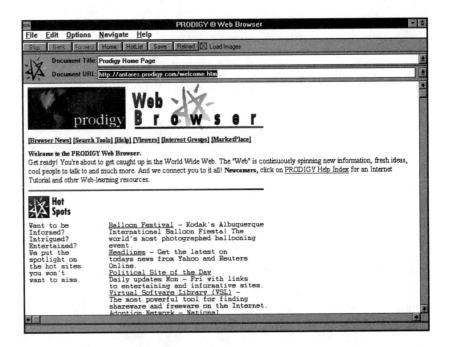

The Least You Need to Know

This chapter prepared you for the HTML ordeal to come by taking you on a 50 cent tour of the Internet and the World Wide Web. You saw, for example, that the Web has become insanely popular in the last couple of years (to the point where the terms "Internet" and "World Wide Web" have become nearly synonymous). The reasons behind this surge in popularity are the HHH of the WWW: handsomeness, hypertext, and HTML. I also ran through a few Web words, such as browser, surf, and URL. Speaking of browsers and surfing, I also showed you how to surf the Web using the Netscape Navigator browser as an example.

Chapter 3

A Brief HTML Web Page Primer

In This Chapter

➤ What in the name of blue blazes is HTML?

➤ A look at what kind of havoc you can wreak with HTML

➤ Answers to pressing HTML questions

➤ A veritable cornucopia of Web page examples that show HTML in its best light

Okay, now that you've got a sense of what the World Wide Web is all about, it's time for me to narrow the focus a little. Specifically, you need to get a handle on this HTML hoo-ha that seems to be such an integral part of Web page construction. What is HTML? Why bother with it? What can you do with it? Why does it sound so darned scary? Will it turn your brain to mush? This chapter will answer all these questions and more as we examine HTML in general terms and look at some examples of what HTML has wrought on the World Wide Web.

Okay, So Just What Is HTML?

I have some good news, and I have some bad news. The bad news is that, as I mentioned in the last chapter, HTML stands for—brace yourself—HyperText Markup Language. (I'll pause for a sec to let you get the inevitable shudders out of the way.)

The goods news, however, is that HTML doesn't stand for Hard To Master Lingo. HTML is, in fact, really a sheep in wolf's clothing: it looks nasty, but it's really not that bad (and, no—it won't turn even a small part of your brain to mush). Basic HTML—which is what 90 percent of all Web pages use—isn't much tougher than reciting the alphabet. It's way easier than programming your VCR (which is, I'm sure, good news for those of you who sport that scarlet letter of modern technology: the flashing 12:00 on your VCR's clock). Heck, you don't even have to memorize anything. The handy reference card at the front of this book (which you can tear out and keep at your side or tape to your cat's forehead) tells you absolutely everything you need to know about HTML.

That's all well and good, I hear you say, but *HyperText Markup Language* isn't exactly a phrase that trips lightly off the tongue; it really does sound intimidating. Well, you're right, it does. So, in the spirit of self-help books everywhere, you need to face your fears and look HTML squarely in the eye. Specifically, let's examine what each element of HyperText Markup Language means in plain English:

HyperText I told you in Chapter 2 that a hypertext link is a special word or phrase in a Web page that "points" to another Web page. When you click on one of these links, your browser transports you immediately to the other Web page, no questions asked. Because these hypertext links are really the distinguishing feature of the World Wide Web, Web pages are often known as hypertext documents. So HTML has the word "HyperText" in it because you use it to create these hypertext documents. (It would be just as accurate to call it WPML—Web Page Markup Language.)

Markup My dictionary defines "markup" as (among other things) "detailed stylistic instructions written on a manuscript that is to be typeset." For our purposes, I can rephrase this definition as follows: "detailed stylistic instructions typed into a text document that is to be published on the World Wide Web." That's HTML in a nutshell. It has a few simple codes for detailing things like making text bold or italic, creating bulleted lists, inserting graphics, and, of course, defining hypertext links. You just type these codes into the appropriate places in an ordinary text document and the World Wide Web automatically displays your page the way you want. In fact, the Web browser software handles all the hard stuff.

Language This may be the most misleading word of them all. Many people interpret this to mean that HTML is a programming language, and they wash their hands of the whole thing right off the bat. "You mean I gotta learn programming to get my two cents worth on the Web?" Not a chance, Vance. HTML has nothing, I repeat nothing, whatsoever to do with computer programming. Rather, HTML is a "language" in the sense that it has a small collection of two- and three-letter combinations and words that you use to specify styles such as bold and italic.

What Can You Do with HTML?

All right, so HTML isn't a Hideous, Terrible, Mega-Leviathan, but rather a Harmless, Tame, and Meek Lapdog. What can you do with such a creature? Well, lots of things, actually. After all, people aren't flocking to the World Wide Web because it's good for their health. Just the opposite, in fact. They're surfing 'til they drop because the Web presents them with an attractive and easily navigated source of info and entertainment (or infotainment, as the wags like to call it). It's HTML that adds the attractiveness and ease of navigation. To see what I mean, the next few sections take you through examples of the basic HTML elements.

You Can Format Text

A high JPM (Jolts Per Minute) count is what turns the crank of your average Web-surfing dude and dudette. Nothing generates fewer jolts (and is harder on the eyes, to boot) than plain, unadorned, text. To liven things up, use different sizes and styles for your Web page text. Happily, HTML is no slouch when it comes to dressing up text for the prom:

➤ You get six different font sizes that you can use for titles, headings, and such.

➤ You can display your Web prose as bold.

➤ You can emphasize things with italics.

➤ You can make text look like it was produced by a typewriter.

➤ You can (as long as you view the page with the Netscape browser) use different font sizes for characters.

The following figure shows examples of each kind of style. (I'll be showing you how to use HTML to format Web page text in Chapter 5, "From Buck-Naked to Beautiful: Dressing Up Your Page." For the extra formatting options available with the Netscape browser, see Chapter 10, "Fooling Around with the Netscape Extensions.")

Some examples of HTML text styles.

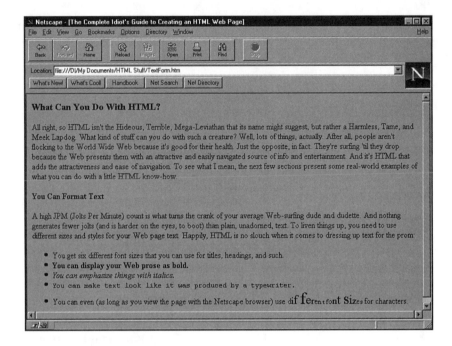

You Can Create Lists of Things

If you're presenting information on your Web page, it'll help if you can display your data in a way that makes sense and is easy to read. In some cases, this means arranging the data in lists, such as the bulleted list shown in the figure above, or in a numbered list. I'll fill you in on how to use HTML to create these kinds of lists and more in Chapter 6, "A Fistful of List Grist for Your Web Page Mill."

You Can Set Up Links to Other Pages

Web sessions aren't true surfin' safaris unless you go take a flying leap or two. I'm speaking, of course, of selecting hypertext links that take you to the far-flung corners of the Web world.

You can give the readers of your Web pages the same kicks by using HTML to create links anywhere you like in a page. You can set up three kinds of links:

➤ To another of your Web pages.

➤ To a different location in the same Web page. This is useful for humongous pages; you could, for example, put a "table of contents" at the top of the page that consists of links to various sections in the document.

➤ To any page, anywhere on the Web.

There are plenty of sites around the World Wide Web that exist only to provide a Web "mouse potato" (like a couch potato, only with a computer) with huge lists of links to pages that are informative, entertaining, or simply "cool." For example, the next screen shows a page from the Yahoo Web site, which boasts tens of thousands of links arranged in dozens of categories (Yahoo is a good place to go if you're looking for Web sites on a particular subject). In this particular case, the page shows a few links to some "useless" Web pages. (Beard research!? Cabbage!?) You'll find out how to use HTML to sprinkle links all over your Web pages in Chapter 7, "Making the Jump to Hyperspace: Adding Links."

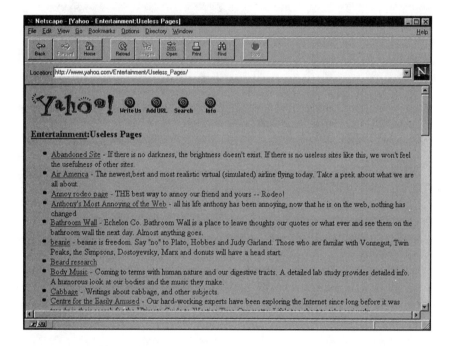

A page from Yahoo showing a few links to some, uh, unusual sites.

You Can Insert Images

Fancy text effects, lists, and lotsa links go a long way toward making a Web page a hit. But for a real crowd-pleasing page, you'll want to throw in an image or two. It could be a picture of yourself, a drawing the kids made, some clip art, or any of the images that are on this book's disk. As long as you have the image in a graphics file, you can use HTML to position the image appropriately on your page. I'll give you the details (as well as info on the types of graphics files you can use) in Chapter 8, "A Picture Is Worth a Thousand

Clicks: Working with Images." (Another of Netscape's innovations is the background image—a picture, pattern, or color that takes the place of the drab gray background you normally see on most Web pages. I'll talk about this in Chapter 10, "Fooling Around with the Netscape Extensions.")

The next figure shows an example page with an image. In this case, it's Netscape Communications' famous Fish Cam. Fish Cam? Yeah. Once every minute, a camera takes a picture of a fish tank and then loads the new picture onto the Web page. Silly? Yes. Cool? Definitely.

Netscape's notorious Fish Cam. The Information SuperWaterway?

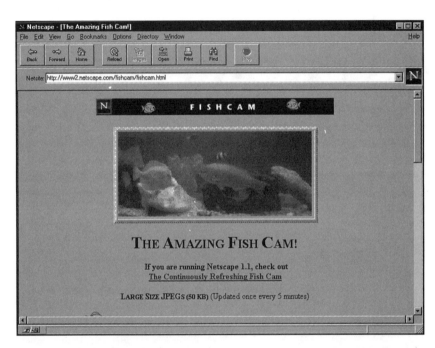

Lights, Camera, Surf!

If you like the Fish Cam, there's no shortage of camera-ready Web pages that'll give you up-to-minute views of anything from ants to piranhas. Here are a few of my fave raves:

Steve's Ant Farm—`http://sec.dgsys/AntFarm.html`

Wearable Wireless Webcam—`http://www.white.media.mit.edu/~steve/netcam.html`

The Tele-Garden—`http://www.usc.edu/dept/garden/`

Adam's Casa—`http://curryco.com/.a/casa.html`

You Can Format Information in Tables

If your Web page needs to show data formatted in rows and columns, you could try using tabs and spaces to line things up all nice and neat. However, you'll groan in disappointment when you view the page in a browser. Why? Because HTML reduces multiple spaces to a single space, and it ignores tabs completely! This sounds like perverse behavior, but it's just the way HTML was set up.

You're not out of luck, though. You can use HTML to create tables to slot your data into slick-looking rows and columns. The next picture shows an example of a table. (Note that, as I write this, only a few browsers know how to display tables. Netscape does, of course, as do the latest versions of NCSA Mosaic and Internet Explorer.) I'll tell you how to use HTML to construct tables in Chapter 11, "Table Talk: Adding Tables to Your Page."

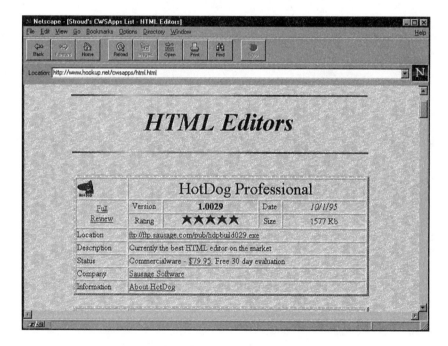

Tables: A blessing for neat freaks everywhere

Pages from All Walks of Web Life

Now that you've got some idea of what HTML can do, wouldn't you like to see the rabbits various Web magicians have pulled from their HTML hats? To that end, the next few sections present some real-world examples of Web pages that show you what you can do with a little HTML know-how. Of course, these examples represent only the smallest subset of the Web world. There are, literally, tens, if not hundreds, of thousands of Web pages out there, and each one is like a digital fingerprint—a unique expression of its creator's individuality.

The Personal Touch: Personal Home Pages

The simplest, and probably the most common, type of Web page is the personal home page. This is a page that an individual sets up to tell the Web world a little bit about himself. They're the Web equivalent of those "Hi! My Name is…" stickers that people wear at parties and receptions. They range from warm and fuzzy ("Welcome, friend, to my home page!"), to downright vainglorious ("Let me tell you everything there is to know about me"), to frighteningly personal ("Dear diary…"). The following figure shows the personal home page for yours truly.

The author's humble HTML home.

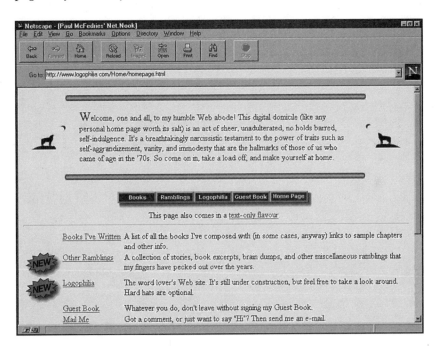

Hobbyists Do It with HTML

Sometimes the hardest thing about putting together a Web page is thinking of something to say. (Although there are plenty of garrulous guys and gals out there for whom this is definitely not a problem!) So what's a body to do about a bad case or Web writer's block? Well, lots of people go with what they know: they talk about their hobbies and interests. Hey, it makes sense. You're more likely to sound enthusiastic and excited about a topic you're keen on, so you're more likely to hold your reader's interest. There are lots of things you can do to fill up your page: introduce the hobby to novices; talk about how you got started; show some samples of your work (depending on the hobby, of course); and include links to related Web pages. The sky's the limit.

As you might imagine, there's no shortage of hobby-related pages on the World Wide Web. You'll find info on everything from amateur radio to millefiori to woodworking. Millefiori!? No, I haven't the faintest idea what it is, either, but the next picture shows a page from someone who does.

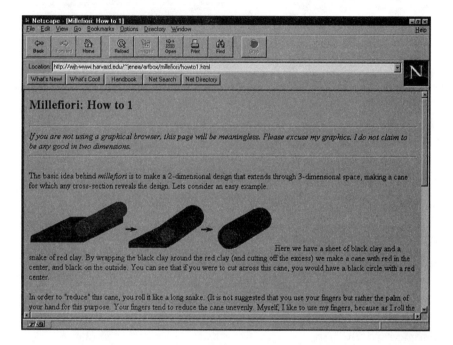

Obscurity is no barrier for Web spinners: a millefiori (?) how-to page.

Not for Bathroom Reading: Electronic Magazines

The Web's marriage of text and graphics meant it was only a matter of time before someone decided to "publish" a Web-based magazine. Now it seems that new electronic magazines (they're also often called e-mags, or e-zines) hit the Web's newsstands every few days. The quality, as you might expect, runs the gamut from professional to pathetic, from slick to sick. But the good ones are very good, with well-written articles, handsome graphics, and some unique approaches to the whole magazine thing. There are, literally, hundreds of e-zines out there, so there's no shortage of reading material. John Labovitz maintains a list of e-zines at the following address:

```
http://www.meer.net/!johnl/e-zine-list/index.html
```

The next screen shows the home page for one of the better e-zines: Urban Desires.

The Urban Desires electronic magazine.

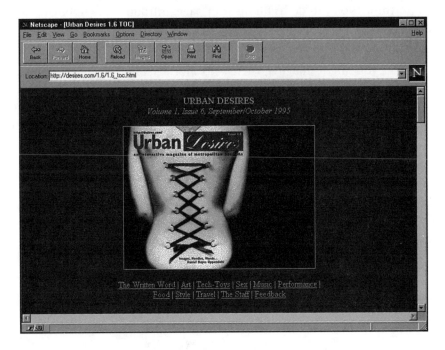

Corporate Culture Hits the Web

One of the biggest engines driving the growth of the World Wide Web is the influx of corporations scrambling to get a "presence" in cyberspace. Companies from mom-and-pop shops to Fortune 500 behemoths are setting up on the Web in anticipation of, well, something. Nobody's quite sure why they need a Web site, but they're happy to put one up, just in case something BIG happens one of these days. Hey, who can blame them? With all the Internet hype floating around these days, no self-respecting CEO is going to be caught with his or her pants down. And, as proof that every corporate entity on the face of the earth has a Web site, I offer you the following figure: the home page of the Polyurethane Foam Association!

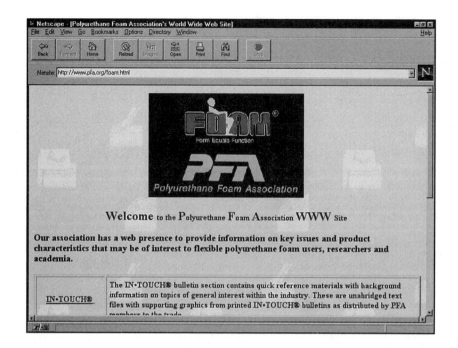

At last, the PFA has its own Web site!

Your Tax Dollars at Work: Government Web Pages

If Big Business is rushing to get on the Web, you better believe Big Brother isn't going to be left behind, either. Yes, governments—local, state, and federal—are putting up Web pages to beat the band. Granted, many of these sites are quite useful. You can use them to contact representatives, read government reports and studies, do research, and more. Some of the pages are even—gasp!—creative. For example, check out the handsome graphics you get when you surf to the home page of the White House (see the next figure).

The Changing Face of HTML: HTML 3.0

As I write this, various Web engineers, programmers, and other geeks are busy putting the finishing touches on a new version of HTML: HTML 3.0. There's no need to panic, however. The advent of HTML 3.0 does *not* mean all the HTML I'll be teaching you in this book isn't worth the paper it's printed on. No, thankfully, HTML 3.0 is an extension of the existing tags, not a replacement of them. I'll be telling you about some of the new features in HTML 3.0 as you work through the next section.

The White House World Wide Web page.

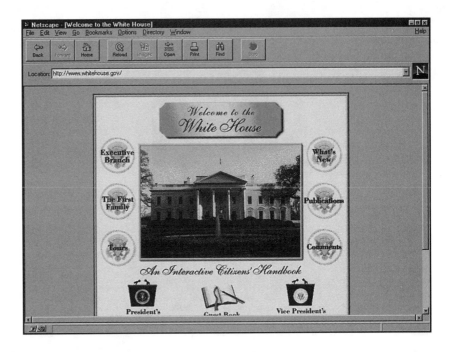

The Least You Need to Know

This chapter gave you a quick overview of HTML. I showed you what it is and why it isn't as scary as it sounds, and you saw quite a few examples of what HTML can do.

So much for the preliminaries. In the next chapter you'll get started with the nuts and bolts of HTML so you can start building your first Web page.

Part 2
Creating Your First HTML Web Page

Okay, I'd say that's quite enough theory for one book! By now you must be chomping at the bit in anticipation of creating a Web page to call your own. Well, I'm happy to say, your big moment is at hand. The six chapters here in Part 2 will take you through the entire Web page production process, from go to whoa. When the dust settles, you'll have an actual, honest-to-goodness, "Look, ma, I'm in cyberspace!" Web page. You will be, in short, a full-fledged Webmeister and the envy of all your pageless friends.

WE'RE GONNA HAVE TO KNOCK OUT THAT WALL...

Laying the Foundation: The Basic Structure of a Web Page

In This Chapter

➤ A laundry list of things you need to get started

➤ A quick course on tags—the building blocks of HTML

➤ The basic blueprint for all Web pages

➤ How to add a title, toss in some text, and split your prose into paragraphs

➤ Your field guide to the most fundamental of HTML flora and fauna

This book's goal is to help you create your own Web pages and thus lay claim to a little chunk of personal cyberspace real estate: a home page away from home, if you will. Before you can live in this humble abode, however, you have to "pour the concrete" that will serve as the foundation for the rest of your digital domicile. In this chapter, I'll be showing you a few HTML basics that constitute the underlying structure of all Web pages.

Getting Started

As you saw in the last chapter, some Web pages look truly spectacular. To achieve these impressive effects, you might think you need to stretch a fancy word processing or page layout program to its limits. Or you might think you have to rush out and spend beaucoup bucks for some kind of highfalutin "HTML generator" that's designed specifically for cranking out Web pages. Nah, you're way off. All you really need for creating a basic page is a lowly text editor. Yes, Windows users, even a brain-dead program like Notepad is more than adequate for doing the HTML thing. (Although, having said all that, there are HTML "editors" that can take some of the drudgery out of page production. I'll talk about some of them in Part 4.)

Surely a plain old run-of-the-mill text editor won't let me create anything resembling those beautiful pages I see on the Web.

Yes, it will—and stop calling me Shirley. 99.9 percent of all the Web pages in the world are really just simple text files.

So why in the name of Sam Hill do those pages look so good? Any text files I've ever met have been ugly with a capital Ugh!

The Web's beauty secret is that it's actually the Web browsers that determine how a page looks. When you surf to a Web page, the browser reads in the text, scours the file for HTML markings, and then displays the page accordingly. So, for example, you can mark in your text file that you want a certain word to appear as bold. When the browser comes to that part of the document, it goes right ahead and formats the word in a bold font. The browser handles all this dirty work behind the scenes, and you never have to give it a second thought (or even a first thought, for that matter).

Crank Out a New Text File

So, to get to the point at long last, all you really need to do to get started is fire up your favorite text editor and launch a new document—if the program doesn't do that for you automatically, as most do. (Of course, that isn't to say there aren't other, equally important, accouterments you may need. For me, a good, strong cup of java is a must. Other optional HTML accessories include the appropriate mood music—something by The Spinners, perhaps?—a copy of *Feel the Fear and Do It Anyway*, and semi-important things like your creativity and imagination.)

If you prefer, it's okay to use a word processor such as Windows' Write, Windows 95's WordPad, or Microsoft Word. One caveat, though: don't try to format the document in any way (such as adding italics or centering paragraphs). Not only do you run the risk of having a browser choke on these extra formatting codes, but every Web browser on the face of the Earth will completely ignore your efforts. Remember, the only way to make a browser do your bidding and display your Web page properly is to use the appropriate HTML codes.

The Edit-Save-Browse Cycle

While slaving away on the text file that will become your Web page, make sure you practice safe computing. That is, make sure you save your work regularly. Keep in mind that most Web browsers only know how to deal with files that end with the .HTML extension (such as MYPAGE.HTML). If your system balks at extensions longer than three characters (for example, if you have a DOS or Windows 3.1 system), just use .HTM, for now. You can always change it after you send the file to the hosting provider's computer. (I'll talk more about this in Chapter 9.)

Using a Word Processor?

If you're using a word processor to create your Web page, make sure you save the document as a plain text file. A Web browser may gag on an HTML page you save in the word processor's native format. Text files normally use a .TXT extension, so make sure you change it to .HTM or .HTML.

By now you've probably figured out the biggest problem associated with fashioning a Web page out of a text file: there's no way to know what the page will look like once it's been foisted onto the Web! Fortunately, all is not lost. Most browsers are more than happy to let you load a text file right from the confines of your computer's hard disk. This means you can test drive your page without first having to put it on the Web. So here's the basic cycle you'll be using to build your pages:

1. Add some text and HTML stuff (I'll define what this "stuff" is in the next section) to your text file.

2. Save the file.

3. Load the file into your browser of choice to see how things look.

4. Lather. Rinse. Repeat steps 1 through 3. Note that once the file is loaded in the browser, you need only choose the program's "Reload" command to see the effects of your changes.

As a public service (it's a tough job but, hey, somebody's gotta do it), I've compiled the appropriate instructions from a few popular browsers for loading a file from your hard disk:

➤ In Netscape, pull down the **File** menu, select the **Open File** command (or you can press **Ctrl+O**), and then choose the file from the Open dialog box that appears. To reload the file, pull down the **View** menu and select **Reload** (or press **Ctrl+R**).

➤ In NCSA Mosaic, select the File menu's **Open Local File** command (or press **Ctrl+L**) and then pinpoint the file in the Open dialog box. To reload the file, select the **Navigate** menu's **Reload** command, or press **R**.

➤ In Microsoft's Internet Explorer, select the File menu's **Open** command (or press **Ctrl+O**), select the **Open File** button in the Open Internet Address dialog box that appears, and then pick out the file you need. You can reload the file by selecting the View menu's **Refresh** command, or by pressing **F5**.

Tag Daze: Understanding HTML's Tags

As I mentioned earlier, the magic of the Web is wrought by browser programs that read text files and then decipher the HTML nuggets that you've sprinkled hither and thither. These HTML tidbits are markers—called *tags*—that spell out how you want things to look. For example, if you want a word on your page to appear in bold text, you surround that word with the appropriate tags for boldfacing text.

In general, tags use the following format:

```
<TAG>The text to be affected by the tag</TAG>
```

The TAG part is a code (usually a one- or two-letter abbreviation, but sometimes an entire word) that specifies the type of effect you want. You always surround these codes with angle brackets <>; the brackets tell the Web browser that it's dealing with a chunk of HTML and not just some random text.

For example, the tag for bold is <B>. So if you want the phrase "BeDazzler Home Page" to appear in bold, you type the following into your document:

```
<B>BeDazzler Home Page</B>
```

The first <B> says to the browser, in effect, "Listen up, Browser Boy! You know the text that comes after this? Be a good fellow and display it in bold." This continues until the browser reaches the </B>. The slash (/) defines this as an end tag; this lets the browser know it's supposed to stop what it's doing. So the </B> tells the browser, "Okay, okay. Ixnay on the oldbay!" As you'll see, there are tags for lots of other effects, including italics, paragraphs, headings, page titles, lists, and lots more. HTML is just the sum total of all these tags.

And Now, Some Actual HTML

Okay, you're ready to get down to some brass HTML tacks. (Halle-freakin'-lujah, I hear you saying.) You'll begin by cobbling together a few HTML tags that constitute the underlying skeleton of all Web pages.

Your HTML files will always lead off with the <HTML> tag. This tag doesn't do a whole heckuva lot except tell any Web browser that tries to read the file that it's dealing with a file that contains HTML knickknacks. Similarly, the last line in your document will always be the corresponding end tag: </HTML>. You can think of this end tag as the HTML equivalent for "The End." So each of your Web pages will start off looking like this:

```
<HTML>
</HTML>
```

The next items serve to divide the document into two sections: the head and the body. The head section is like an introduction to the page. Web browsers use the head to glean various types of information about the page. Although there are a number of items that can appear in the head section, the only one that makes any real sense to us mere mortals is the title of the page, which I'll talk about in the next section.

To define the head, you add a <HEAD> tag and a </HEAD> tag immediately below the <HTML> tag you typed in earlier. So your Web page should now look like this:

```
<HTML>
<HEAD>
</HEAD>
</HTML>
```

The body section is where you enter the text and other fun stuff that will actually appear on the Web page. To define the body, you place a <BODY> tag and a </BODY> tag after the head section (that is, below the </HEAD> tag), as follows:

```
<HTML>
<HEAD>
</HEAD>
<BODY>
</BODY>
</HTML>
```

Hmm. It's not exactly a work of art, is it? On the excitement scale, these opening moves rank right up there with watching the grass grow and tuning in to C-SPAN on a slow news day. Well, just file it under "Necessary Evils" and move on.

Techno Talk

A Not-So-Necessary Evil?

To relieve some of the inevitable boredom of these early stages of Web page creation, you'll find some help on the disk that comes with this book. I've included a file named SKELETON.HTM that contains all the tags that make up the bare bones of a Web page. You can use this file as a template each time you start a new Web page.

A Page by Any Other Name: Adding a Title

If you try loading your Web page into a browser, you'll just get a whole lot of nothing-ness because you haven't given the browser anything meaty into which it can sink its teeth. The first snack you can offer a hungry browser program is the title of the Web page. The page's title is just about what you might think it is: the overall name of the page (not to be confused with the name of the file you're creating). If someone views the page in a graphical browser (such as Netscape or Mosaic), the title appears in the title bar of the browser's window.

The <TITLE> Tag

To define a title, you surround the text with the <TITLE> and </TITLE> tags. For example, if you want the title of your page to be "My Home Sweet Home Page," you enter it as follows:

```
<TITLE>My Home Sweet Home Page</TITLE>
```

Note that you always place the title inside the head section, so your basic HTML document now looks like so:

```
<HTML>
<HEAD>
<TITLE>My Home Sweet Home Page</TITLE>
</HEAD>
<BODY>
</BODY>
</HTML>
```

The following figure shows this document loaded into the Windows 95 version of Netscape Navigator. Notice how the title appears in the window's title bar.

The page title ⎯

The body text will appear here.

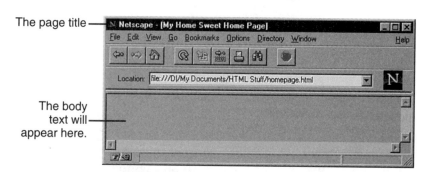

Most Windows Web browsers display the page title in the window's title bar (duh).

Title Dos and Don'ts

Here are a few things to keep in mind when thinking of a title for your page:

➤ Do make sure your title describes what the page is all about.

➤ Don't make your title too long. If you do, the browser may chop it off because there's not enough room to display it in the title bar. 50 or 60 characters are usually the max.

➤ Do use titles that make sense when someone views them out of context. For example, if someone really likes your page, she may add it to her list of bookmarks (hey, it could happen). The browser will display the page title in the bookmark list, so it's important that the title makes sense when she looks at her bookmarks later on.

➤ Don't use titles that are cryptic or vague. Titling a page "Link #42" or "A Page" may make sense to you, but your readers may not appreciate it.

Fleshing Out Your Page with Text

With your page title firmly in place, you can now think about putting some flesh on your Web page's bones by entering the text you want to appear in the body of the page. For the most part, you can simply type the text between the <BODY> and </BODY> tags, like so:

```
<HTML>
<HEAD>
<TITLE>My Home Sweet Home Page</TITLE>
</HEAD>
<BODY>
This text appears in the body of the Web page.
</BODY>
</HTML>
```

Before you start typing willy-nilly, however, there are a few things you should know:

➤ You might think you can line things up and create some interesting effects by stringing together two or more spaces. Ha! Web browsers will chew up all those extra spaces and spit them out into the nether regions of cyberspace. Why? Well, the philosophy of the Web is that you can use only HTML tags to lay out a document. So a run of multiple spaces (or white space, as it's called) is verboten. (There is a trick you can use to get around this, however: the <PRE> tag. I'll tell you about it in the next chapter.)

➤ Tabs, too, fall under the rubric of white space. You can enter tabs all day long, but the browser will ignore them completely.

➤ Another thing that browsers like to ignore is the carriage return. It may sound reasonable to the likes of you and me that pressing Enter starts a new paragraph, but not in the HTML world. I'll talk more about this in the next section.

➤ If HTML documents are just plain text, does that mean you're out of luck if you need to use characters such as ©, ™, and £? Luckily, no, you're not. HTML has special codes for these kinds of characters, and I'll talk about them in the next chapter.

More Character Assassinations

Note, too, that the angle bracket characters < and > are out of bounds because you use them to identify tags. Again, if you need to use them, there are some special codes that'll get the job done.

➤ Word processor users—it bears repeating here—it's not worth your bother to format your text. The browser will cheerfully ignore even the most elaborate formatting jobs because, as usual, browsers only understand HTML-based formatting. (And besides, a document with formatting is, by definition, not a pure text file, so a browser may bite the dust trying to load it.)

How to Do Paragraphs

As I mentioned above, carriage returns aren't worth a hill of beans in the World Wide Web. If you type one line, press **Enter**, and then type a second line, the browser will simply run the two lines together, side by side.

If a new paragraph is what you need, you have to stick the browser's nose in it, so to speak, by using the <P> tag. For example, consider the following text:

```
<HTML>
<HEAD>
<TITLE>My Home Sweet Home Page</TITLE>
</HEAD>
<BODY>
This text appears in the body of the Web page.
This is the second line (sort of).
<P>
This is the third line.
</BODY>
</HTML>
```

Hey, Where's the </P> Tag?

You might have noticed that I didn't use a </P> tag to mark the end of the <P> tag. What gives? Well, the </P> tag exists, but no one ever uses it. Why? Because the end of one paragraph automatically implies the beginning of the next one, so there's no need to toss in the </P>.

The following figure shows how this looks in the browser. As you can see, the first two lines appear beside each other, despite the fact that they're on separate lines in the original text. However, the third line sits nicely in its own paragraph thanks to the <P> tag that precedes it.

You need to use the <P> tag to create paragraphs in HTML.

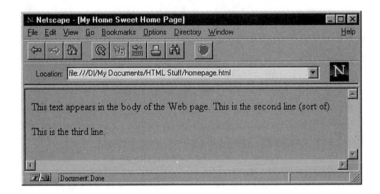

The Least You Need to Know

This chapter got you started on your way to earning your Web Master merit badge by showing you the basic HTML structure of a Web page. Here's the highlight reel:

➤ The only thing you need to get started with your Web page is a text editor (such as Windows' Notepad) and a brand new text file.

➤ HTML is nothing but a series of tags that take the form <TAG>*text*</TAG>.

➤ All Web pages begin with the <HTML> tag and end with the </HTML> tag.

➤ There are two sections in an HTML document. The first section is the head, and you define it by the <HEAD> and </HEAD> tags. The second section is the body, and you surround it by the <BODY> and </BODY> tags.

➤ You wedge the title of your Web page in between the <TITLE> and </TITLE> tags, and plop the whole thing inside the head section.

➤ Your Web page text goes inside the body section. If you need to separate your prose into paragraphs, use the <P> tag.

Chapter 5

From Buck-Naked to Beautiful: Dressing Up Your Page

In the early, pre-text stages of the Web-page production process, your page is essentially naked. It passes its days exposed to the elements, shivering and teeth-chatteringly cold. Brrr. To put some color in your page's cheeks and prevent it from catching its death, you need to clothe it with the text you want everyone to read.

These new text garments may be warm, but they aren't much to look at. I mean, face it, a plain-text Web page just doesn't present your prose in the best light. I'm definitely talking Worst Dressed List here.

However, this really doesn't matter for those times when you're just kicking around the Web house. At this stage, you're the only one who sees your Web page, so you usually don't care how it looks. But what about when it's time to go out on the town? What do you do when you want the rest of the Web world to see your creation? Heck, you can't send your Web page out into cyberspace looking like that!

Before your page has its coming-out party, you need to dress it up in clothes appropriate for the occasion. You need, in short, to format your text so it looks its best. This chapter will be your Web page fashion consultant as it examines the various ways you can use HTML to beautify your words.

Sprucing Up Your Text

The first of our Web page makeover chores will be to examine some tags that alter the look of individual words and phrases. The next few sections fill you in on the details.

Yer Basic Text Formatting Styles

The good news about text formatting is that most browsers only support four kinds: **bold**, *italic*, monospace, and underline. (Underlining is relatively new, so not all browsers may support it. However, the latest versions of the Big Three—Netscape, NCSA Mosaic, and Internet Explorer—are all on friendly terms with underlining.) The bad news is that HTML has about a billion different tags that produce these styles. However, I'll take mercy on you and only let you in on the easiest tags to use. The following table shows the tags that produce each of these formats.

Text style	Begin tag	End tag
Bold	<B>	</B>
Italic	<I>	</I>
Underline	<U>	</U>
Monospace	<TT>	</TT>

Here's a sample HTML document that shows each of these styles in action. The figure shows how the styles look when viewed with Internet Explorer.

```
<HTML>
<HEAD>
<TITLE>Yer Basic Text Formatting Styles</TITLE>
</HEAD>
<BODY>
<U>My Excellent Bookstore Adventure</U>
<P>
The other day, I went to a unique bookstore called
<TT>Mary, Mary, Quite Contrary</TT>. There were
<I>tons</I> of unexpected delights, including, believe
it or not, a <B>Self-Helpless</B> section! For real.
I saw titles like <I>Got a 50-Cent Head? Here's How To
```

```
Get a Ten Dollar Haircut!</I> and <I>A Few Geese Shy of
a Gaggle—And Proud Of It!</I>
</BODY>
</HTML>
```

Alternative Text Tags

Just in case you're a glutton for punishment, here's a rundown of some of the alternative tags you can use for these text styles:

Text style	Alternative tags
Bold	<STRONG>
Italic	<EM> or <CITE>
Monospace	<CODE> or <KBD>

Unfortunately, there's no way to predict how a given browser will display these styles, so I don't recommend using them.

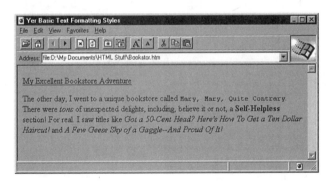

A Web page showing the four basic text formatting styles.

Keep in mind that this book's disk includes all the HTML examples you'll read about in the book. (For instructions on installing the disk, see the appendix called "The Goodies on the Disk" at the back of this book.) This will help make your Web-building chores easier because you can use the examples to get started with your own pages. To get your mitts on the example I used above, look for the file named BOOKSTOR.HTM on the disk. If the disk is missing or damaged, or if you don't have a Windows system, you can get the examples from my Web site at the following URL:

```
http://www.mcfedries.com/books/cightml/
```

55

Combining Text Formats

You should note, as well, that most (but by no means all) modern browsers are perfectly happy to let you combine these text styles. So, for example, if you need bold italic text, you can get it by throwing the <B> and <I> tags together, like so:

```
<B><I>This'll give you, like, bold italic text</I></B>
```

Accessorizing: Displaying Special Characters

You might think because HTML is composed in text-only documents (documents that include only the characters and symbols you can peck out from your keyboard), non-standard characters such as ¢ and ¥ would be taboo. It's true that there's no way to add these characters to your page directly, but the Web wizards who created HTML thought up a way around this limitation. Specifically, they came up with special codes (called—a name only a true geek would love—*character entities*) that represent these and other oddball symbols.

These codes come in two flavors: a *character reference* and an *entity name*. Character references are basically just numbers, while the entity names are friendlier symbols that describe the character you're trying to display. For example, you can display the cents sign (¢) using either the ¢ character reference, or the ¢ entity name, as shown here:

```
Got a 50&#162; Head? Here's How To Get a $10 Haircut!
```

or

```
Got a 50&cent; Head? Here's How To Get a $10 Haircut!
```

The next table lists a few other popular characters and their corresponding codes. You'll find a more complete list at the back of the book—see the "HTML Codes for Cool Characters" appendix.

Using Entity Names? Proceed with Caution

You should know that, as I write this, the exact makeup of all the entity names is not yet set in stone (although it's pretty darn close), so many browsers don't support them yet. If you use entity names, you might want to run your page through a few popular browsers to make sure things look reasonable.

Symbol	Character Reference	Entity name
<	&#060;	&lt;
>	&#062;	&gt;
¢	&#162;	&cent;
£	&#163;	&pound;
¥	&#165;	&yen;
©	&#169;	&copy;
®	&#174;	&reg;
°	&#176;	&deg;
1/4	&#188;	&frac14;
1/2	&#189;	&frac12;
3/4	&#190;	&frac34;
×	&#215;	&times;

Sectioning Your Page with Headings

Like chapters in a book, many Web page creators divide their contents into several sections. To help separate these sections and so make life easier for the reader, you can use headings. Ideally, these headings act as mini-titles that convey some idea of what each section is all about. To make these titles stand out, HTML has a series of heading tags that display text in larger, bold fonts. There are six heading tags in all, ranging from <H1>—which uses the largest font— down to <H6>—which uses the smallest font.

What's with all the different headings? Well, the idea is that you use them to outline your document. As an example, consider the headings I've used in this chapter and see how I'd format them in HTML.

The overall heading, of course, is the chapter title, so I'd display it using the <H1> tag. The first main section is the one titled "Sprucing Up Your Text," so I'd give its title an <H2> heading. That section contains three subsections, "Yer Basic Text Formatting Styles," "Combining Text Formats," and "Accessorizing: Displaying Special Characters." I'd give each of these titles an <H3> heading. Then I come to the section

Check This Out...

Netscape Knows Text
Netscape Navigator supports a few other text tricks, including adjusting the size of fonts for individual characters. I'll spell everything out in Chapter 10, "Fooling Around with the Netscape Extensions."

called "Sectioning Your Page With Headings." This is another main section of the chapter, so I'd go back to an <H2> tag for its title, and so on.

The following HTML document (look for HEADINGS.HTM on the disk) shows how I'd format all the section titles for this chapter, and the next figure shows how they appear in Netscape (notice how I don't need to use a <P> tag to display headings on separate lines; that's handled automatically):

```
<HTML>
<HEAD>
<TITLE>A Text Formatting and Headings Extravaganza</TITLE>
</HEAD>
<BODY>
<H1>From Buck-Naked to Beautiful: Dressing Up Your Page</H1>
<H2>Sprucing Up Your Text</H2>
<H3>Yer Basic Text Formatting Styles</H3>
<H3>Combining Text Formats</H3>
<H3>Accessorizing: Displaying Special Characters</H3>
<H2>Sectioning Your Page With Headings</H2>
<H2>A Few More Formatting Features</H2>
<H3>Handling Preformatted Text</H3>
<H3>Them's the Breaks: Using &lt;BR&gt; for Line Breaks</H3>
<H3>Inserting Horizontal Lines</H3>
</BODY>
</HTML>
```

Examples of HTML's heading tags.

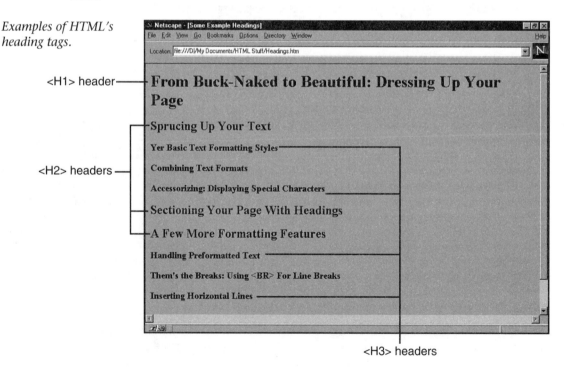

58

A Few More Formatting Features

I'll finish off this chapter by taking you through three more formatting tags that should serve you in good stead throughout your career as a Web engineer. You use these tags for displaying preformatted text, inserting line breaks, and displaying horizontal lines. The next few sections give you the details.

Handling Preformatted Text

Remember when I told you in the last chapter that Web browsers ignore white space (multiple spaces and tabs) as well as carriage returns? Well, I lied. Sort of. You see, all browsers normally *do* spit out these elements, but you can talk a browser into swallowing them whole by using the <PRE> tag. The "PRE" part is short for "preformatted," and you normally use this tag to display preformatted text exactly as it's laid out. Here, "preformatted" means text in which you use spaces, tabs, and carriage returns to line things up.

Let's look at an example. Here's an HTML document where I've set up two chunks of text in a pattern that uses spaces and carriage returns. The first bit of doggerel doesn't make use of the <PRE> tag, but I've surrounded the second poem with <PRE> and </PRE>. The next screen shows the results. Notice that the lines from the first poem are strung together, but that when the browser encounters <PRE>, it displays the white space and carriage returns faithfully.

Check This Out...

<PRE> Text Is Ugly!

You'll notice one other thing about how the browser displays text that's ensconced within the <PRE> and </PRE> tags: it formats the text in an ugly monospaced font. There is, unfortunately, no way to avoid this.

```
<HTML>
<HEAD>
<TITLE>The &lt;PRE&gt; Tag</TITLE>
</HEAD>
<BODY>
<H3>Without the &lt;PRE&gt; Tag:</H3>
          Here's
        some ditty
      Specially done
    to lay it out all
  Formatted and pretty.
Unfortunately, that is all
  This junk really means
    Because I admit I
```

```
             couldn't scrawl
                Poetry for
                   beans.
   <P>
   <H3>With the &lt;PRE&gt; Tag:</H3>
   <PRE>
                Here's
             some ditty
          Specially done
       to lay it out all
    Formatted and pretty.
 Unfortunately, that is all
    This junk really means
          Because I admit I
             couldn't scrawl
                Poetry for
                   beans.
   </PRE>
   </BODY>
   </HTML>
```

How preformatted text appears in Netscape.

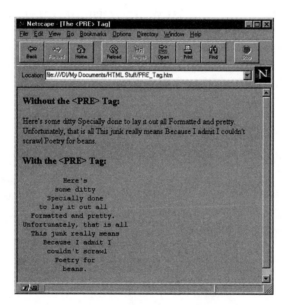

Them's the Breaks: Using <BR> for Line Breaks

As you saw in the last chapter, you use the <P> tag when you need to separate your text into paragraphs. When a browser trips over a <P> tag, it starts a new paragraph on a separate line and inserts an extra, blank line after the previous paragraph. However, what if you don't want that extra line? For example, you might want to display a list of items with each item on a separate line and without any space between the items. (Actually, there are better ways to display lists than the method I'll show you here; see Chapter 6, "A Fistful of List Grist for Your Web Page Mill.")

Well, you could use the <PRE> tag, but your text would appear in the ugly, monospaced font. A better solution is to separate your lines with <BR>, the line break tag. When a browser encounters <BR> it starts a new line, but it doesn't toss in an extra, blank line. Here's an example (it's the file named LINEBRKS.HTM on the disk):

```
<HTML>
<HEAD>
<TITLE>Yer Basic Text Formatting Styles</TITLE>
</HEAD>
<BODY>
<H2>My Excellent Bookstore Adventure</H2>
<HR>
The other day, I went to a unique bookstore called
<TT>Mary, Mary, Quite Contrary</TT>. There were
<I>tons</I> of unexpected delights, including, believe
it or not, a <B>Self-Helpless</B> section! For real.
Here's a list of just some of the great titles I saw:
<P>
Got a 50&#162; Head? Here's How To Get a $10 Haircut!<BR>
A Few Geese Shy of a Gaggle--And Proud Of It!<BR>
The Seven Habits of Highly Ineffective Couch Potatoes<BR>
Dieting? No, Sorry, You're <I>Way</I> Too Late For That!<BR>
"Dumb and Dumber": A Yahoo Way of Knowledge
</BODY>
</HTML>
```

In the list of books, I added the <BR> tag to the end of each line (except the last one; I don't need it there). As you can see in the following figure, Netscape dutifully displays each line separately, with no space in between.

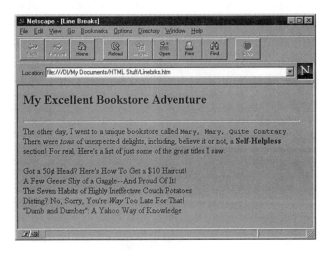

Use the <BR> tag to force a line break in your text.

Inserting Horizontal Lines

The eagle-eyed among you noticed a horizontal line extending across the Netscape screen shown above. What gives? Well, while you weren't looking, I surreptitiously inserted an <HR> tag into the HTML text. <HR> (which stands for "horizontal rule") produces a line across the page, which is a handy way to separate sections of your document. (Netscape, as usual, accepts a few extra attributes for the <HR> tag. I'll let you in on them in Chapter 10.)

Web Page Fashion Tips

The HTML elements I discussed in this chapter (and many of the ones I'll be talking about in subsequent chapters) can make a Web page actually look worse if you misuse or overuse them. If you're interested in making your pages look their best, be sure to read Chapter 12, "The Elements of Web Page Style," where I discuss the dos and don'ts of Web page design.

The Least You Need to Know

This chapter showed you a few ways to dress up your Web page for a night on the town. Let's take a fond look back at some of the chapter's more memorable moments:

➤ The four main tags for text styles are <B> for bold, <I> for italic, <U> for underline, and <TT> for monospace. You're free to combine these tags to apply multiple styles to the same text.

➤ You can use special codes (either character references or entity names) to display non-standard characters such as ¢ and ¥. See the table in the back of the book for a list of these codes.

➤ If you have multiple sections in your page, use the heading tags—<H1> through <H6>—to format the section titles and set up an outline structure.

➤ You can display white space and carriage returns in preformatted text by enclosing it with the <PRE> and </PRE> tags.

➤ To create a line break, use the <BR> tag.

➤ To run a horizontal line across the page, use the <HR> tag.

A Fistful of List Grist for Your Web Page Mill

Are you making a list and checking it twice? Gonna find out who's naughty and...oops, drifted off to the North Pole for a second! But if you do want to include a list of things in your Web page, what's the best way to go about it? You saw in the last chapter how you can use the
 (line break) tag to display items on separate lines. That works well enough, I guess, but hold your list horses—there's a better way. HTML has a few tags that are specially designed to give you much more control over your list-building chores. In fact, HTML offers no less than three different list styles: numbered lists, bulleted lists, and definition lists. This chapter takes you through the basics of each list type and provides you with plenty of examples.

Putting Your Affairs in Order with Numbered Lists

If you want to include a numbered list of items—it could be a top ten list, bowling league standings, or any kind of ranking—don't bother adding in the numbers yourself. Instead, you can use HTML ordered lists to make the Web browser generate the numbers for you.

Ordered lists use two types of tags:

➤ The entire list is surrounded by the <OL> and </OL> tags.

➤ Each item in the list is preceded by the <LI> (list item) tag.

The general setup looks like this:

```
<OL>
<LI>First item.
<LI>Second item.
<LI>Third item.
<LI>You get the idea.
</OL>
```

Here's an example (see NUMLIST1.HTM on the disk):

```
<HTML>
<HEAD>
<TITLE>Numbered Lists - Example #1</TITLE>
</HEAD>
<BODY>
<H3>My Ten Favorite U.S. City Names</H3>
<OL>
<LI>Toad Suck, Arkansas
<LI>Panic, Pennsylvania
<LI>Dismal, Tennessee
<LI>Boring, Maryland
<LI>Hell, Michigan
<LI>Two Egg, Florida
<LI>Muck City, Alabama
<LI>Rambo Riviera, Arkansas
<LI>King Arthur's Court, Michigan
<LI>Buddha, Indiana
</OL>
</BODY>
</HTML>
```

Notice how I didn't include any numbers before each list item. However, when I display this document in a browser (see the following figure), the numbers get inserted automatically. Pretty slick, huh?

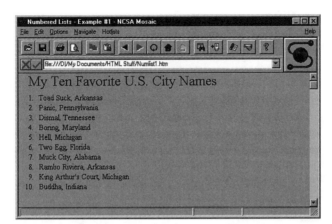

How the numbered list appears in the Mosaic browser (it will look pretty much the same in any browser).

Spice Up Your List Items

Your list items don't have to be just plain text, so you're free to go crazy and insert other HTML tags. For example, you could use <B> and </B> to boldface a word or two in the item, you could use a heading tag to increase the font size of the item, or you could make an item a hypertext link to another Web page (I'll discuss this linking stuff in the next chapter).

The items you toss into your numbered lists don't have to be short words and phrases, however. For example, if you're explaining how to perform a certain task, a numbered list is the perfect way to take your readers through each step. Here's a more involved example (it's NUMLIST2.HTM on the disk) that uses a numbered list to explain how to juggle:

```
<HTML>
<HEAD>
<TITLE>Numbered Lists - Example #2</TITLE>
</HEAD>
<BODY>
<H3>The Complete Idiot's Guide to Juggling</H3>
<HR>
Here are the basic steps for the most fundamental of juggling
moves - the three-ball cascade:
<OL>
<LI>Place two balls in your right hand, one in front of the other,
and hold the third ball in your left hand.
<LI>Of the two balls in your right hand, toss the front one towards
your left hand in a smooth arc. Make sure the ball doesn't spin and
that it goes no higher than about eye level.
```

```
<LI>Once the first ball has reached the top of its arc, you need to
release the ball in your left hand. Throw it towards your right hand,
making sure it flies <I>under</I> the first ball. Again, watch that
the ball doesn't spin or go higher than eye level.
<LI>Now things get a little tricky (!). Soon after you release the
second ball, the first ball will approach your left hand (gravity
never fails). Go ahead and catch the first ball.
<LI>When the second ball reaches its apex, throw the third ball
(the remaining ball in your left hand) under it.
<LI>At this point, it just becomes a game of catch-and-throw-under,
catch-and-throw-under. Keep repeating steps 1-5 and, before you know
it, you'll be a juggling fool. (However, I'd recommend holding off
on the flaming clubs until you've practiced a little.)
</OL>
</BODY>
</HTML>
```

As you can see, most of the items are quite long; although, it's kind of hard to tell where each <LI> item begins and ends. However, as shown in the next figure, the list looks pretty good when viewed in a Web browser (this time I'm using Netscape).

Numbered lists are perfect for outlining the steps in a procedure.

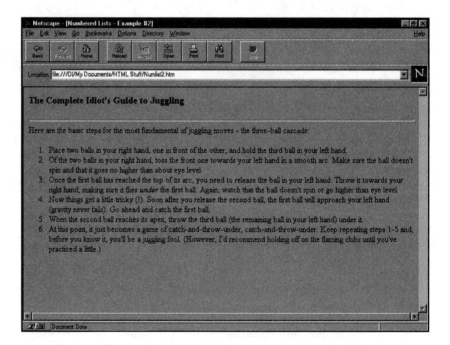

Numbered Lists in HTML 3.0

HTML 3.0 includes a few snazzy options for numbered lists. For example, starting the list with <OL CONTINUE> tells the browser to start this list's numbers where the previous list left off. Similarly, <OL SEQNUM> lets you specify which number to start with (for example, <OL SEQNUM=10>). Also, you can use a new <LH> tag to specify a title for the list. Netscape also has a few extra numbered list goodies (these extras are called "Netscape extensions"). See Chapter 10 to learn about the Netscape extensions for numbered lists.

Scoring Points with Bulleted Lists

Numbered lists, of course, aren't the only kinds of lists. If you just want to enumerate a few points, a bulleted list may be more your style. They're called "bulleted" lists because a Web browser displays a cute little dot or square (depending on the browser) called a *bullet* to the left of each item.

The HTML tags for a bulleted list are pretty close to the ones you saw for a numbered list. As before, you precede each list item with the same <LI> tag, but you enclose the entire list with the <UL> and </UL> tags. Why <UL>? Well, what the rest of the world calls a bulleted list, the HTML powers-that-be call an *unordered list*. Yeah, that's real intuitive. Ah well, here's how they work:

```
<UL>
<LI>First bullet point.
<LI>Fifty-seventh bullet point.
<LI>Sixteenth bullet point.
<LI>Hey, whaddya want-it's an unordered list!
</UL>
```

Here's an HTML document (look for BULLETED.HTM on the disk) that demonstrates how to use the bulleted list tags:

```
<HTML>
<HEAD>
<TITLE>Bulleted List Example</TITLE>
</HEAD>
<BODY>
<H3>Products I'd Like To See</H3>
<UL>
<LI>Water-resistant sponge
<LI>Self-soiling oven
```

```
<LI>Tineless fork
<LI>Silent alarm clock
<LI>Inflatable dartboard
<LI>Teflon bath mat
<LI>Helium-filled paperweight
<LI>Flame-retardant firewood
<LI>Sandpaper bathroom tissue
<LI>Water-soluble dishcloth
</UL>
</BODY>
</HTML>
```

The next figure shows how the NCSA Mosaic browser renders this file, snazzy bullets and all.

A typical bulleted list.

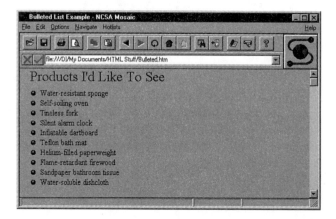

HTML 3.0's Bulleted Lists

When HTML 3.0 finally arrives (and the Web browsers support it), you can have lots of fun with bulleted lists. You can specify one of dozens of bullet styles (called, believe it or not, dingbats) by adding DINGBAT to the <UL> tag (for example, <UL DINGBAT=folder> will give you a bullet that looks like a file folder). You can specify your own bullets by adding SRC to the <UL> tag. For example, if you have an image named MyBullet.gif, you could use it as a bullet like so: <UL SRC="MyBullet.gif">. If you don't want any bullets at all, start the list with <UL PLAIN>.

Definition Lists

The final type of list is called a *definition list.* People used it, originally, for dictionary-like lists where each entry had two parts: a term and the definition of the term. As you'll see, though, definition lists are useful for more than just definitions.

To mark the two different parts of each entry in these lists, you need two different tags. The term is preceded by the <DT> tag, and the definition is preceded by the <DD> tag, like so:

```
<DT>Term<DD>Definition
```

You can, if you like, put the <DT> part and the <DD> part on separate lines, but I prefer this style (and either way, they end up looking the same in the browser). You then surround the whole list with the <DL> and </DL> tags to complete your definition list. Here's how the whole thing looks:

```
<DL>
<DT>A Term<DD>Its Definition
<DT>Another Term<DD>Another Definition
<DT>Yet Another Term<DD>Yet Another Definition
<DT>Etc.<DD>Abbreviation of a Latin phrase that means "and so forth."
</DL>
```

Let's look at a for instance. The HTML document shown next (you'll find it on the disk in the file named DEFNLIST.HTM) uses a definition list to outline a few words and phrases and their definitions. (Notice that I've applied boldfacing to all the terms; this helps them stand out more when the browser displays them.)

```
<HTML>
<HEAD>
<TITLE>Definition List Example</TITLE>
</HEAD>
<BODY>
<H3>Some Techno-Terms You Should Know</H3>
<DL>
<DT><B>Barney Page</B><DD>A Web page that tries to capitalize on a
current craze.
<DT><B>Bit-Spit</B><DD>Any form of digital correspondence.
<DT><B>Byte-Bonding</B><DD>When computer users discuss things that
nearby noncomputer users don't understand. See also <I>geeking out</I>.
<DT><B>Clickstreams</B><DD>The paths a person takes as she negotiates
various Web pages.
<DT><B>Cobweb Page</B><DD>A Web page that hasn't been updated in a while.
```

```
<DT><B>Geek</B><DD>Someone who knows a lot about computers and very
little about anything else.
<DT><B>Geeking Out</B><DD>When <I>geeks</I> who are <I>byte-bonding</I>
start playing with a computer during a non-computer-related social event.
<DT><B>Luser</B><DD>A "loser user." Someone who doesn't have the faintest
idea what they're doing and, more importantly, refuses to do anything about
it.
<DT><B>Nerd</B><DD>A <I>geek</I> totally lacking in personal hygiene and
social skills.
</DL>
</BODY>
</HTML>
```

The following screen shows how the definition list appears in the Netscape scheme of things.

A few definitions arrayed, appropriately enough, in a definition list.

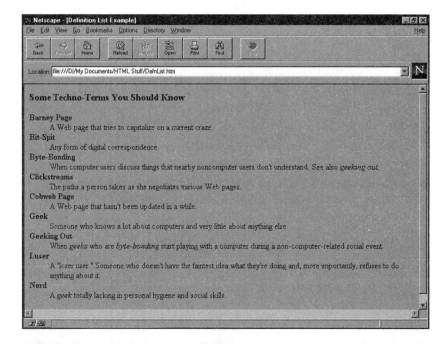

More Than Just Definitions

You'll often see people using definition lists for things other than definitions. Some Web welders like to use the term (the <DT> part) as a section heading and the definition (the <DD> part) as the section text. You can also leave out the term and just use the <DD> tag by itself. This is handy for those times when you need indented text (say, if you're quoting someone at length).

Combining Lists Inside Lists

The three types of HTML lists should stand you in good stead for most of your Web page productions. However, you're free to mix and match various list types to suit the occasion. Specifically, it's perfectly legal to plop one type of list inside another (this is called *nesting lists*). For example, suppose you have a numbered list that outlines the steps involved in some procedure. If you need to augment one of the steps with a few bullet points, you could simply insert a bulleted list after the appropriate numbered list item.

As an example, I'll take the definition list from the last section and toss in both a numbered list and a bulleted list. Here's the result (I've lopped off some of the lines to make it easier to read; you can find the full document on the disk in the file named COMBO.HTM):

```
<DL>
<DT><B>Barney Page</B><DD>A Web page that tries to capitalize on a
current craze. Recent subjects of Barney pages are:

<UL>
<LI>O.J. Simpson
<LI>Windows 95
<LI>1996 Presidential election
</UL>

<DT><B>Bit-Spit</B><DD>Any form of digital correspondence.
<DT><B>Byte-Bonding</B><DD>When computer users discuss things that
nearby noncomputer users don't understand. Here are the three stages
of byte-bonding that inevitably lead to <I>geeking out</I>:

<OL>
<LI>"Say, did you see that IBM ad where the nuns are talking about surfing
the Net?"
<LI>"Do you surf the Net?"
<LI>"Let's go surf the Net!"
</OL>

<DT><B>Clickstreams</B><DD>The paths a person takes as she negotiates
various Web pages.
...
</DL>
```

After the first definition list entry—the one for Barney Page—I've inserted a bulleted list that gives a few examples. (I've added blank lines above and below the bulleted list to make it stand out better. Note that I added these lines for cosmetic purposes only; they don't affect how the page appears in the browser.) Then, after the third definition list entry—Byte-Bonding—I've put in a numbered list. The following screen shows how all this looks when a browser gets hold of it.

HTML is more than happy to let you insert lists inside each other.

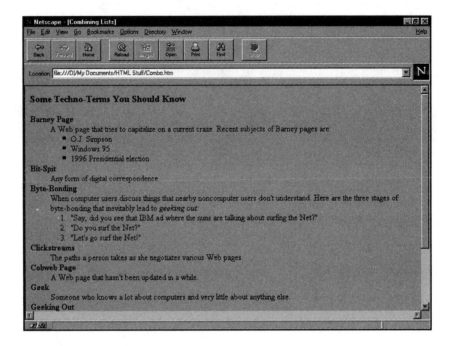

The Least You Need to Know

This chapter took you through the wacky world of HTML lists. You may not need to use them all that often, but they can really come in handy. Just to make sure all this sinks in (where it sinks to is your business), here's a recap of some of the sights you saw along the way:

➤ Numbered lists are useful for rankings, procedures, and people who just like to count things. Each item is preceded by a <LI> tag, and the whole list is bracketed by the <OL> and </OL> tags.

➤ Bulleted lists let you display point-form comments in your Web page. Again, each item gets an <LI> tag out front, and the list sits inside <UL> and </UL> tags.

➤ Definition lists are useful for dictionary-style entries, or even for document sections (where the term is the section heading and the definition is the section text). Use the <DT> tag for the term, the <DD> tag for the definition, and surround everything with the <DL> and </DL> tags.

➤ It's no problem combining one type of list inside another type (or even, for that matter, the same type).

Chapter 7

Making the Jump to Hyperspace: Adding Links

In This Chapter

➤ Some URL fundamentals

➤ Creating links to other Web pages

➤ Creating links to other locations in your Web page

➤ Creating links that send e-mail messages

➤ Easy hypertext help that'll have your Web pages fully linked in no time flat

There is, of course, no shortage of buzzwords buzzing around the Internet community. Words such as *bandwidth*, *domain*, and *protocol* are bandied about like so many linguistic Ping-Pong balls. My vote for the current champ in the Most Overused Buzzword category is *interactive*. Everything's "interactive this" or "interactive that." Sheesh! These people must hate watching TV, because they can't *interact* with it (or else they sit on their couches with visions of interactive TV set-top boxes and Gilligan's Island reruns on-demand dancing in their heads).

Still, as a Web page publisher, you've gotta give the people what they want, right? Unfortunately, truly interactive Web pages are still on the bleeding edge of Web technology (I'll talk about some of this stuff in Chapter 14, "Hack to the Future: What's Ahead for HTML and the Web"). And the semi-interactive Web pages that are quite common (they're called *forms*) can't be created without recourse to some heavy-duty programming, and so are well beyond the scope of this book (aren't you glad to hear *that*).

However, there is a way to throw at least a small interactive bone to the readers of your Web creations: give 'em a few hypertext links that they can follow to the four corners of the Web world (or even just to another part of your own cyberspace plot). It's an easy way to give your pages a dynamic feel that'll have people coming back for more. This chapter explains links and shows you how to put the "hypertext" into HTML.

The URL of Net: A Cyberspace Address Primer

Before the hypertext festivities commence, there's a bit of background info I need to slog through for you. As I mentioned in Chapter 2, a *hypertext link* is a special word or phrase in a Web page that, when the user clicks on it, takes her to a different Web document (or to an FTP site, or whatever). I also mentioned in Chapter 2 that each Web page (and, indeed, any Internet resource) has its own address, called a *Uniform Resource Locator* (or URL, for short).

When you combine these two factoids, you realize that for a hypertext link to work properly, you need to know the correct address of the resource to which you're linking. And to do that, you need to understand the anatomy of these URL things. Unfortunately, the whole URL concept seems to have been invented by some insane Geek of Geeks who never believed normal human beings would actually use the darn things. They're long, they're confusing, they're messy, and they're almost impossible to type correctly the first time. Not to worry, though; I've gone *mano a mano* with this URL foofaraw, and I've come up with a plan that's designed to knock some sense into the whole mess.

The idea is that, like journalists and their 5 Ws (who, what, where, when, and why), you can reduce any URL to 3 Ws (who, what, and where) and an H (how). So the basic form of any URL ends up looking like so:

```
How://Who/Where/What
```

Hmm. I'm definitely talking serious weirdness here, so let's see what the heck I mean by all that:

How   The first part of a URL specifies how the data is going to be transferred across Net lines. This is called the *protocol* and, luckily, mere mortals like you and I don't need to concern ourselves with the guts of this stuff. All you need to know is which protocol each resource uses, which is easy. For example, the World Wide Web uses something called HTTP (I'll tell you which protocols other resources use later in this chapter). So the "how" part of a URL is the protocol, followed by a colon (:) and two slashes (//). (I told you this stuff was arcane; it makes alchemy look like "The Cat In the Hat.") So a Web page URL always starts like so (lowercase letters are the norm, but they're not necessary):

```
http://
```

Who   Calling the next part the "who" of a URL is, I admit, a bit of a misnomer because there's no person involved. Instead, it's the name of the computer where the resource is located—in geek circles, this is called the *host name*. (This is the part of an Internet address that has all those dots you're always hearing, such as ncsa.uiuc.edu or www.yahoo.com.) For example, my home page is located on a computer named www.logophilia.com. You just tack this "who" part onto the end of the "how" part, as shown here:

```
http://www.logophilia.com
```

Where   The next part of the address specifies where the resource is located on the computer. This generally means the directory the resource is stored in; the directory may be something like /pages or /pub/junk/software. My home page is in my personal directory, which is /Home. (To get your own directory, you need to sign up with a company that puts pages on the Web; see Chapter 9 for details.) So now you just staple the directory onto the URL and then add another slash on the end, for good measure:

```
http://www.logophilia.com/Home/
```

What   Almost there. The "what" part is just the name of the file you want to use. For a Web page, you use the name of the document that contains the HTML codes and text. The file containing my home page is called homepage.html, so here's the full URL:

```
http://www.logophilia.com/Home/homepage.html
```

Check This Out...

Make Sure You're on the Case

I mentioned earlier that you can use uppercase or lowercase letters (the latter are normally used) for the "how" part of a URL. The same is true for the "who" part, but case is crucial when entering the directory and filename. Most Internet computers use an operating system called UNIX, which is notoriously finicky about uppercase versus lowercase. If you enter even a single letter in a directory or filename in the wrong case, you won't get to where you want to go.

Got all that? Yeah, I know—it's as clear as mud. Well, have no fear. If you can keep the how, who, where, and what idea in your head, it'll all sink in eventually.

Getting Hyper: Creating Links in HTML

Okay, with that drivel out of the way, it's time to put your newfound know-how to work (assuming, that is, I haven't scarred you for life!). To wit, this section shows you how to use HTML to add hypertext links to your Web page.

The HTML tags that do the link thing are <A> and </A>. (Why "A"? Well, as you'll find out later on—see the section "Anchors Aweigh: Internal Links"—you can create special links called *anchors* that send your readers to other parts of the same document, instead of to a different document.) The <A> tag is a little different from the other tags you've seen (you just knew it would be). Specifically, you don't use it by itself but, instead, you shoehorn into it the URL of your link. Here's how it works:

```
<A HREF="URL">
```

Here, HREF stands for *Hypertext REFerence*. Just replace *URL* with the actual URL of the Web page you want to use for the link (and, yes, you have to enclose the address in quotation marks). Here's an example:

```
<A HREF="http://www.logophilia.com/Home/homepage.html">
```

Now you can see why I made you suffer through all that URL poppycock earlier: it's crucial for getting the <A> tag to work properly.

You're not done yet, though; not by a long shot (insert groan of disappointment here). What are you missing? Right, you have to give the reader some descriptive link text on which to click. Happily, that's easier done than said because all you do is insert the text between the <A> and </A> tags, like so:

```
<A HREF="URL">Link text goes here</A>
```

Need an example? You got it (see the file LINK2.HTM on the disk):

```
Why not head to my
<A HREF="http://www.logophilia.com/Home/homepage.html">home page</A>?
```

Here's how it looks in a Web browser. Notice how the browser highlights and underlines the link text and when I point my mouse at the link, the URL I specified appears in the status bar.

How the hypertext link appears in Mosaic.

The URL of my home page appears in the browser's status bar.

The link that will take you to my home page.

Hypertext links are generally divided into two categories: external and internal. An *external link* is one that sends the person who clicks it to a different document. You have two choices here: you can link to a Web page in a different directory or on a different system (I call this a "faraway" link), or you can link to a Web page in the same directory as the current page (I call this a "nearby" link). An *internal link* (an anchor) sends the reader to a different part of the same document. The next few sections describe each type of link.

External Links to Faraway Pages

The most common type of link is one that whisks the reader off to a page at some other Web site. Many Webmeisters use these kinds of external links to provide their readers with a quick method of surfing to related sites. For example, if you're putting together a page extolling the virtues of, say, the Helsinki Formula, you may want to include some links to pages about Helsinki or Finland or even The Man From U.N.C.L.E. For these types of links, make sure your <A> tag includes the full address of the new location, as described in the preceding section.

Lots of pages also include links that point to the author's fave rave Web sites and to those sites that the author deems "cool." These so-called "hot lists" are a popular item on home pages, and they can be fun for surfers (providing, of course, they share the Web page creator's taste in what's cool).

Check This Out...

An Easy Way to Create a "Hot Links" Page

Most modern browsers enable you to store your favorite Web pages as bookmarks that you can call up anytime. The good news is that these browsers usually store all your bookmarks in an HTML document! (In Netscape, for example, bookmarks are stored in a file named BOOKMARK.HTM. In NCSA Mosaic version 2, the Advanced Hotlist Manager's File menu has an Export to HTML File command.) You can use this document as a starting point for your hot links page.

External Links to Nearby Pages

When putting together Web pages, the operating principle is "Bet you can't create just one!" That is, people usually get so juiced by getting a page on the Web that they're inspired to do it once more from the top. It's not at all unusual for a prolific Websmith to have five, ten, or even 20 different pages!

Chances are that if you create more than one Web page at least a few of your pages will be related, so you'll probably want to include links that take your readers to other examples of your Web handiwork. You'll probably store all your Web pages in the same directory, so the how, who, and where parts of the URL will be the same as the current document. For example, compare the URL of my home page with the URL of another HTML file I use called guestbook.html:

```
http://www.logophilia.com/Home/homepage.html
http://www.logophilia.com/Home/guestbook.html
```

As you can see, the two addresses are identical right up to (but not including) the filenames. This is good because if I want to include a link to guestbook.html in my home page, I only have to include the filename in the <A> tag. That's right: if you're creating a link to a document in the same directory, you can simply lop off the how, who, and where parts of the URL. Here's how such a link looks:

```
Please sign my <A HREF="guestbook.html">Guest Book</A>
```

Anchors Aweigh: Internal Links

Most of your HTML pages will probably be short and sweet, and the Web surfers who drop by will have no trouble navigating their way around. But if, like me, you suffer from a bad case of terminal verbosity combined with bouts of extreme longwindedness, you'll end up with Web pages that are lengthy, to say the least. Rather than force your readers to scroll through your tome-like creations, you can set up links to various sections of the document. You can then assemble these links at the top of the page to form a sort of "hypertable of contents."

Unlike the links you've looked at so far, internal links don't connect to a different document. Instead, they link to a special version of the <A> tag—called an anchor—that you've inserted somewhere in the same document. To understand how anchors work, think of how you might mark a spot in a book you're reading. You might dog-ear the page, attach a Post-It note, or place something between the pages such as a bookmark or your cat's tail.

An anchor performs the same function: it "marks" a particular spot in a Web page, and you can then use a regular <A> tag to link to that spot.

I think an example is in order. Suppose I want to create a hypertext version of this chapter. (As a matter of fact, I did! Look for the file named CHAPTER7.HTM on the disk.) To make it easy to navigate, I want to include a table of contents at the top of the page that includes links to all the section headings. My first chore is to add anchor tags to each heading. Here's the general format for an anchor:

```
<A NAME="Name">Anchor text goes here</A>
```

As you can see, an anchor tag looks a lot like a regular hypertext link tag. The only difference is that the HREF part is replaced by NAME="*Name*"; *Name* is the name you want to give the anchor. You can use whatever you like for the name, but most people choose relatively short names to save typing. For example, this chapter's first section is titled "The URL of Net: A Cyberspace Address Primer." If I want to give this section the uninspired name Section1, I use the following anchor:

```
<A NAME="Section1">The URL of Net: A Cyberspace Address Primer</A>
```

Now, when I set up my table of contents, I can create a link to this section by using a regular <A> tag (with the HREF thing) that points to the section's name. And, just so a Web browser doesn't confuse the anchor name with the name of another document, I preface the anchor name with a number sign (#). Here's how it looks:

```
<A HREF="#Section1">The URL of Net: A Cyberspace Address Primer</A>
```

Just so you get the big picture, here's an excerpt from the HTML file for this chapter (the figure shows how it looks in a browser):

```
<H3>Hypertable of Contents:</H3>
<DL>
  <DD><A HREF="#Section1">The URL of Net: A Cyberspace Address Primer</A>
  <DD><A HREF="#Section2">Getting Hyper: Creating Links in HTML</A>
  <DL>
    <DD><A HREF="#Section2a">External Links to Faraway Pages</A>
    <DD><A HREF="#Section2b">External Links to Nearby Pages</A>
    <DD><A HREF="#Section2c">Anchors Aweigh: Internal Links</A>
  </DL>
  <DD><A HREF="#Section3">Creating an E-Mail Link</A>
  <DD><A HREF="#Section4">The Least You Need to Know</A>
</DL>
<HR>
[Rambling introduction goes here]
<A NAME="Section1"><H2>The URL of Net: A Cyberspace Address Primer</H2></A>
```

The hypertext version of this chapter.

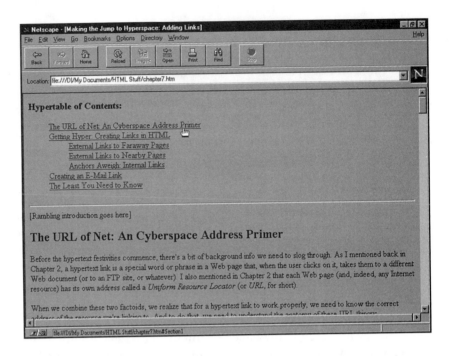

Dropping Anchor in Other Pages

Although you'll mostly use anchors to link to sections of the same Web page, there's no law against using them to link to specific sections of other pages. All you do is add the appropriate anchor to the other page and then link to it by adding the anchor's name (preceded, as usual by #) to the end of the page's filename. For example, here's a tag that sets up a link to a section named Grumpy in an HTML file named dwarves.html:

```
<A HREF="dwarves.html#Grumpy">Info on Grumpy</A>
```

Creating an E-Mail Link

As I mentioned earlier, there's no reason a link has to lead to a Web page. In fact, all you have to do is alter the "how" part of a URL, and you can connect to most other Internet services, including FTP and UseNet.

In this section, however, I'll concentrate on the most common type of non-Web link: e-mail. In this case, someone clicking on an e-mail link will be presented with a screen (assuming their browser supports this kind of link, which most recent browsers do) they can use to send a message to your e-mail address. Now that's interactive!

This type of link is called a *mailto link* because you include the word `mailto` in the `<A>` tag. Here's the general form:

```
<A HREF="mailto:YourEmailAddress">The link text goes here</A>
```

Here, `YourEmailAddress` is your Internet e-mail address. For example, suppose I want to include an e-mail link in one of my Web pages. My e-mail address is paul@logophilia.com, so I'd set up the link as follows:

```
You can write to me at my
<A HREF="mailto:paul@mcfedries.com">e-mail address.</A>
```

The next figure shows how it looks in NSCA Mosaic.

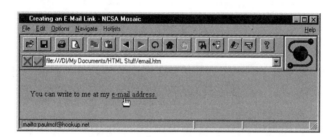

A Web page with an e-mail link.

How to Link to Other Net Resources

If you want to try your hand at linking to other Net resources, here's a rundown of the type of URLs to use:

Resource	URL
FTP (directory)	ftp://Who/Where/
FTP (file)	ftp://Who/Where/What
Gopher	gopher://Who/
UseNet	news:*newsgroup.name*
Telnet	telnet://Who

Note that who, where, and what are the same as I defined them earlier in this chapter. Also, *newsgroup.name* is just the name of the newsgroup that has articles you want to see. Note that not all browsers support all of these resources.

The Least You Need to Know

This chapter gave you the lowdown on using HTML to include hypertext links in your Web pages. Here's a review of today's top stories:

➤ To make URLs easier to figure out, you can break them down into four sections: how (the protocol, such as http, followed by ://); who (the host name, such as www.logophilia.com); where (the directory, such as /Home/); and what (the filename, such as homepage.html).

➤ The basic structure of an HTML hypertext link is `<A HREF="URL">Link text</A>`.

➤ If the page you're linking to is in the same directory as the current document, you can get away with specifying only the filename in the link's URL.

➤ To create an anchor, use the following variation on the `<A>` tag theme: `<A NAME="Name">Anchor text</A>`.

➤ To set up a link to the anchor, use this tag: `<A HREF="#Name">Link text</A>`.

➤ E-mail links use the `mailto` form of the `<A>` tag: `<A HREF="mailto:EmailAddress">Link Text</A>`.

A Picture Is Worth a Thousand Clicks: Working with Images

In This Chapter

➤ A quick look at some image basics

➤ Using the <IMG> tag to insert an image on your Web page

➤ How to make text and images get along together

➤ Turning an image into a hypertext link

➤ Adding the finishing touches to your Web page with icons, bullets, buttons, and other graphical glad rags

You've probably seen those TV ads proclaiming in no uncertain terms (true hipsters are never uncertain about their hipness) that "image is everything." You know they couldn't put it on TV if it wasn't true (!), so you need to think about what kind of image your Web pages present to the outside world.

You've seen how tossing a few text tags, a list or two, and a liberal dose of links can do wonders for drab, lifeless pages. But face it: anybody can do that kind of stuff. If you're looking to make your Web abode really stand out from the crowd, you need to go graphical with a few well-chosen images. To that end, this chapter gives you the ins and outs of images, including some background info on the various graphics formats, tags for inserting images, how to turn an image into a hypertext link, and lots more.

Images: Some Semi-Important Background Info

Before you get down to brass tacks and start trudging through the HTML tags that'll plop pictures onto your pages, there are a few things I need to discuss. Not to worry, though; it's nothing that's overly technical. (That, of course, would be contrary to Idiot's Guide bylaw 4.17c: "Thou shalt not cause the eyes of thy readers to glaze over with interminable technical claptrap.") Instead, I'll just look at a few things that'll help you choose and work with images, and that should help make all this stuff a bit clearer.

No, Images Aren't Text, But That's Okay

First off, let me answer the main question that's probably running through your mind even now about all this graphics rumpus:

If the innards of a Web page are really just text and HTML tags, then how in the name of h-e-double-hockey-sticks am I supposed to get an image in there?

Hey, that's a darn good question. Here's the easy answer: you don't.

Huh?

Yeah. As you'll see later on (in the section "The Nitty-Gritty, At Last: The <IMG> Tag"), all you'll really be doing is, for each image you want to use, adding a tag to the document that says, in effect, "Yo! Insert image here." That tag specifies the name of the graphics file, so the browser just opens the file and displays the image.

Well, I should say that the browser *probably* displays the image. Different browsers handle graphics in different ways, so you need to make allowances:

➤ Some browsers (such as Lynx) are ham-fisted when it comes to graphics, so they display only text. There are things you can do to make life easier for the users of these browsers, however, and I'll talk about them in the section titled "Handling Graphically-Challenged Text Browsers."

➤ If the browser knows how to handle an image, it displays it in the Web page without kicking up a fuss. These kinds of graphics are called *inline images*, and they're the preferred kind for most Webmeisters. As long as you use the right type of graphics format (which I'll talk about in the next section), most modern browsers display your graphics inline.

➤ If the browser balks at your image, you have to hope the reader has set up her browser to use some kind of graphics program to display the image in a separate window. These are called *external images*, and they're a poor substitute for inline images. Again, you can avoid this fate by using the right kinds of graphics.

Graphics Formats: Can't We All Just Get Along?

Some computer wag once said that the nice thing about standards is that there are so many of them! Graphics files are no exception. It seems that every geek who ever gawked at a graphic has invented his own format for storing them on disk. And talk about alphabet soup! Why, there are images in GIF, JPEG, BMP, PCX, TIFF, DIB, EPS, and TGA formats, and those are just off the top of my head. How's a budding Web page architect supposed to make sense of all this acronymic anarchy?

Well, my would-be Web welders, I bring tidings of great joy. You can toss most of that graphic traffic into the digital scrap heap, because the Web has standardized on just two formats, one of which is used in 90 percent of all Web imagery! Oh happy day!

The format that Web creators use almost exclusively in Web pages is GIF (which, just so you know, stands for Graphics Interchange Format). All graphical browsers are fully GIF-aware, so they display these images within a Web page without getting all hot and bothered. This means you can include GIF files in your Web pages willy-nilly, safe in the knowledge that the vast majority of your readers will be able to see the pics in all their glory.

GIFs: Not a Royalty-Pain-In-the-You-Know-What, After All

The GIF format was invented by CompuServe, and it takes advantage of compression technology from a company called Unisys. You might have heard some hubbub at the end of 1994 to the effect that Unisys was going to start enforcing its technology patent and charge royalties for the use of GIFs. That tempest turned out to be teapot-based, and in the end nothing much changed. So, in case you were wondering, you're free to use GIFs all you want in your Web pages. (Provided, of course, you're not infringing the copyright of the artist who created the image. Stay tuned for more on this.)

The other format that's becoming increasingly popular on the Web is JPEG (which gets its name from the Joint Photographic Experts Group that invented it; gee, don't they sound like a fun bunch of guys to hang out with?). The main advantage of JPEG files is that, given the same image, they're smaller than GIFs, so they take less time to download. Unfortunately, only a few browsers (such as Netscape and Mosaic) know how to handle JPEG images inline, so you're probably better off sticking with GIFs for now. The only exception is for digitized photographs and other high-quality images. The GIF format doesn't display these graphics very well, so JPEG is almost always a better choice.

How Do I Get Graphics?

The text part of a Web page is, at least from a production standpoint, a piece of cake for most folks. After all, even the most pathetic typist can peck out at least a few words a minute. Graphics, on the other hand, are another kettle of digital fish entirely. Creating a snazzy logo or eye-catching illustration requires a modicum of artistic talent, which is a bit harder to come by than basic typing skills.

However, if you have such talent, then you're laughing: just create the image in your favorite paint program and save it in GIF format. (If your program gives you several GIF options, use GIF87 or, even better, GIF89, if possible. If the software doesn't know GIF from a hole in the ground, I'll show you how to convert the file in the next section.)

The non-artists in the crowd will have to obtain their graphics goodies from some other source. Fortunately, there's no shortage of images floating around. Here are some ideas:

➤ Many software packages (including Microsoft Office and most paint and illustration programs) come with clip art libraries. Clip art is professional-quality artwork that you can freely incorporate in your own designs. If you don't have a program that comes with its own clip art, most software stores have CD-ROMs for sale that are chock-full of clip art images.

➤ Grab an image from a Web page. When your browser displays a Web page with an image, the corresponding graphics file is stored temporarily on your computer's hard disk. Most browsers have a command that lets you save that file permanently. Here are some examples:

> **Netscape**—Right-click on the graphic and choose **Save this Image as** from the menu that appears.

> **NCSA Mosaic**—Right-click on the image, choose **Save Image** from the menu, and then choose **Remote Site Format**.

> **Internet Explorer**—Right-click on the graphic and then select **Save Picture As** from the shortcut menu.

➤ Take advantage of the many graphics archives on the Internet. There are sites all over the Net that store dozens, even hundreds, of images. I'll give you some specifics in Chapter 13, "Some HTML Resources on the Web."

➤ If you have access to a scanner, you can use it to digitize photos, illustrations, doodles, or whatever. Alternatively, if you have a fax modem and fax software, and you don't mind a black and white picture, you can send yourself an image as a fax. You capture the fax using your software and then load the image into a graphics program for editing.

The Copyright Conundrum

Don't forget that many images are the property of the individuals who created them in the first place. Unless you're sure the picture is in the public domain, you'll need to get permission from the artist before using it. This is particularly true if your Web page has a commercial slant.

➤ Use the images that come with this book. I've included a few small GIFs on this book's disk that I hope will come in handy. The following screen displays a few of these graphics along with their filenames.

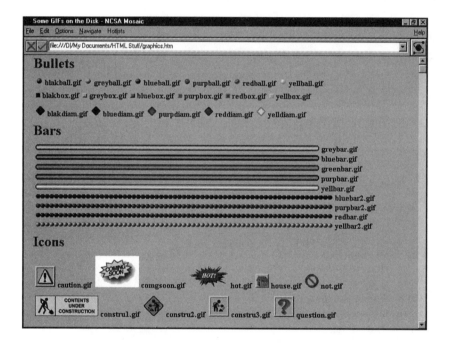

Some of the sample images that are included at no extra cost on this book's disk.

Converting Graphics to GIF Format

What do you do if you've got the perfect image for your Web page, but it's not in GIF format? No sweat. There are plenty of programs out there that do nothing but convert graphics files from one format to another. In fact, I've included one of them on this book's disk. It's called LView, and it does the job as pretty as you please. Here's how:

1. Start LView. (If LView isn't installed yet, see "The Goodies on the Disk," at the back of the book for instructions.) If you get a warning telling you that the current graphics mode is not suited for 24-bit images, nod your head knowingly and select **OK** to continue.

2. Pull down the **File** menu and select the **Open** command to display the Open File dialog box.

3. In the List files of type box, select the graphics format that the file currently uses. For example, if the file is in BMP format, you select Windows (***.bmp, *.dib**).

4. Find the file you want to convert, highlight it in the File name list, and then select **OK**. LView opens the file.

5. Select the File menu's **Save as** command. (If the image is small, you might see only the "F" of the File menu. In this case, you can still pull down the menu normally, or you can maximize the window to get the full menu names.) LView displays the Save File As dialog box.

6. In the Save file as type box, select the **GIF 87a (*.gif)** option.

7. Enter a name for the file in the File name text box. (Make sure you keep the ".gif" extension. Also, if you're running Windows 95, you can avoid confusion later on by entering the name entirely in lowercase letters; don't include any spaces in the name, either.)

8. Select **OK**. LView saves the graphic in GIF format.

The Nitty-Gritty, At Last: The <IMG> Tag

Okay, enough of that. Let's get the lead out and start squeezing some images onto our Web pages. As I mentioned earlier, there's an HTML code that tells a browser to display an image: the <IMG> tag. Here's how it works:

```
<IMG SRC="filename">
```

Here, "SRC" is short for "source" and *filename* is the name of the graphics file you want to display. For example, suppose you have an image named logo.gif. To add it to your page, you use the following line:

```
<IMG SRC="logo.gif">
```

Let's check out a real world example. I'm constantly tinkering with my home page, modifying existing pages, pruning dead wood (I do a lot of that!), and adding new stuff. Until my new pages are ready, however, I don't subject my visitors to them. Instead, I just display a generic page (I call it the "Procrastination Page") that tells people the new module isn't quite ready for prime time just yet.

If you'd like something similar for your Web pages, here's some HTML code that'll do the job (look for the file named UNDERCON.HTM on the disk):

```
<HTML>
<HEAD>
<TITLE>Detour!</TITLE>
</HEAD>
<BODY>
<IMG SRC="constru1.gif">
<H2>Web Work In Progress!</H2>
<HR>
Sorry for all the mess, but I haven't quite got around to
implementing this section yet. Hopefully I'll have everything
up and running real soon.
<P>
<A HREF="homepage.html">Click here to go back to my home page.</A>
</BODY>
</HTML>
```

To emphasize the "work in progress" feel, this page includes a small graphic (constru1.gif) that says "Contents Under Construction" and shows a construction worker in action (see the next screen). Note, too, that the page includes a link that gives the reader an easy way to get back to your home page. (In the <A> tag, make sure you change "homepage.html" to the appropriate name of your home page; see Chapter 7 if you need a refresher course on this link stuff.)

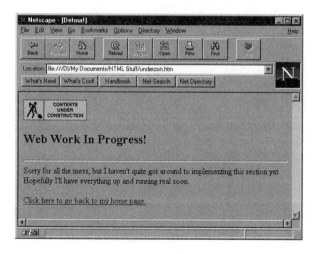

A Web page to use as a substitute for pages you're still slaving away at.

Good Uses for Images on Your Web Page

Images are endlessly useful, and they're an easy way to give your page a professional look and feel. Although I'm sure you can think of all kinds of ways to put pictures to work, here are a few suggestions:

➤ A company logo on a business-related page

➤ Graphics from an ad

➤ Drawings done by the kids in a paint program

➤ Charts and graphs

➤ Fancy-schmancy fonts

➤ Your signature

➤ Using a graphic line in place of the <HR> tag

➤ Using graphic bullets to create a better bulleted list

You might be wondering how to do that last item. Well, there are a number of ways to go about it, but the one I use is to create a definition list (see Chapter 6) and precede each item in the list with a graphic bullet. For example, the file redball.gif on the disk is a small, red, 3-D sphere. To use this as a "bullet," you put together a definition list, like so:

```
<DL>
<DD><IMG SRC="redball.gif">First item
<DD><IMG SRC="redball.gif">Second item
<DD><IMG SRC="redball.gif">Third item
</DL>
```

Check This Out...

Graphics Are Slooooooowwwwww

Although graphics have a thousand-and-one uses, that doesn't mean you should include a thousand-and-one images in each page. Bear in mind that many of your readers will be accessing your site from a slow modem link, so graphics will take forever to load. If you have too many images, most folks will give up and head somewhere else.

Aligning Text and Images

In the "Work In Progress" example you saw earlier, the image appears on a line by itself. However, that only happened because I used a heading tag—<H2>—immediately after the <IMG> tag, and heading tags always start on a fresh line. However, if you insert an image inside regular page text, the browser will display the image and the text on the same line. (Now you know why images that appear in a Web page are called *inline images*.)

This is all very reasonable, but you might run into problems with tall images, because the bottom of the image is aligned with the bottom of the line. If you prefer your text to appear at the top of the image, or even in the middle, the <IMG> tag has an extra ALIGN attribute that you can use. Here's how it works:

```
<IMG SRC="filename" ALIGN=TOP¦MIDDLE¦BOTTOM>
```

Here, ¦MIDDLE¦BOTTOM means you use either TOP, MIDDLE, or BOTTOM to specify the alignment you want. The following HTML listing (ALIGN.HTM) gives you a demo (the next screen shows the results):

```
<HTML>
<HEAD>
<TITLE>Aligning Text and Images</TITLE>
</HEAD>
<BODY>
<IMG SRC="constru1.gif" ALIGN=TOP>This text appears at the top of the
  image.
<P>
<IMG SRC="constru1.gif" ALIGN=MIDDLE>This text appears in the middle of
  the image.
<P>
<IMG SRC="constru1.gif" ALIGN=BOTTOM>This text appears at the bottom of
  the image.
</BODY>
</HTML>
```

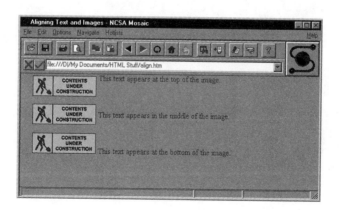

The <IMG> tag's ALIGN options.

91

Handling Graphically Challenged Text Browsers

As I mentioned earlier, some browsers are text-only and wouldn't know how to display a graphics file if it bit them in the face. Instead, they usually just display [IMAGE] in the spot where your <IMG> tag appears, and then they wash their hands of this whole graphics rigmarole.

That looks pretty ugly (and not particularly descriptive, either), so you should have mercy on the image-deprived users of such browsers. How? Well, the <IMG> tag has an extra ALT attribute you can throw in to provide some alternative text that appears in place of the image. Here's the general format:

```
<IMG SRC="filename" ALT="[alternative text]">
```

Here, *alternative text* is whatever text you want to use instead of the graphic. For example, if you have a picture of your hometown in your page, you can display [A lovely pic of my hometown] (it's traditional to enclose these things in square brackets) with the following line:

```
<IMG SRC="hometown.gif" ALT="[A lovely pic of my hometown]">
```

In most cases, though, it's best not to trouble text-only Web surfers with descriptions of images. So most Web authors display a blank instead of a description, like so:

```
<IMG SRC="hometown.gif" ALT=" ">
```

Check This Out...

Another Reason to Use ALT

If you think the number of Internauts using text-only browsers is too small for you to bother with the ALT attribute, here's another reason: Most graphical browsers allow you to turn off the display of images. This feature is a favorite among people with slow Internet connections, so there may be more people in "text mode" than you think.

Images Can Be Links, Too

You might think that Web page images are all show and no go, but I assure you they can "go" with the best of them. Specifically, I mean you can use them as hypertext links, just like regular text. The reader just clicks on the image, and he/she goes off to whatever corner of the Web you specify.

Designating an image as a hypertext link is not a whole lot different from using text (which I covered in the last chapter). You use the same <A> tag, but you insert an <IMG> tag between the <A> and </A>, like this:

```
<A HREF="URL"><IMG SRC="filename"></A>
```

For example, it's often a good idea to include a link back to your home page from all of your other Web pages. This makes it easy for your readers to start over again. Here's a document (BACKHOME.HTM on the disk) that sets up an image of a house as the link back to the home page:

```
<HTML>
<HEAD>
<TITLE>Images Can Be Links, Too</TITLE>
</HEAD>
<BODY>
Click on this house <A HREF="homepage.html"><IMG SRC="house.gif"></A>
to return to my home page.
</BODY>
</HTML>
```

The next screen shows how it looks. Notice how the browser displays a border around the image to identify it as a link. If you prefer not to see this border, add BORDER=0 to your <IMG> tag:

```
<IMG SRC="house.gif" BORDER=0>
```

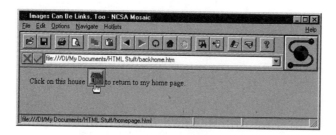

An image masquerading as a hypertext link.

The Least You Need to Know

This chapter showed you how to turn your Web pages into veritable works of art by adding an image or two. Here's the *Reader's Digest* condensed version of what happened:

➤ Inline images appear directly in a Web page. External images can only be viewed by using a separate graphics program.

➤ There are billions and billions of graphics formats floating around, but only two are used extensively on the Web: GIF and JPEG (and the vast majority of sites use GIFs).

➤ Other than your own artistic endeavors, graphics are available from clip art libraries, other Web pages, Internet archives, via scanner or fax, and on the disk that accompanies this book.

➤ If you have a non-GIF graphic, use the LView program that comes on the disk to convert it into GIF format.

➤ To add an image to your Web page, include the `<IMG SRC="filename">` tag, where *filename* is the name of the graphics file.

➤ To make an image a hypertext link, use the <A> tag and replace the usual link text with an <IMG> tag: `<A HREF="URL"><IMG SRC="filename"></A>`.

GOD HELP US.

idiot's
THE PAGE!
★ ★ ★ ★ ★

Chapter 9

Publishing Your Page on the Web

In This Chapter

➤ A rundown of the various choices for publishing your page

➤ A review of some companies that will put your pages on the Web (page hosting providers)

➤ How to get your Web pages to the provider

➤ Advertising your page

➤ A blow-by-blow description of the whole Web page publishing thing

I've covered a lot of ground in the past few chapters, and no doubt you've worked liked the proverbial Trojan applying the electronic equivalent of spit and polish to buff your Web page to an impressive sheen. However, there's still one task you need to perform before you can cross "Make Web Page" off your to-do list. I'm talking, of course, about getting your page published on the Web so surfers the world over can eyeball your creation.

This chapter shows you how to help your Web pages emigrate from their native land (your hard disk) to the New World (the Web). I'll show you how to best prepare them for the journey, how to select a mode of transportation and an ultimate destination, and how to settle your pages once they've arrived.

A Plethora of Web Publishing Possibilities

The third most common question posed by Web page publishing neophytes is "Where the heck do I put my page when I'm done?" (The most common question, in case you're wondering, is "How do I get started?" The second most common question is "Why is Jerry Lewis so popular in France?") If you've asked that question yourself, then you're doing okay because it means you're clued into something crucial: Just because you've created a Web page and you have an Internet connection, it doesn't mean your page is automatically a part of the Web.

The reasons for this are mind-numbingly technical, but the basic idea is that people on the Net have no way of "getting to" your computer and, even if they did, your computer isn't set up to hand out documents (such as Web pages) to visitors who ask for them. (Yes, it is possible to get your machine to do this, but it requires a Ph.D. in programming, electrical engineering, and geekhood.)

Computers that can do this are called *servers* (because they "serve" stuff out to the Net), and computers that specialize in distributing Web pages are called *Web servers*. So, to get to the point at long last, your Web page isn't on the Web until you store it on a Web server. (Since this computer is, in effect, playing "host" to your pages, such machines are also called *Web hosts*. Companies that run these Web hosts are called *hosting providers*.)

Okay, that's all more or less reasonable. Now, just how does one go about finding one of these Web server thingamajigs? Well, the answer to that depends on a bunch of factors, including the type of page you have, how you got connected to the Internet in the first place, and how much money you're willing to shell out for the privilege. In the end, you have three choices:

➤ Use your existing Internet provider

➤ Try to find a free hosting provider

➤ Sign up with a commercial hosting provider

Use Your Existing Internet Provider

If you access the Internet via a corporate or educational network, your institution may have its own Web server that you can use. If you get your Net jollies through an access provider, ask them if they have a Web server available. Many providers will put up personal pages free of charge.

Try to Find a Free Hosting Provider

If you qualify, there are a few hosting providers that will bring your Web pages in from the cold out of the goodness of their hearts. What do I mean by "qualify?" Well, in most cases, these services are open only to specific groups, such as students, artists, non-profit organizations, less fortunate members of the Partridge Family, and so on. The following table lists a few of these do-gooder services that you might want to check out.

One-Click Host Shopping

For your shopping convenience, I've gathered all the info you see here and in the next few sections and created a Web page with the appropriate links. To check out a company, open the page in your favorite browser, click on the link, and you're there! Look for the file named WEBHOSTS.HTM on the disk.

Who Does It	How To Get There	Who's Eligible
Allfaiths Press	http://www.ssp-ii.com/ssp/Allfaiths/	Religious organizations
Beverly Hills	http://www.geopages.com/cgi-bin/	Anyone!
Internet CurBet Communications	main/homestead/http://www.curbet.com/donate.html	Non-profit groups in Virginia
Esoteric Source Providers	http://www.value.net/~esoteric/	Writers "of meta physical subjects"
MarketNet	http://mkn.co.uk/HELP/USERS/FREEPAGE	Anyone!
Nitehawk	http://www.nitehawk.com/	Anyone (up to 200KB of storage)
The Student Center	http://www.infomall.org/studentcenter/	Students
USA Online	http://USAonline.com/	Artists and programmers (see the next figure)
Vive Web Connections	http://www.vive.com/connect/	Non-profit organizations, schools, community centers

USA Online offers free Web hosting for artists and programmers.

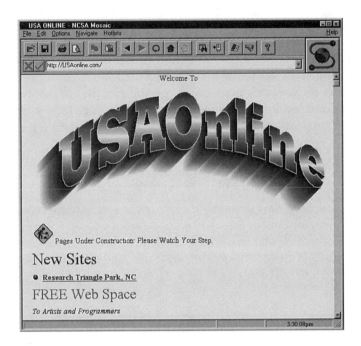

Sign Up with a Commercial Hosting Provider

For personal and business-related Web pages, most Web artisans end up renting a chunk of a Web server from a commercial hosting provider. You normally fork over a setup fee to get your account going, and then you're looking at a monthly fee that gets you two things:

➤ **A specified amount of storage on the Web server for your files**—The amount of acreage you get determines the amount of info you can store. For example, if you get a 1MB (megabyte) limit, you can't store more than 1MB worth of files on the server. HTML files don't take up much real estate, but large graphics sure do, so you'll need to watch your limit.

➤ **A specified amount of bandwidth**—*Bandwidth* is a measure of how much data the server serves. For example, suppose the HTML file for your page is 1KB (kilobyte) and the graphics associated with the page consume 9KB. If someone accesses your page, the server ships out a total of 10KB; if ten people access the page, the total bandwidth is 100KB. Caveat emptor: Most providers charge you an extra fee for exceeding your bandwidth limitation, so check this out before signing up.

The world's capitalists—efficient free-market types that they are—smelled plenty of money to be had once the explosive growth of the Web became apparent. This means there's certainly no shortage of Web hosting providers available. In fact, there are hundreds of the darn things. To see a list of most of them, point your favorite browser to the following URL:

```
http://www.yahoo.com/Business_and_Economy/Companies/
Internet_Presence_Providers/
```

The following table provides you with a random sampling of just some of the ones you can check out:

Who Does It	How To Get There	The Skinny
Aquila BBS	`http://www.aquila.com/`	Setup fee: $49 Monthly fee: $19.95 Storage: 20MB Bandwidth: 100MB Notes: Also offers plans for small and large businesses.
Clever dot Net	`http://clever.net/self/index.html`	Setup fee: None Monthly fee: $18.50 Storage: 10MB Bandwidth: 200MB Notes: See the next figure.
Lynk	`http://www.lmg.com/`	Setup fee: None Monthly fee: $15 Storage: 5MB Bandwidth: No limit Notes: $75.00 for six months.
NetHomes	`http://www.nethomes.com/`	Setup fee: None Monthly fee: $5 (includes 14-day free trial) Storage: 1MB Bandwidth: 5MB Notes: Includes a "file manager" that makes it easy to transfer files to the site.
Nitehawk	`http://www.nitehawk.com/`	Setup fee: None Yearly fee: $12 for 1MB, $40 for 5MB Storage: 1MB or 5MB Bandwidth: No limit Notes: Nitehawk is free up to200KB of storage (see above); additional storage: $10 per MB per year.

continues

continued

Who Does It	How To Get There	The Skinny
PRONET	http://www.pronett.com/	Setup fee: None Monthly fee: $19.95 Storage: one page, two pics Bandwidth: No limit Notes: Monthly fee is for a single page with two images. Has a do-it-yourself Web page creator.
Wix	http://www.wix.com/	Setup fee: $50 Monthly fee: $20 Storage: 1MB Bandwidth: 500 hits per day Notes: A "hit" is recorded each time a browser accesses your page.

The Clever dot Net Web hosting service is a commercial hosting provider.

What happens when you sign up with one of these providers? Well, after you establish your account, the Web administrator will create two things for you: a directory on the server computer that you can use to store your Web page files, and your very own URL. (This is also true if you're using a Web server associated with your corporate or school network.)

The directory usually takes one of the following forms:

```
/usr/login/
/usr/users/login/
/usr/login/www-docs/
```

In each case, *login* is the login name or user name that the provider assigns to you. Your URL will normally take the following shape:

```
http://provider/~login/default.html
```

Here, *provider* is the host name of your provider (for example, www.nethomes.com), *login* is your login name (note the tilde (~) in front), and *default* is the recommended name for your home page (which is usually either index.html or default.html).

Why the Default Name for a Home Page?

Why do hosting providers often insist that your home page have a certain name? Well, they need to allow for someone trying to access your URL without specifying an HTML document (if they don't know the name of your home page, for example). For example, suppose your provider's host name is www.host.com and your login name is biff. Now suppose someone uses the following URL to access your site:

```
http://www.host.com/~biff/
```

The server has to display something, so it will usually look for a default HTML file (such as index.html). If your home page is named something else, the reader may get an ugly listing of the files in your directory, or even an error.

A Pre-Trip Checklist

Once you decide on a hosting provider, you're just about ready to transfer your files to your directory on your hosting provider's server. Before you do that, however, you need to do the look-before-you-leap thing. That is, you need to give your files the once-over to make sure everything's on the up-and-up. Here's a short checklist to run through:

➤ HTML isn't hard, but it's fussy, persnickety stuff. If you miss even the smallest part of a single tag, your entire page could look like a real dog's breakfast. To avoid this, recheck your tags to make sure they look right. In particular, make sure that each tag's opening angle bracket (<) has a corresponding closing angle bracket (>), that links and <IMG> tags have two sets of quotation marks ("/"), and that tags such as <B>, <I>, <U>, <H1>, <OL>, <UL>, <DL>, and <A>, have their appropriate closing tags (</B>, </I>, and so on).

Putting Your Page into Analysis

If you want to give your page a thorough HTML check, there are resources on the Web that'll do the dirty work for you. These so-called HTML "analyzers" check your page for improper tags, mismatched brackets, missing quotation marks, and more. One of the best is called Weblint (because it picks the lint off your Web pages). To try it out, point your browser to the following site:

```
http://www.unipress.com/weblint/
```

Copy your entire HTML code and then paste it in the DATA box near the bottom of the Weblint screen. Select Check it, and Weblint goes to work. After a few seconds, a new page appears with a complete analysis of your page. It's the easy way to good HTML mental health!

➤ URLs are easy to mistype, so double check all your links. The best way to do this is to load the page into a browser and then try clicking on the links.

➤ Different browsers have different ways of interpreting your HTML codes. To make sure your Web page will look good to a large percentage of your readers, load the page into as many different browsers as you can.

➤ One of the advantages of using a word processor to create HTML files is that you usually have access to a spell checker. If so, make sure you use it to look for spelling gaffes in your page. You might want to add all the HTML tags to your custom dictionary so they don't constantly trip up the spell checker. In any case, you should always reread your text to make sure things make sense and are at least semi-grammatical.

➤ Create a list of all the files you need. This includes not only the HTML documents, but also any graphics files referenced in your pages. This way, you can easily make sure you don't miss any files during the transfer.

➤ Make backup copies of all your files before beginning the transfer. If anything untoward should happen while you're sending your files, you'll be able to recover gracefully.

Okay, Ship It!

Now, at long last, you're ready to get your page on the Web. To proceed, you have two choices:

➤ If the Web server is on your company's or school's network, you'll send the files over the network to the directory set up by your system administrator.

➤ Otherwise, you'll send the files to the directory created for you on the hosting provider's Web server.

In the latter case, you need to use the Internet's FTP (File Transfer Protocol) service. For this portion of the show, you'll use the WS_FTP software that comes on the disk with this book. This is a Windows FTP program that makes it easy to send files from your computer to the Web server. The next couple of sections show how to configure and use WS_FTP to get the job done.

Setting Up the FTP Program

Before you can send anything to the Web server, you have to tell WS_FTP how to find it and which directory to use. Thankfully, you only have to do this once, and you're set for life. Here's how it's done:

1. Start WS_FTP. You see the Session Profile dialog box appear.

2. In the Profile Name text box, enter a name for this profile (something like "My Web Directory" is just fine).

3. In the Host Name text box, enter the host name of your provider (for example, www.logophilia.com).

4. Make sure the Host Type box says Automatic detect.

5. Enter your login name in the User ID box and your password in the Password box. (Note that, for security reasons, the password appears as asterisks.)

6. In the Remote Host text box, enter the Web server directory that was assigned to you (such as /usr/login/).

7. In the Local PC box, enter the drive and directory on your computer that contains your Web page files.

8. Select **Save** to store your settings. The next figure shows an example of a completed dialog box.

An example of a completed Session Profile dialog box.

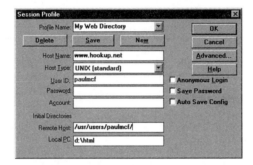

Sending the Files Via FTP

With WS_FTP ready for action, you can get down to it. Here are the basic steps to follow to send your files to the Web server via FTP:

1. If you haven't done so already, establish a connection with your regular Internet access provider.

2. In WS_FTP's Session Profile dialog box, select **OK** to connect to the hosting provider's Web server. (If the Session Profile dialog box isn't on-screen, select the **Connect** button.) Once you log in to the server, the WS_FTP window shows your computer's files at the top (the Local System box) and your Web server files at the bottom (the Remote System box).

3. Your first task is to select all the files you want to send. The easiest way to do this is to hold down the **Ctrl** key, move your mouse into the **Local System** box, and then click on each file that you're sending. When you finish selecting the files, release the **Ctrl** key.

4. If you're sending non-text files (such as graphics), make sure the **Binary** option is activated.

5. Click the **Send** button. WS_FTP sends the files one by one to the Web server.

Extending Your File Extensions

Some browsers don't know how to handle files that end with the .HTM extension and prefer to see .HTML, instead. To avoid problems, you should rename all your .HTM files so they end with .HTML. To do this with WS_FTP, click on the file in the **Remote System** box, click on **Rename**, enter the new name, and then select **OK**.

6. Once the files have arrived safely, click the **Close** button to shut down the connection.

To make sure everything's working okay, plug your URL into your browser and give your page a test surf. If all goes well, then congratulations are in order because you've officially earned your Webmeister stripes!

Getting the Word Out: Advertising Your Page

Okay, your page is floating out there in Webspace. Now what? How are people supposed to know that your new cyberhome is up and running and ready for visitors? Well, people won't beat a path to your door unless you tell them how to get there. For starters, you can spread the news via word of mouth, e-mail notes to friends and colleagues, and by handing out your shiny, new business cards that have your home page URL plastered all over them. Also, it's worth checking to see if your hosting provider has a section devoted solely to announcing new customer pages.

For the Internet at large, however, you'll need to engage in a bit of shameless self-promotion. While there's no central database of Web pages, there are a few spots you can use to get some free publicity for your new page. These include UseNet newsgroups, "What's New" pages, Web directories, Web search engines, mailing lists, and more. The best place to get a complete rundown of all these sources is the article titled "FAQ: How to Announce Your New Web Site." You can eyeball this article in either of the following locales:

➤ In the comp.infosystems.www.announce newsgroup.

➤ On the Web at `http://ep.com/faq/webannounce.html`.

Good luck!

The Least You Need to Know

This chapter completed your course on creating your first Web page by showing you how to get your page out onto the Net. Here's a quick review before the final exam:

➤ To allow others access to your Web pages, you have to store them on a computer called a Web server. Web servers are maintained either on your corporate or school network, or by a company called a hosting provider.

➤ If you can't get access to a Web server through your existing network or service provider, you'll either need to find a free hosting provider, or you'll need to rent space with a commercial hosting provider.

➤ Before sending out your pages, check your HTML codes and your spelling, try the page in different browsers, and make backup copies of your files.

➤ You send your Web page files to your hosting provider's computer using FTP (File Transfer Protocol).

➤ Once you properly set up your page, the Net has quite a few resources you can use to advertise your page. The article titled "FAQ: How to Announce Your New Web Site," gives you the details.

Part 3
A Grab Bag of Web Page Wonders

The HTML hoops I made you jump through in Part 2 will stand you in good stead for the majority of your Web page projects. In fact, you now have enough HTML trivia crammed into your brain to keep you going strong for the rest of your career as a Web author. But that doesn't mean you should rip out the rest of this book and turn it into confetti. Heck no. You still have quite a few nuggets of HTML gold to mine, and that's just what you'll do here in Part 3. Think of the next few chapters as page-bound piñatas, stuffed full of various HTML candies and toys. You'll whack each one with a stick (metaphorically speaking, of course) to spill out things like cool Netscape extensions (Chapter 10), tables (Chapter 11), advice on proper Web page style (Chapter 13), Net-based resources for Web spinners (Chapter 14), and lots more.

Fooling Around with the Netscape Extensions

In This Chapter

➤ Changing the size and color of text

➤ Adding some variety to your numbered lists and bulleted lists

➤ A few enhancements for graphics files

➤ Setting a different background color

➤ A veritable cornucopia of cool HTML add-ons designed for the Netscape browser

If you'll indulge me a little bit (yes, again; you didn't realize you'd need the patience of a saint when you began this book, did you?), I'd like to approach the subject of this chapter obliquely with a little metaphoric meandering. To wit, I want you to think of the basic HTML tags you've looked at so far as the equivalent of a pizza. No, really. Think of a plain, no-frills, garden-variety pie: dough, tomato sauce, cheese, maybe a pepperoni slice or two. Tasty? Sure. Exciting? Well, not really. To give your taste buds a real workout, you need to add some substance to the pizza in the form of tomatoes, mushrooms, peppers, or whatever.

HTML is the same way. The basic tags produce good pages, to be sure, but your control over those pages is limited. To remedy this, the Netscape programmers have added a few more ingredients to the HTML pizza. These so-called *Netscape extensions* come in two flavors:

➤ Brand new tags

➤ Tags that improve upon existing tags

This chapter presents you with a menu of most of the Netscape extensions for your Web page dining pleasure.

The Pizza Metaphor: A Warning Before You Begin

I have no qualms about wringing a metaphor to death, so let's stick with the pizza analogy a bit longer. The best thing you can say about the basic pizza described above is that most people would be hard pressed to find fault with such a simple creation (vegetarians can do without the pepperoni on their half).

Think of what happens, however, if you start adding a few ingredients. You'll probably keep most folks happy with things like tomatoes and mushrooms, but they'll start dropping like flies once you get into exotic fare such as anchovies, pineapple, and artichokes. In other words, you can add stuff to the basic pizza, but you run the risk of offending some people's palates.

In the Web world, almost all browsers are comfortable ingesting any of the HTML tags you've looked at so far. However, many of the Netscape extensions can give unwary browsers a bad case of heartburn. There are, as you'll see, some exceptions, but you should know that if you use these extras in your Web pages, you can only be sure that those people viewing them with Netscape will see them properly. There are three ways to handle this situation:

➤ Create two versions of your pages: one that uses the Netscape appendages, and one that doesn't. The idea is that you show surfers the Netscape version first, but include a link to the non-Netscape page. (You see this kind of setup all the time on the Web.)

➤ Use only the "safe" extensions. Netscape designed many of their extras so that most browsers will simply ignore them. Using only these tags will prevent problems, but your pages may look ugly in another browser.

➤ Ignore non-Netscape browsers altogether. Something like 60 or 70 percent of all Web wanderers use the Netscape browser, so you can figure that a large chunk of your visitors won't have any problems.

Text Extensions

In standard HTML, the only way to display your text in a different font size is to use one of the heading tags (such as <H1>). Unfortunately, you can't use heading tags to adjust the size of individual characters, because headings always appear on a line by themselves. To fix this, Netscape created two new tags: <FONT> and <BASEFONT>, which I'll discuss in the next couple of sections. I'll also show you how to change the color of your text.

The <FONT> Tag

The <FONT> tag adjusts the size of any text placed between <FONT> and its corresponding end tag, </FONT>. Here's how it works:

```
<FONT SIZE=size>Affected text goes here</FONT>
```

The *size* part is a number that pinpoints how big you want the text to appear, where 3 is the size of standard-issue text. You can use any number between 1 (tiny) and 7 (gargantuan). Here's an example (see FONTSIZE.HTM on the disk):

```
<HTML>
<HEAD>
<TITLE>Text Extensions</TITLE>
</HEAD>
<BODY>
<H1>Using Netscape's &lt;FONT&gt; Tag</H1>
<HR>
<FONT SIZE=7>This text uses a font size of 7.</FONT><BR>
<FONT SIZE=6>This text uses a font size of 6.</FONT><BR>
<FONT SIZE=5>This text uses a font size of 5.</FONT><BR>
<FONT SIZE=4>This text uses a font size of 4.</FONT><BR>
<FONT SIZE=3>This text uses a font size of 3 (normal).</FONT><BR>
<FONT SIZE=2>This text uses a font size of 2.</FONT><BR>
<FONT SIZE=1>This text uses a font size of 1.</FONT><BR>
<HR>
<FONT SIZE=7>Y</FONT>ou can mix and match sizes:
<BR>
Here at Shyster & Son Brokerage, you'll see your investments
<FONT SIZE=7>s<FONT SIZE=6>h<FONT SIZE=5>r<FONT SIZE=4>i
<FONT SIZE=3>n<FONT SIZE=2>k</FONT> while our commissions
<FONT SIZE=4>g<FONT SIZE=5>r<FONT SIZE=6>o<FONT SIZE=7>w!</FONT>
</BODY>
</HTML>
```

The following figure shows the results as they appear in Netscape. Load this same file into any other browser (except the latest version of Internet Explorer), and all you'll see is regular text!

111

Examples of Netscape's <FONT> extension.

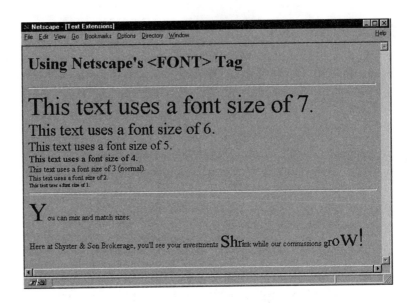

The <BASEFONT> Tag

I mentioned above that the standard font size in a Netscape document is 3. This is called the *base font*, and it's not set in stone. To change it, use the <BASEFONT> tag:

```
<BASEFONT SIZE=size>
```

Once again, *size* is a number between 1 and 7 that specifies the base font size you want. For example, if you enter <BASEFONT=7> at the top of your document (the top of the body section, that is), then all the text will appear with font size 7.

You may be wondering what the heck's the big deal with <BASEFONT>. After all, couldn't you just insert a <FONT SIZE=7> tag at the top of the document? Good point. (Gee, you are paying attention, aren't you?) The beauty (if beauty is the right term) of base fonts is that they enable you to set up relative font sizes. A relative font size is one that's so many sizes larger or smaller than the base font. Here's an example:

```
<BASEFONT=6>
This text is displayed in the base font size. However
<FONT SIZE=-2>these three words</FONT> were displayed in
a font size that was two sizes smaller than the base font.
```

The <FONT SIZE=-2> tag tells Netscape to display the text in a font size that's two sizes smaller than the base font (to get larger fonts, you'd use a plus sign (+), instead). Since I specified a base font of 6, the text up to the </FONT> tag appears with a font size of 4.

Why not simply use <FONT SIZE=4>, instead? Well, suppose you plaster your document with dozens of font changes and then, when you display it in Netscape, the fonts look too small. If you're using explicit font sizes, you have to painstakingly adjust each <FONT> tag. However, if you're using relative font sizes, you only have to change the <BASEFONT> tag.

Font Size Fun in HTML 3.0

The HTML 3.0 specification doesn't support the <FONT> tag. Instead, it uses <BIG> for larger text (larger, that is, than whatever the current font size is) and <SMALL> for smaller text. You can also use <SUB> to get subscripts and <SUP> to get superscripts. By the way, Netscape 2.0 supports these new tags, so they may be the best way to produce different font sizes.

Changing the Color of Your Page Text

Browsers display your text in basic black, which is readable but not all that exciting. To put some color in your text's cheeks, Netscape extended the <BODY> tag with a new TEXT attribute:

```
<BODY TEXT="#nnnnnn">
```

The *nnnnnn* part is a number that specifies the color you want to use. (Note, however, that colored text looks best on a background other than the normal, boring gray. I'll show you how to change the background color later in this chapter.) The following table lists the appropriate values for some common colors.

If you use this value...	You get this color...
#000000	Black
#FFFFFF	White
#FF0000	Red
#00FF00	Green
#0000FF	Blue
#FF00FF	Magenta
#00FFFF	Cyan
#FFFF00	Yellow

You also can see a "clickable palette" of colors by pointing your browser to the following site:

```
http://www.bga.com/~rlp/dwp/palette/palette.html
```

Just click on one of the color squares, and a page appears that tells you the appropriate code to use.

Changing Link Colors

Netscape also has extensions that enable you to specify colors for the links you include in your page. Here's how it works:

```
<BODY LINK="#nnnnnn" VLINK="#nnnnnn" ALINK="#nnnnnn">
```

Use LINK to specify the color of new links (links the reader has never clicked on before); use VLINK to set up a color for visited links; use ALINK to set up a color for active links. (An active link is a link you've clicked on and are waiting for the page to display.)

The Dreaded <BLINK> Tag

For some unfathomable reason, Netscape created a <BLINK> tag that causes text to blink on and off when viewed in a browser:

```
<BLINK>This text is @#$&% blinking!</BLINK>
```

The head Netscape programmer (an otherwise upstanding fellow named Marc Andreeson) claims this tag was put in "as a joke." Hah! This is, far and away, the single most annoying effect in all of HTML. Oh sure, it might sound cool (and it is—for about five seconds), but it's truly an eyesore. Also, it's been known to send Web surfers into paroxysms of rage. I beg you, I implore you: Don't use this tag!

List Extensions

If you're planning to use a lot of numbered lists or bulleted lists, Netscape offers a couple of simple enhancements that can give your pages some variety. To wit, you can specify an alternative numbering scheme in a numbered list, and you can specify a different type of bullet in a bulleted list.

Using a Different Numbering Scheme in Numbered Lists

As you learned back in Chapter 6, you enclose a numbered list with the <OL> and </OL> tags, and use <LI> at the beginning of each item. For each <LI> tag, the browser includes a number to the left of the item, where the first item is 1, the second is 2, and so on.

Netscape has an extension to the <OL> tag that enables you to define a different numbering scheme. Here's how it works:

```
<OL TYPE=type>
```

Here, *type* is one of the following characters:

Type	Numbering scheme	Example
1	Standard numbers	1, 2, 3
a	Lowercase letters	a, b, c
A	Uppercase letters	A, B, C
i	Small Roman numerals	i, ii, iii
I	Large Roman numerals	I, II, III

Here's an example (see OLTYPE.HTM on the disk):

```
<HTML>
<HEAD>
<TITLE>Numbered List Extensions</TITLE>
</HEAD>
<BODY>
<H3>Using Netscape's &lt;OL TYPE=<I>type</I>&gt; Tag</H3>
<OL TYPE=a>
<LI>Win.
<LI>Place.
<LI>Show.
</OL>
<HR>
<OL TYPE=A>
<LI>Gold.
<LI>Silver.
<LI>Bronze.
</OL>
<HR>
<OL TYPE=i>
<LI>Miss America.
<LI>First runner-up.
<LI>Second runner-up.
```

115

```
</OL>
<HR>
<OL TYPE=I>
<LI>Picard.
<LI>Riker.
<LI>Data.
</OL>
<HR>
</BODY>
</HTML>
```

The next picture shows how Netscape handles the various types. Just so you know, other browsers will cheerfully ignore the TYPE attribute when they stumble across it.

Netscape's extension to the <OL> tag in action.

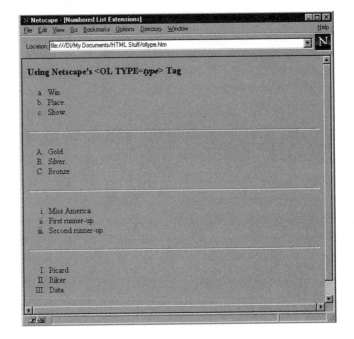

Changing the Bullet Type in Bulleted Lists

Netscape's basic bulleted-list bullet is a small circle. The best way to get a better bullet, in my not-so-humble opinion, is to use an <IMG> tag that references some cool bullet-like image. (I told you how to do this in Chapter 8.) If you prefer to leave graphics out of it, Netscape's <UL> tag for bulleted lists has an extra TYPE attribute:

```
<UL TYPE=type>
```

In this case, *type* can be either disc (the standard bullet), circle, or square. Here's a for-instance (look for ULTYPE.HTM on the disk):

```
<HTML>
<HEAD>
<TITLE>Bulleted List Extensions</TITLE>
</HEAD>
<BODY>
<H3>Using Netscape's &lt;UL TYPE=<I>type</I>&gt; Tag</H3>
<HR>
<UL TYPE=disc>
<LI>Compact disc.
<LI>Disc jockey.
<LI>Disc brake.
</UL>
<HR>
<UL TYPE=circle>
<LI>This "circle" type looks suspiciously like a square.
<LI>What's the problem, do you think?.
<LI>I guess somebody at Netscape failed geometry.
</UL>
<HR>
<UL TYPE=square>
<LI>Square root.
<LI>Three square meals.
<LI>Times square.
</UL>
</BODY>
</HTML>
```

And here's how it looks from Netscape's point of view. (Again, other browsers will simply shun the TYPE attribute when they see it inside a <UL> tag.)

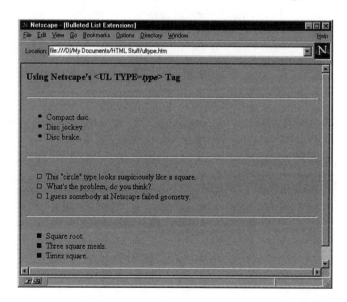

Netscape's TYPE extension to the <UL> tag enables you to choose from any of three different bullet styles.

Graphics Extensions

You saw back in Chapter 8, "A Picture Is Worth a Thousand Clicks: Working with Images," how a few well-chosen graphics can do wonders for your pages. Netscape has some extra graphics goodies that can help your images display faster and can enhance the overall look of your page. The next two sections tell all.

Specifying Image Height and Width

When surfing Web sites that contain graphics, have you ever wondered why it sometimes takes quite a while before anything appears on the screen? Well, one of the biggest delays is that most browsers won't display the entire page until they've calculated the height and width of all the images. The ever-intrepid Netscapers realized this, of course, and decided to do something about it. "What if," they asked themselves, "there was some way to tell the browser the size of each image in advance? That way, the browser wouldn't have to worry about it and things would show up on-screen much faster."

**Displaying <
and >** Notice how I forced Netscape to display a less-than sign (<) by using the character code < and to display a greater-than sign (>) by using the code >.

Thus was born an extension to the <IMG> tag: the HEIGHT and WIDTH attributes:

```
<IMG SRC="filename" WIDTH=x HEIGHT=y>
```

Here, *filename* is, as usual, the name of the graphics file, *x* is the width of the graphic, and *y* is its height. Both dimensions are measured in *pixels* (which is short for *picture elements*), which are the tiny dots that make up the picture on your screen. For example, the graphic image named HOT.GIF that comes on this book's disk is 79 pixels wide and 43 pixels tall. How do I know? I used the LView program (the graphics viewer that comes on the disk). All you have to do is use LView to open the graphics file, and the program tells you the file's size in the title bar (if it's not visible, try maximizing the LView window). You'll see something like this:

```
HOT.GIF: 79x43x4
```

The first number (79) is the width; the second number (43) is the height; the third number (4) is the number of colors the image uses (which you can safely ignore).

Alternatively, you can express the width and height as percentages of the screen. For example, the following line displays the image BLUEBAR.GIF so its width always takes up 90 percent of the screen:

```
<IMG SRC="bluebar.gif" WIDTH=90%>
```

The advantage here is that, no matter what size screen someone is using, the graphic will always take up the same amount of room across the screen. As proof, check out the next two figures showing the BLUEBAR.GIF image with WIDTH set to 90 percent. As you can see, the image always usurps 90 percent of the available width, no matter how big the Netscape window. (Note, too, that since I didn't specify the HEIGHT, Netscape adjusts the height in proportion to the increase or decrease of the width.)

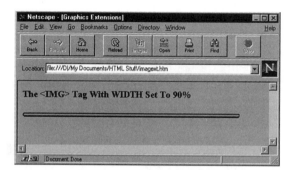

The BLUEBAR.GIF image in a relatively narrow window.

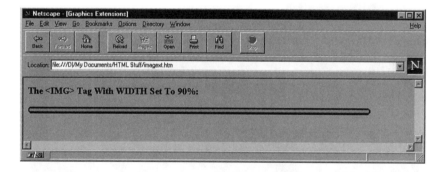

The same image in a wider window.

Netscape and HTML 3.0 Agree for Once!

You'll be happy to know that the <IMG> tag's HEIGHT and WIDTH attributes are also endorsed by HTML 3.0. This means they'll be adopted by most browsers before too long, so you can use them with impunity.

119

Setting the Background

When it appears in a browser, your Web page text and graphics float in a sea of dull, drab gray. It's about as exciting as a yawning festival. One of Netscape's most welcome extensions is the ability to change the background color your page appears on to whatever suits your style. The guts of your page appears within the body, so it makes sense that this extension is part of the <BODY> tag:

```
<BODY BGCOLOR="#nnnnnn">
```

Yes, you're right: the *nnnnnn* part is the same as what you saw earlier in this chapter when I talked about changing the color of text. (You can use the same values that I outlined, as well.) The next figure shows the Internet Hockey Pool page that uses a black background. Black text would, of course, be impossible to read on this background, so the author rightly chose to use white text.

A page that uses a black background.

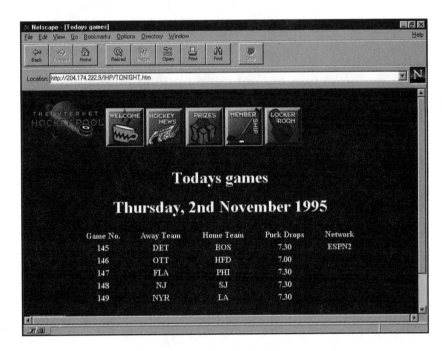

Instead of a color, Netscape also enables you to specify an image to use as the background (similar to the way Windows lets you cover the desktop with wallpaper). This doesn't have to be (nor should it be) a large image. Netscape takes smaller graphics and *tiles* them so they fill up the entire screen. The secret to background images is the <BODY> tag's new BACKGROUND attribute:

```
<BODY BACKGROUND="filename">
```

Here, *filename* is the name of the graphics file you want to use.

In general, I recommend sticking with just a different background color. Tiled background images take longer to load, and they can make text devilishly difficult to read. On the other hand, many new browsers understand the BACKGROUND attribute, but not the BGCOLOR attribute. So a compromise solution is to create a small graphics file that displays only the background color you want to use and then reference that file using BACKGROUND.

Extra Extensions

To round out my extended coverage of Netscape's extensions, this section looks at two more innovations that should come in handy: centering text and a new, improved <HR> (horizontal rule) tag.

Centering Paragraphs

Centering text and graphics is a time-honored way to give reports and brochures a professional look and feel. To provide the same advantage to your Web pages, Netscape's <CENTER> tag gives you centering capabilities for your page headings, paragraphs, lists, and even graphics. Here's how <CENTER> works:

```
<CENTER>
[Headings, text, and graphics that you
want centered go here.]
</CENTER>
```

The previous figure shows an example of the <CENTER> tag at work.

How the Rest of the Web World Centers Stuff

Netscape's <CENTER> tag is a nice, simple way to shift things to the middle of a page. The folks who created HTML 3.0 preferred to complicate things, for some reason (ah, bureaucracy). Their solution was to create a new ALIGN attribute for the <P> tag and the heading tags. For example, to center the next paragraph, you use the following variation on the <P> tag theme:

```
<P ALIGN=CENTER>
```

Similarly, you can center, say, an <H1> heading like so:

```
<H1 ALIGN=CENTER>
```

The only advantage to this approach is that you can also use either LEFT or RIGHT with the ALIGN attribute.

A Better Horizontal Rule

To conclude your look of the Netscape extensions, I'll examine various enhancements to the <HR> tag. <HR>, you'll recall, displays a horizontal rule across the page. Netscape's <HR> extensions allow you to change the line's size, width, alignment, and more. Here's a rundown:

<HR> Extension	What It Does
<HR WIDTH=*x*>	Sets the width of the line to *x* pixels.
<HR WIDTH=*x*%>	Sets the width of the line to *x* percent of the screen.
<HR SIZE=*n*>	Sets the thickness of the line to *n* units (where the default thickness is 1 unit).
<HR ALIGN=LEFT>	Aligns the line with the left margin.
<HR ALIGN=CENTER>	Centers the line.
<HR ALIGN=RIGHT>	Aligns the line with the right margin.
<HR NOSHADE>	Displays the line as a solid line (instead of appearing etched into the screen).

The Least You Need to Know

This chapter took you on a tour of the various Netscape extensions to HTML. Here are a few of the tourist attractions you saw during the trip:

➤ Use <FONT SIZE=*size*> to specify a font size. To set the size for all your text, use <BASEFONT SIZE=*size*>.

➤ To get a different text color, use <BODY TEXT="#*nnnnnn*">. The <BODY> tag also supports the BGCOLOR attribute, which specifies the color of the background.

➤ You can use a different numbering scheme in your numbered lists by using <OL TYPE=*type*>. To get different bullets in a bulleted list, use <UL TYPE=*type*>.

➤ Your page graphics will load quicker if you specify a HEIGHT and WIDTH in the <IMG> tag.

➤ To center text, paragraphs, headings, and graphics, use the <CENTER> tag.

Chapter 11

Table Talk: Adding Tables to Your Page

In This Chapter

➤ What is a table and why are they useful?

➤ Creating simple tables

➤ Ever-so-slightly advanced tables

➤ Netscape's table extensions

➤ Tons of table tips and techniques

In this chapter, you'll learn a bit of computer carpentry as I show you how to build and work with *tables*. Don't worry if you can't tell a hammer from a hacksaw; the tables we'll be dealing with are purely electronic. An HTML table is a rectangular grid of rows and columns on a Web page, into which you can enter all kinds of info, including text, numbers, links, and even images. This chapter tells you everything you need to know to build your own table specimens.

What Is a Table?

Despite their name, HTML tables aren't really analogous to the big wooden thing you eat on every night. Instead, as I've said, a table is a rectangular arrangement of rows and columns on your screen. The picture below shows an example table.

An HTML table in a Web document.

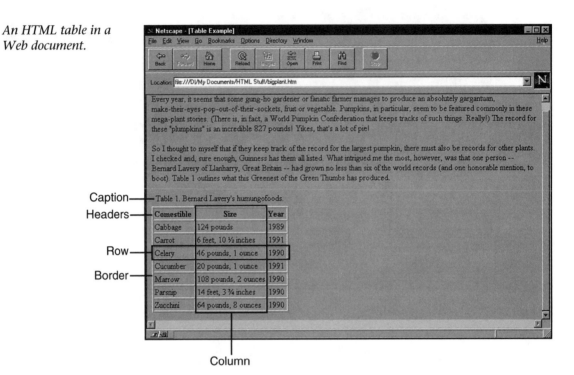

Caption ——

Headers ——

Row ——

Border ——

Column

To make sure you understand what's going on (that's my job, after all), let's check out a bit of table lingo:

Row   A single "line" of data that runs across the table. In the example shown above, there are 8 rows in all.

Column   A single vertical section of data. The previous example has 3 columns.

Cell   The intersection of a row and column. The cells are where you enter the data that appears in the table.

Caption   This is text that appears (usually) above the table and is used to describe the contents of the table.

Headers   The first row of the table. The headers are optional, but many people use them to label each column.

Borders   These are the lines that surround the table and each cell.

Nothing too rocket-science-y there.

Wait a minute. Way back in Chapter 5, you showed me how to use the <PRE> tag to make text line up all nice and neat. So why use a table when <PRE> can do a similar job?

Good question. Here are just a few advantages that tables bring to the, uh, table:

➤ Getting text to line up using <PRE> is frustrating at best, and a hair-pulling, head-pounding, curse-the-very-existence-of-the-@#$%#&!-World-Wide-Web chore at worst. With tables, though, you can get your text to line up like boot camp recruits with very little effort (and without having to yell orders at the top of your lungs).

➤ Each table cell is self-contained. You can edit and format the contents of a cell without disturbing the arrangements of the other table elements.

➤ The text "wraps" inside each cell, making it a snap to create multiple-line entries.

➤ Tables can include not only text, but images and links as well.

➤ Most text tags (such as <B>, <I>, <H1>, etc.) are fair game inside a table, so you can format the table to suit your needs. Recall that text stuck between <PRE> and </PRE> is displayed in an ugly, typewriter-like font.

Are tables another one of those Netscape extension thingys you mentioned in the last chapter?

Nope. Netscape was the first browser to understand tables, but they've been around long enough that new releases of most big-time browsers (including NCSA Mosaic and Internet Explorer) are fluent in tables.

Check This Out...

Providing Text Alternatives for Tables

Text-only browsers (such as Lynx) and most older browsers wouldn't know a table from a tubal ligation. The good news is that these browsers ignore all table-related HTML tags. The bad news is that your page ends up looking like a dog's breakfast of jumbled text. Web tailors concerned about this usually add a link to the page that takes surfers to a text-only version of the table. You construct these textual tables using simple characters such as -, =, and | for the borders, like so:

```
+—————————————————+
|Comestible |      Size           |Year|
|===========+====================+====|
|Cabbage    |124 pounds          |1989|
|Carrot     |6 feet, 10 1/2 inches|1991|
+—————————————————+
```

Web Woodworking: How to Build a Table

Okay, it's time to put the table pedal to the HTML metal and start cranking out some of these table things. The next few sections take you through the basic steps. As an example, I'll show you how I created the table you saw earlier.

The Simplest Case: A One-Row Table

Your tables will always begin with the following basic container:

```
<TABLE>
</TABLE>
```

All the other table tags fit between these two tags. There are two things you need to know about the <TABLE> tag:

➤ If you want your table to show a border, use the <TABLE BORDER> tag instead of <TABLE> (you still close the table with the </TABLE> tag, though).

➤ If you don't want a border, just use <TABLE>.

After you do that, most of your remaining table chores will involve the following 4-step process:

1. Add a row.

2. Divide the row into the number of columns you want.

3. Insert data into each cell.

4. Repeat steps 1–3 until done.

To add a row, you toss a <TR> (table row) tag and a </TR> tag (its corresponding end tag) between <TABLE> and </TABLE>:

```
<TABLE BORDER>
<TR>
</TR>
</TABLE>
```

Now you divide that row into columns by placing the <TD> (table data) and </TD> tags between <TR> and </TR>. Each <TD></TD> combination represents one column (or, more specifically, an individual cell in the row), so if you want a three-column table, you'd do this:

```
<TABLE BORDER>
<TR>
<TD></TD>
<TD></TD>
```

```
<TD></TD>
</TR>
</TABLE>
```

Now you enter the row's cell data by typing text between each <TD> tag and its </TD>
end tag:

```
<TABLE BORDER>
<TR>
<TD>Cabbage</TD>
<TD>124 pounds</TD>
<TD>1989</TD>
</TR>
</TABLE>
```

Remember that you can put any of the following within the <TD> and </TD> tags:

➤ Text

➤ HTML text-formatting tags (such as <B> and <I>)

➤ Links

➤ Lists

➤ Images

Images? Sure! Tables are a great way for text and graphics to get along with each other
and not step on each other's electronic toes. For example, I wanted my home page to
have an introductory paragraph surrounded by an image on each side. This is impossible
with other HTML commands, but tables make it a snap. Here's a snippet of my home
page HTML file, and the screen below shows how it looks.

```
<TABLE>
<TR>
<TD><IMG SRC="lonewolf.jpg" ALT=" "></TD>
<TD><FONT SIZE=5>W<FONT SIZE=3>elcome, one and all, to my humble Web
abode! This digital domicile (like any personal home page worth its
salt) is an act of sheer, unadulterated, no holds barred,
self-indulgence. It's a breathtakingly narcissistic testament to the
power of traits such as self-aggrandizement, vanity, and immodesty
that are the hallmarks of those of us who came of age in the '70s.
So come on in, take a load off, and make yourself at home.</TD>
<TD><IMG SRC="lonewolf2.jpg" ALT=" "></TD>
</TR>
</TABLE>
```

As you can see, the first column displays the image lonewolf.jpg; the second column is
the introduction; and the third column is another image: lonewolf2.jpg. Note, too, that
these kinds of tables look best without a border.

Use tables to help your text and graphics live in blissful HTML harmony.

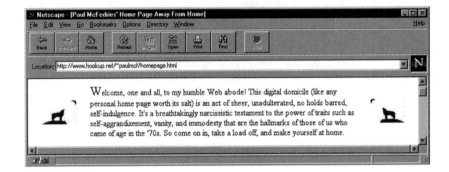

Shortcuts for Table Style

Since one row ends where another begins (or where the table itself ends), many HTML hounds don't bother with the </TR> tag. Also, since one column ends where another begins, it's okay to bypass the </TD> tags. Finally, you'll often see a row's <TD> tags placed on one line to emphasize that these cells are on a single row.

Adding More Rows

When your first row is firmly in place, you simply repeat the procedure for the other rows in the table. For our example table, here's the HTML that includes the data for all the rows:

```
<TABLE BORDER>
<TR>
<TD>Cabbage</TD><TD>124 pounds</TD><TD>1989</TD>
</TR>
<TR>
<TD>Carrot</TD><TD>6 feet, 10 &#189; inches</TD><TD>1991</TD>
</TR>
<TR>
<TD>Celery</TD><TD>46 pounds, 1 ounce</TD><TD>1990</TD>
</TR>
<TR>
<TD>Cucumber</TD><TD>20 pounds, 1 ounce</TD><TD>1991</TD>
</TR>
<TR>
<TD>Marrow</TD><TD>108 pounds, 2 ounces</TD><TD>1990</TD>
</TR>
<TR>
<TD>Parsnip</TD><TD>14 feet, 3 &#190; inches</TD><TD>1990</TD>
</TR>
```

```
<TR>
<TD>Zucchini</TD><TD>64 pounds, 8 ounces</TD><TD>1990</TD>
</TR>
</TABLE>
```

Creating a Row of Headers

If your table displays stats, data, or other info, you'll make your readers' lives easier by including labels at the top of each column that define what's in the column. (You don't need a long-winded explanation; in most cases a word or two should do the job.) To define a header, use the <TH> and </TH> tags within a row, like so:

```
<TR>
<TH>First Column Header</TH>
<TH>Second Column Header</TH>
<TH>And So On, Ad Nauseum</TH>
<TR>
```

As you can see, the <TH> tag is a lot like the <TD> tag. The difference is that the browser displays text that appears between the <TH> and </TH> tags as bold and centered within the cell. This helps the reader differentiate the header from the rest of the table data. Remember, though, that headers are optional; you can bypass them if your table doesn't need them.

Here's how I added the headers for the example you saw at the beginning of the chapter:

```
<TABLE BORDER>
<TR>
<TH>Comestible</TH><TH>Size</TH><TH>Year</TH>
<TR>
etc.
</TABLE>
```

Including a Caption

The last basic table element is the caption. A caption is a short description (a sentence or two) that tells the reader the purpose of the table. You define the caption with the <CAPTION> tag (duh):

```
<CAPTION ALIGN=where>Caption text goes here.</CAPTION>
```

Here, *where* is either TOP or BOTTOM; if you use TOP, the caption appears above the table; if you use BOTTOM, the caption appears—you guessed it—below the table. Here's the <CAPTION> tag from the example (for the complete document, look for BIGPLANT.HTM on the disk):

```
<TABLE BORDER>
```

131

```
<CAPTION ALIGN=TOP>Table 1. Bernard Lavery's humungofoods.</CAPTION>
etc.
</TABLE>
```

Table Refinishing: More Table Tidbits

The tags we've eyeballed so far are enough to let you build tables that are sturdy, if not altogether flashy. If that's all you need, you can safely ignore the rest of the dreck in this chapter. However, if you'd like a tad more control over the layout of your tables, the next few sections take you through a few refinements that can give your tables that certain *je ne sais quoi.*

Aligning Text Within Cells

The standard-issue alignment for table cells is left-aligned for data (<TD>) cells and centered for header (<TH>) cells. Not good enough? No sweat. Just shoehorn an ALIGN attribute inside the <TD> or <TH> tag and you can specify the text to be left-aligned, centered, or right-aligned. Here's how it works:

```
<TD ALIGN=alignment>
<TH ALIGN=alignment>
```

In both cases, *alignment* can be LEFT, CENTER, or RIGHT. That's not bad, but there's even more alignment fun to be had. You can also align your text vertically within a cell. This comes in handy if one cell is quite large (because it contains either a truckload of text or a relatively large image) and you'd like to adjust the vertical position of the other cells in the same row. In this case, you use the VALIGN (vertical alignment) attribute with <TD> or <TH>:

```
<TD VALIGN=vertical>
<TH VALIGN=vertical>
```

Here, *vertical* can be TOP, MIDDLE (the default alignment), or BOTTOM. Here's an example document (TBLALIGN.HTM on the disk) that demos each of these alignment options:

```
<HTML>
<HEAD>
<TITLE>Table Alignment</TITLE>
</HEAD>
<BODY>
<TABLE BORDER>
<CAPTION>Aligning Text Within Cells:</CAPTION>
<TR>
<TD></TD>
<TD ALIGN=LEFT>Left</TD>
```

```
<TD ALIGN=CENTER>Center</TD>
<TD ALIGN=RIGHT>Right</TD>
</TR>
<TR>
<TD><IMG SRC="constru1.gif">
<TD VALIGN=TOP>Top o' the cell</TD>
<TD VALIGN=MIDDLE>Middle o' the cell</TD>
<TD VALIGN=BOTTOM>Bottom o' the cell</TD>
</TR>
</TABLE>
</BODY>
</HTML>
```

The figure below shows how the table looks with Internet Explorer.

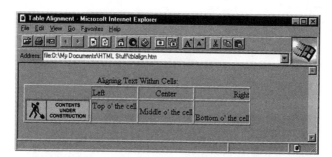

The various and sundry cell alignment options.

Spanning Text Across Multiple Rows or Columns

The data we've entered into our table cells so far has been decidedly monogamous. That is, each hunk of data has used up only one cell. But it's possible (and perfectly legal) for data to be bigamous (take up two cells) or even polygamous (take up three or more cells). Such cells are said to *span* multiple rows or columns, which can come in quite handy for headers and graphics.

Let's start with spanning multiple columns. To do this, you need to interpose the COLSPAN (column span) attribute into the <TD> or <TH> tag:

```
<TD COLSPAN=cols>
<TH COLSPAN=cols>
```

Check This Out...

Running Cells on Empty
Did you notice that the top left corner of the table is empty? I did this just by placing a <TD> tag and </TD> tag side by side, with nothing in between. Note that, in the browser, the cell appears "filled in." If you want a truly empty cell, use this tag combo, instead: <TD>
</TD>.

In this case, *cols* is the number of columns you want the cell to span. Here's a simple example (TBLSPAN1.HTM on the disk) that shows a cell spanning two columns:

```
<HTML>
<HEAD>
<TITLE>Spanning Text Across Multiple Columns</TITLE>
</HEAD>
<BODY>
<TABLE BORDER>
<CAPTION>The Spanning Thing — Example #1 (COLSPAN)</CAPTION>

<TR>
<TD COLSPAN=2>This item spans two columns</TD>
<TD>This one doesn't</TD>
</TR>

<TR>
<TD>The 1st Column</TD>
<TD>The 2nd Column</TD>
<TD>The 3rd Column</TD>
</TR>

</TABLE>
</BODY>
</HTML>
```

The figure below shows how it looks in Netscape.

A cell that spans two columns.

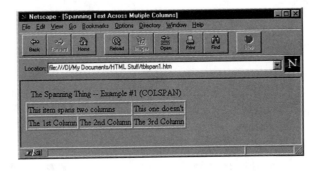

Spanning multiple rows is similar, except that you substitute ROWSPAN for COLSPAN in <TD> or <TH>:

```
<TD ROWSPAN=rows>
<TH ROWSPAN=rows>
```

The *rows* value is the number of rows you want the cell to span. Here's an example (TBLSPAN2.HTM on the disk) that shows a cell spanning two rows:

```
<HTML>
<HEAD>
<TITLE>Spanning Text Across Multiple Rows</TITLE>
</HEAD>
<BODY>
```

```
<TABLE BORDER>
<CAPTION>The Spanning Thing — Example #2 (ROWSPAN)</CAPTION>

<TR>
<TD ROWSPAN=2>This item spans two rows</TD>
<TD>The 1st Row</TD>
</TR>

<TR>
<TD>The 2nd Row</TD>
</TR>

<TR>
<TD>This one doesn't</TD>
<TD>The 3rd Row</TD>
</TR>

</TABLE>
</BODY>
</HTML>
```

The picture below shows the result.

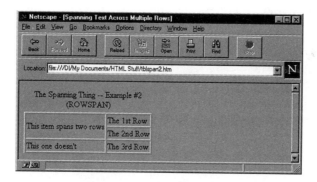

A cell that spans two rows.

Netscape's Table Extensions

For our final table trick, we'll pull a few more Netscape extensions out of our HTML hat. (In case you missed them, I went through a boatload of Netscape niceties in Chapter 10, "Fooling Around with the Netscape Extensions.") For tables, Netscape browsers support no less than five table extras:

The border size   To change the thickness of the table border, Netscape lets you assign a value to the <TABLE> tag's BORDER attribute. (Note that this applies only to the part of the border that surrounds the outside of the table; the inner borders aren't affected.) For example, to display your table with a border that's five units thick, you'd use the following:

```
<TABLE BORDER=5>
```

The width of the table Netscape usually does a pretty good job of adjusting the width of a table to accommodate the current window size. If you need your table to be a particular width, however, Netscape accepts a WIDTH attribute for the <TABLE> tag. You can either specify a value in pixels or, more likely, a percentage of the available window width. For example, to make sure your table always usurps 75 percent of the window width, you'd use this version of the <TABLE> tag:

```
<TABLE WIDTH=75%>
```

The width of a cell You can also specify the width of an individual cell by adding the WIDTH attribute to a <TD> or <TH> tag. Again, you can either specify a value in pixels or a percentage of the entire table. (Note that all the cells in the column will adopt the same width.) In this example, the cell takes up 50 percent of the table's width:

```
<TD WIDTH=50%>
```

The amount of space between cells By default, browsers allow just two units of space between each cell (vertically and horizontally). To bump that up, use Netscape's CELLSPACING attribute for the <TABLE> tag. Here's an example that increases the cell spacing to 10:

```
<TABLE CELLSPACING=10>
```

The amount of space between a cell's contents and its border Browsers like to cram data into a cell as tightly as possible. To that end, they leave a mere one unit of space between the contents of the cell and the cell border. (This space is called the *cell padding*.) To give your table data more room to breathe, use the <TABLE> tag's CELLPADDING attribute. For example, the following line tells the browser to reserve a full ten units of padding above, below, left, and right of the content in each cell:

```
<TABLE CELLPADDING=10>
```

Here's a Web page that shows you a fer-instance for each of these extensions (see TBLNETSC.HTM on the disk):

```
<HTML>
<HEAD>
<TITLE>Netscape's Table Extensions</TITLE>
</HEAD>
<BODY>
```

```
<B>&lt;TABLE BORDER=5&gt;</B>
<TABLE BORDER=5>
<TR>
<TD>One</TD>
<TD>Two</TD>
<TD>Buckle my shoe</TD>
</TR>
</TABLE>

<P>
<B>&lt;TABLE WIDTH=75%&gt;</B>
<TABLE BORDER WIDTH=75%>
<TR>
<TD>Three</TD>
<TD>Four</TD>
<TD>Shut the door</TD>
</TR>
</TABLE>

<P>
<B>&lt;TD WIDTH=50%&gt;</B>
<TABLE BORDER>
<TR>
<TD WIDTH=50%>WIDTH=50%</TD>
<TD>Normal width</TD>
<TD>Normal width</TD>
</TR>
</TABLE>

<P>
<B>&lt;TABLE CELLSPACING=10&gt;</B>
<TABLE BORDER CELLSPACING=10>
<TR>
<TD>Eeny</TD>
<TD>Meeny</TD>
<TD>Miney</TD>
<TD>Mo</TD>
</TR>
</TABLE>

<P>
<B>&lt;TABLE CELLPADDING=10&gt;</B>
<TABLE BORDER CELLPADDING=10>
<TR>
<TD>Veni</TD>
<TD>Vidi</TD>
<TD>Vici</TD>
</TR>
</TABLE>

</BODY>
</HTML>
```

137

When you load this file into Netscape, you'll see the tables shown in the following figure.

Examples of Netscape's table extensions.

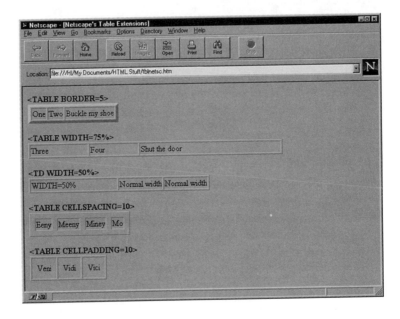

The Least You Need to Know

This chapter showed you the ins and outs of creating World Wide Web tables in HTML. Admittedly, tables are a bit more convoluted than the simple tags we've looked at so far. So, just to help things sink in, here's a quick review:

➤ A table is a rectangular grid of rows and columns.

➤ Tables are better than using <PRE> tags to lay out text because tables are easier to work with, you can include images and links, and you can use tags to format the text with, say, bolding and italics.

➤ All your table text and tags fit inside the <TABLE> and </TABLE> tags. Use <TABLE BORDER> if you want to display a border around the table.

➤ Each row is defined by the <TR> and </TR> tags, and you create a cell using the <TD> and </TD> tags.

➤ To turn a cell into a header (bold, centered text), use <TH> and </TH> instead of <TD> and </TD>.

➤ To include a descriptive caption with the table, use the <CAPTION ALIGN=*where*> tag, in which *where* is either TOP or BOTTOM.

➤ The <TD> and <TH> tags let you specify different horizontal and vertical alignments. For the horizontal alignment, use <TD ALIGN=*alignment*> or <TH ALIGN=*alignment*>, where *alignment* is LEFT, CENTER, or RIGHT. For the vertical alignment, use <TD ALIGN=*vertical*> or <TH ALIGN=*vertical*>, where *vertical* is TOP, MIDDLE, or BOTTOM.

➤ To span a cell across multiple columns, use <TD COLSPAN=*cols*>, where *cols* is the number of columns to span. To span a cell across multiple rows, use <TD ROWSPAN=*rows*>, where *rows* is the number of rows to span.

➤ Netscape has a number of extensions that work with the <TABLE> tag. These include the attributes BORDER (to change the border size), WIDTH (to specify the table width), CELLSPACING (to change the amount of space between each cell), and CELLPADDING (to change the amount of space between each cell's contents and the cell border).

Chapter 12

Need Feedback? Create a Form!

In This Chapter

➤ An introduction to forms

➤ Populating your form with buttons, boxes, and other bangles

➤ Where to find the programs that make your form run

➤ Almost everything you need to know to create great forms

Back in Chapter 7, "Making the Jump to Hyperspace: Adding Links," I showed you how to use hypertext links to add a semblance of interactivity to your pages. However, beyond this basic level of interaction lies a whole genre of Web pages called *forms*.

Where, Oh Where Are This Chapter's Examples?

Because the book's disk had already shipped to production by the time I wrote this chapter, none of these form examples will be on the disk. However, all is not lost. I'll put all the examples on my Web site and you'll be able to pick them up from there. Here's where to go:

```
http://www.logophilia.com/Books/CIGHtml/examples.html
```

What Is a Form, Anyway?

Most modern programs will toss a dialog box in your face if they need to extract some information from you. For example, selecting a program's "Print" command will most likely result in some kind of "Print" dialog box showing up. The purpose of this dialog box will be to pester you for information such as the number of copies you want, the pages you want to print, and so on.

A form is simply the Web-page equivalent of a dialog box. It's a page populated with text boxes, drop-down lists, and command buttons to get information from the reader. For example, the picture below shows a form from my Web site. This is a "guest book" that people "sign" when they visit my Web abode. Although most new browsers can handle forms, some older browsers may choke on them.

A form used as a guest book.

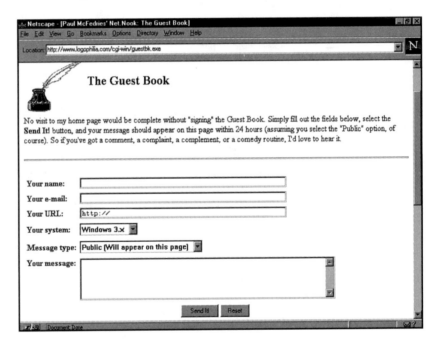

Of course, guest books are only the beginning of what you can do with forms. If you put out a newsletter or magazine, you can use forms to gather information from subscribers; if your Web site includes pages with restricted access, you can use a form to get a person's user name and password for verification; if you have information in a database, you can use a form to have people specify what type of information they want to access.

Creating Forms

You create forms using special HTML tags, and it's pretty easy to set up a form. (The problem, however, is getting hold of the information that the reader types into the form. Unfortunately, this requires some programming, so it's well beyond the scope of a humble book such as this. So what's a poor, programming-challenged Web wizard to do? Check out the section titled "Oh Say, Can You CGI?" later on in this chapter.)

To get started, enter the <FORM> and </FORM> tags. These can be inserted anywhere inside the body of the page. You place all the other form-related tags (which I'll show you in the rest of this chapter) between <FORM> and </FORM>.

The <FORM> tag always includes a couple of extra goodies that tell the Web server how to process the form. Here's the general format:

```
<FORM ACTION="url" METHOD=METHOD>
</FORM>
```

Here, the ACTION attribute tells the browser where to send the form's data. This will almost always be a program (or *script*, as they're often called) that processes the data and then performs some kind of action (hence the name). The *url* part is the URL of the Web page that contains the program.

The METHOD attribute tells the browser how to send the form's data to the URL specified with ACTION. You have two choices here for *METHOD*: POST and GET. Although both work in most cases, GET tends to cause errors in large forms. Therefore, you should always use the POST method.

Let's bring all this gobbledygook down to earth with a concrete example. You can test your forms by using one of the NCSA's public scripts. There's one for the POST method and one for the GET method. Here's how to use the POST method version:

```
<FORM ACTION="http://hoohoo.ncsa.uiuc.edu/htbin-post/post-query" METHOD=POST>
```

Here's how to use the GET method version:

```
<FORM ACTION="http://hoohoo.ncsa.uiuc.edu/htbin/query" METHOD=GET>
```

You can try this out once you build yourself a working form. Speaking of which, the next few sections take you through the basic form elements.

Making It Go: The Submit Button

Most dialog boxes, as you probably know from hard-won experience, have an OK button. Selecting this button says, in effect, "All right, I've made my choices. Now go put everything into effect." Forms also have command buttons, and they come in two flavors: "submit" buttons and "reset" buttons.

A submit button (I'll talk about the reset button in the next section) is the form equivalent of an OK dialog box button. When the reader clicks on the submit button, the form
data is shipped out to the program specified by the <FORM> tag's ACTION attribute.
Here's the simplest format for the submit button:

```
<INPUT TYPE=SUBMIT>
```

As you'll see, most form elements use some variation on the <INPUT> tag and, as I
said before, you place all these tags between <FORM> and </FORM>. In this case, the
TYPE=SUBMIT attribute tells the browser to display a command button labeled **Submit
Query** (or, on some browsers, **Submit** or **Send**). Note that each form can have just one
submit button.

If the standard **Submit Query** label is a bit too stuffy for your needs, you can make up
your own label, as follows:

```
<INPUT TYPE=SUBMIT VALUE="Label">
```

Here, *Label* is the label that will appear on the button. In the following example
(SUBMIT.HTM), I've inserted a submit button with the label "Make It So!", and the
following figure shows how it looks in a browser.

```
<HTML>
<HEAD>
<TITLE>Submit Button Custom Label Example</TITLE>
</HEAD>
<BODY>
<H3>An example of a custom label for a submit button:</H3>
<FORM ACTION="http://hoohoo.ncsa.uiuc.edu/htbin-post/post-query" METHOD=POST>
<INPUT TYPE=SUBMIT VALUE="Make It So!">
</FORM>
</BODY>
</HTML>
```

*A submit button with
a custom label.*

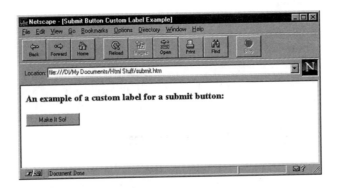

Starting Over: The Reset Button

If you plan on creating fairly large forms, you can do your readers a big favor by including a reset button somewhere on the form. A reset button clears all the data from the form's fields and re-enters any default values that you specified in the fields. (I'll explain how to set up default values for each type of field as we go along.) Here's the tag you use to include a reset button:

```
<INPUT TYPE=RESET>
```

This creates a command button labeled "Reset." Yes, you can create a custom label by tossing the VALUE attribute into the <INPUT> tag, as in the following example:

```
<INPUT TYPE=RESET VALUE="Start From Scratch">
```

Using Text Boxes for Single-Line Text

For simple text entries, such as a person's name or address, use text boxes. These are just rectangles within which the reader can type whatever he or she likes. Here's the basic format for a text box:

```
<INPUT TYPE=TEXT NAME="Field Name">
```

In this case, *Field Name* is a name you assign to the field that's unique among the other fields in the form. For example, to create a text box the reader can use to enter their first name (let's call it "First"), you'd enter the following:

```
<INPUT TYPE=TEXT NAME="First">
```

For clarity, you'll also want to precede each text box with a label that tells the reader what kind of information to type in. For example, the following line precedes a text box with "First Name:" so the reader knows to type in their first name:

```
First Name: <INPUT TYPE=TEXT NAME="First">
```

Here's some HTML code (TEXTBOX.HTM) that utilizes a few text boxes to gather some information from the reader:

```
<HTML>
<HEAD>
<TITLE>Text Box Example</TITLE>
</HEAD>
<BODY>
<H3>Please tell me about yourself:</H3>
<FORM ACTION="http://hoohoo.ncsa.uiuc.edu/htbin-post/post-query" METHOD=POST>
First Name: <INPUT TYPE=TEXT NAME="First">
<P>
```

```
Last Name: <INPUT TYPE=TEXT NAME="Last">
<P>
Nickname: <INPUT TYPE=TEXT NAME="Nickname">
<P>
Stage Name: <INPUT TYPE=TEXT NAME="Stage">
<P>
<INPUT TYPE=SUBMIT VALUE="Just Do It!">
<INPUT TYPE=RESET VALUE="Just Reset It!">
</FORM>
</BODY>
</HTML>
```

The following figure shows how it looks in Netscape:

*A form with a few
text boxes.*

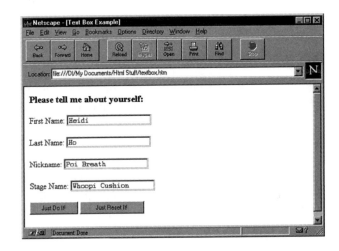

If you run this form (that is, if you select the Just Do It! button), the data is sent to the
NCSA's public server. Why? Because I included the following line:

```
<FORM ACTION="http://hoohoo.ncsa.uiuc.edu/htbin-post/post-query" METHOD=POST>
```

You'd normally replace this ACTION attribute with one that points to a program that will
do something to the data. You don't have such a program right now, so it's safe just to
use the NCSA's server for testing purposes. Remember that this server doesn't do much of
anything except send your data back to you. If everything comes back okay (i.e., there are
no error messages), then you know your form is working properly. Just so you know what
to expect, the following figure shows the page that gets returned to you. Notice how the
page shows the names of the fields followed by the value the user entered.

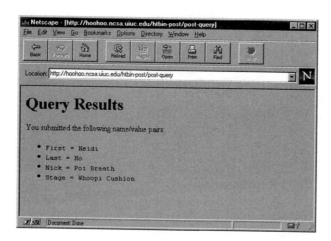

An example of the page that's returned when you send the form data to the NCSA public server.

Text boxes also come with the following bells and whistles:

Setting the default value If you'd like to put some pre-fab text into the field, include the VALUE attribute in the <INPUT> tag. For example, suppose you want to know the URL of the reader's home page. To include *http://* in the field (since most URLs begin with this), you'd use the following tag:

```
<INPUT TYPE=TEXT NAME="URL" VALUE="http://">
```

Setting the size of the box To determine the length of the text box, use the SIZE attribute. (Note that this attribute affects only the size of the box, not the length of the entry; for the latter, see the MAXLENGTH attribute, below.) For example, the following tag displays a text box that's 40 characters long:

```
<INPUT TYPE=TEXT NAME="Address" SIZE=40>
```

Limiting the length of the text In a standard text box, the reader can type away until their fingers are numb. If you'd prefer to restrict the length of the entry, use the MAXLENGTH attribute. For example, the following text box is used to enter a person's age and restricts the length of the entry to 3 characters:

```
<INPUT TYPE=TEXT NAME="Age" MAXLENGTH=3>
```

Using Text Areas for Multi-Line Text

If you want to give your readers lots of room to type their hearts out, or if you need multi-line entries (such as an address), you're better off using a *text area* than a text box. A text area is also a rectangle that accepts text input, but text areas can display two or more lines at once. Here's how they work:

```
<TEXTAREA NAME="Field Name" ROWS=TotalRows COLS=TotalCols WRAP>
</TEXTAREA>
```

Here, *Field Name* is a unique name for the field, *TotalRows* specifies the total number of lines displayed, and *TotalCols* specifies the total number of columns displayed. The WRAP attribute tells the browser to wrap the text onto the next line whenever the user's typing hits the right edge of the text area. (The WRAP attribute is supported by most browsers, but not all of them.) Note, too, that the <TEXTAREA> tag requires the </TEXTAREA> end tag. (If you want to include default values in the text area, just enter them—on separate lines, if necessary—between <TEXTAREA> and </TEXTAREA>.)

The following HTML tags (TEXTAREA.HTM) show a text area in action, and the following figure shows how it looks in a browser.

```
<HTML>
<HEAD>
<TITLE>Text Area Example</TITLE>
</HEAD>
<BODY>
<H3>Today's Burning Question</H3>
<HR>
<FORM ACTION="http://hoohoo.ncsa.uiuc.edu/htbin-post/post-query" METHOD=POST>
First Name: <INPUT TYPE=TEXT NAME="First Name">
<P>
Last Name: <INPUT TYPE=TEXT NAME="Last Name">
<P>
Today's <I>Burning Question</I>: <B>Why is Jerry Lewis so popular in
France?</B>
<P>
Please enter your answer in the text area below:
<BR>
<TEXTAREA NAME="Answer" ROWS=10 COLS=60 WRAP>
</TEXTAREA>
<P>
<INPUT TYPE=SUBMIT VALUE="I Know!">
<INPUT TYPE=RESET>
</FORM>
</BODY>
</HTML>
```

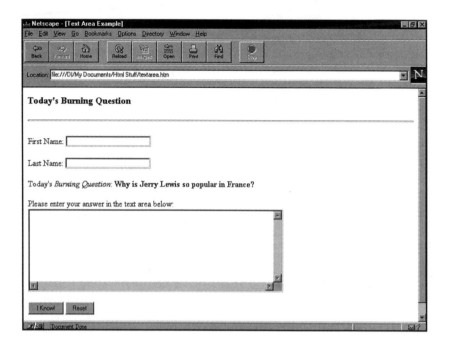

An example of a text area.

Toggling an Option On and Off with Check Boxes

If you want to elicit yes/no or true/false information from your readers, check boxes are a lot easier than having the user type in the required data. Here's the general format for an HTML check box:

```
<INPUT TYPE=CHECKBOX NAME="Field Name">
```

As usual, *Field Name* is a unique name for the field. You can also add the attribute CHECKED to the <INPUT> tag, which tells the browser to display the check box "pre-checked." Here's an example:

```
<INPUT TYPE=CHECKBOX NAME="Species" CHECKED>Human
```

Notice in the above example that I placed some text beside the <INPUT> tag. This text is used as a label that tells the reader what the check box represents. Here's a longer example (CHECKBOX.HTM) that uses a whole mess of check boxes. The following figure shows how it looks (I've checked a few of the boxes so you can see how they appear):

```
<HTML>
<HEAD>
<TITLE>Check Box Example</TITLE>
</HEAD>
<BODY>
<H3>Welcome to Hooked On Phobics!</H3>
<HR>
<FORM ACTION="http://hoohoo.ncsa.uiuc.edu/htbin-post/post-query" METHOD=POST>
What's <I>your</I> phobia? (Please check all that apply):
<P>
<INPUT TYPE=CHECKBOX NAME="Ants">Myrmecophobia (Fear of ants)<BR>
<INPUT TYPE=CHECKBOX NAME="Bald">Peladophobia (Fear of becoming bald)<BR>
<INPUT TYPE=CHECKBOX NAME="Beards">Pogonophobia (Fear of beards)<BR>
<INPUT TYPE=CHECKBOX NAME="Bed">Clinophobia (Fear of going to bed)<BR>
<INPUT TYPE=CHECKBOX NAME="Chins">Geniophobia (Fear of chins)<BR>
<INPUT TYPE=CHECKBOX NAME="Flowers">Anthophobia (Fear of flowers)<BR>
<INPUT TYPE=CHECKBOX NAME="Flying">Aviatophobia (Fear of flying)<BR>
<INPUT TYPE=CHECKBOX NAME="Purple">Porphyrophobia (Fear of the color
purple)<BR>
<INPUT TYPE=CHECKBOX NAME="Teeth">Odontophobia (Fear of teeth)<BR>
<INPUT TYPE=CHECKBOX NAME="Thinking">Phronemophobia (Fear of thinking)<BR>
<INPUT TYPE=CHECKBOX NAME="Vegetables">Lachanophobia (Fear of vegetables)<BR>
<INPUT TYPE=CHECKBOX NAME="Fear">Phobophobia (Fear of fear)<BR>
<INPUT TYPE=CHECKBOX NAME="Everything">Pantophobia (Fear of everything)<BR>
<P>
<INPUT TYPE=SUBMIT VALUE="Submit">
<INPUT TYPE=RESET>
</FORM>
</BODY>
</HTML>
```

Some check box examples.

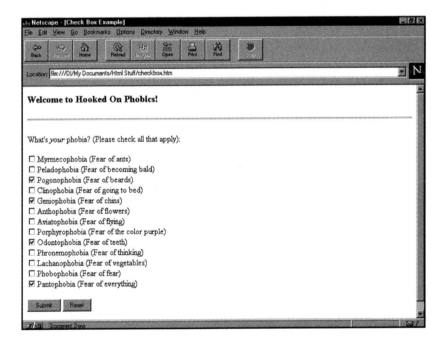

Multiple Choice Options: Radio Buttons

Instead of yes/no choices, you might want your readers to have a choice of three or four options. In this case, radio buttons are your best bet. With radio buttons, the user gets two or more options, but they can pick only one. Here's the general format:

```
<INPUT TYPE=RADIO NAME="Field Name" VALUE="Value">
```

Field Name is the usual field name, except in this case you supply the same name to *all* the radio buttons. That way, the browser knows which buttons are grouped together. *Value* is a unique text string that specifies the value of the option when it's selected. In addition, you can also add CHECKED to one of the buttons to have the browser activate the option by default. The following HTML document (RADIOBTN.HTM) puts a few radio buttons through their paces, as shown in the following figure.

```
<HTML>
<HEAD>
<TITLE>Radio Button Example</TITLE>
</HEAD>
<BODY>
<H3>Survey</H3>
<HR>
<FORM ACTION="http://hoohoo.ncsa.uiuc.edu/htbin-post/post-query" METHOD=POST>
Which of the following best describes your current salary level:
<UL>
<INPUT TYPE=RADIO NAME="Salary" VALUE="Salary1" CHECKED>Below the poverty line<BR>
<INPUT TYPE=RADIO NAME="Salary" VALUE="Salary2">Living wage<BR>
<INPUT TYPE=RADIO NAME="Salary" VALUE="Salary2">Comfy<BR>
<INPUT TYPE=RADIO NAME="Salary" VALUE="Salary2">DINK (Double Income, No Kids)<BR>
<INPUT TYPE=RADIO NAME="Salary" VALUE="Salary2">Rockefellerish<BR>
</UL>
Which of the following best describes your political leanings:
<UL>
<INPUT TYPE=RADIO NAME="Politics" VALUE="Politics1" CHECKED>So far left, I'm right<BR>
<INPUT TYPE=RADIO NAME="Politics" VALUE="Politics2">Yellow Dog Democrat<BR>
<INPUT TYPE=RADIO NAME="Politics" VALUE="Politics3">Right down the middle<BR>
<INPUT TYPE=RADIO NAME="Politics" VALUE="Politics4">Country Club Republican<BR>
<INPUT TYPE=RADIO NAME="Politics" VALUE="Politics5">So far right, I'm left<BR>
</UL>
<P>
<INPUT TYPE=SUBMIT VALUE="Submit">
<INPUT TYPE=RESET>
</FORM>
</BODY>
</HTML>
```

A form that uses radio buttons for multiple-choice input.

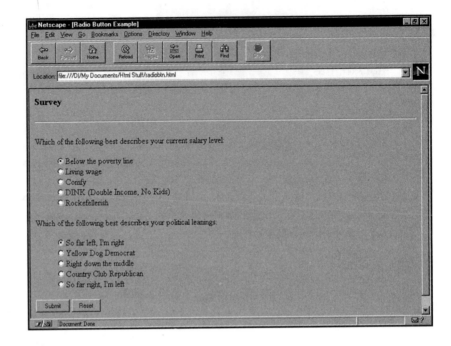

Selecting From Lists

Radio buttons are a great way to give your readers multiple choices, but they get unwieldy if you have more than about five or six options. For longer sets of options, you're better off using lists, or *selection* lists as they're called in the HTML world. Selection lists are a wee bit more complex than the other form tags we've looked at, but not by much. Here's the general format:

```
<SELECT NAME="Field Name" SIZE=Items>
<OPTION>First item text</OPTION>
<OPTION>Second item text</OPTION>
<OPTION>And so on...</OPTION>
</SELECT>
```

As I'm sure you've guessed by now, *Field Name* is the unique name for the list. For the SIZE attribute, *Items* is the number of items you want the browser to display. If you omit SIZE, the list becomes a drop-down list. If SIZE is 2 or more, the list becomes a rectangle with scroll bars for navigating the choices. Also, you can insert the MULTIPLE attribute into the <SELECT> tag. This tells the browser to allow the user to select multiple items from the list.

Between the <SELECT> and </SELECT> tags are the <OPTION></OPTION> tags; these define the list items. If you add the SELECTED attribute to one of the items, the browser selects that item by default.

To get some examples on the table, the following document (LISTS.HTM) defines no less than three selection lists. The following figure shows what the Netscape browser does with them.

```
<HTML>
<HEAD>
<TITLE>Selection List Example</TITLE>
</HEAD>
<BODY>
<H3>Putting On Hairs: Reader Survey</H3>
<HR>
<FORM ACTION="http://hoohoo.ncsa.uiuc.edu/htbin-post/post-query" METHOD=POST>
Select your hair color:<BR>
<SELECT NAME="Color">
<OPTION>Black</OPTION>
<OPTION>Blonde</OPTION>
<OPTION SELECTED>Brunette</OPTION>
<OPTION>Red</OPTION>
<OPTION>Something neon</OPTION>
<OPTION>None</OPTION>
</SELECT>
<P>
Select your hair style:<BR>
<SELECT NAME="Style" SIZE=7>
<OPTION>Bouffant</OPTION>
<OPTION>Mohawk</OPTION>
<OPTION>Page Boy</OPTION>
<OPTION>Permed</OPTION>
<OPTION>Shag</OPTION>
<OPTION SELECTED>Straight</OPTION>
<OPTION>Style? What style?</OPTION>
</SELECT>
<P>
Hair products used in the last year:<BR>
<SELECT NAME="Products" SIZE=5 MULTIPLE>
<OPTION>Gel</OPTION>
<OPTION>Grecian Formula</OPTION>
<OPTION>Mousse</OPTION>
<OPTION>Peroxide</OPTION>
<OPTION>Shoe black</OPTION>
</SELECT>
<P>
<INPUT TYPE=SUBMIT VALUE="Hair Mail It!">
<INPUT TYPE=RESET>
</FORM>
</BODY>
</HTML>
```

153

A form with a few selection list examples.

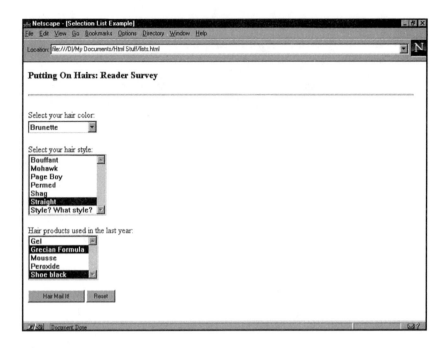

Oh Say, Can You CGI?

All this form folderol is fine, but what good is a form if it doesn't really do much of anything? That is, why bother building a fancy form if you have no way to get the data? Unfortunately, as I mentioned earlier, grabbing form data and manipulating it is a programmer's job. Specifically, you have to use something called the *Common Gateway Interface*, or CGI for short. CGI is a method of transferring form data in a manner that makes it relatively easy to incorporate into a program and then massage it all you need. Easy, that is, if you have the requisite nerdskills.

Well, I may not have room to teach you how to program forms, and you may not have the inclination in any case, but that doesn't mean you're totally stuck. The next few sections give you some ideas for getting your forms to do something useful.

Ask Your Provider

Many people want to add simple guest books and feedback mechanisms to their sites, but they don't want to have to bother with the programming aspect. So, in response to their customers' needs, most Web hosting providers make some simple CGI scripts (programs) available to their customers. For example, one common type of script grabs form data, extracts the field names and values, and sends them to an e-mail address you specify.

Check with the provider's administrator or webmaster to see if they have any CGI scripts that you can use. And if you haven't settled on a provider yet, you should ask in advance if they have CGI programs available.

The Hire-a-Nerd Route

A more expensive alternative is to hire the services of a CGI wizard to create a custom program for you. Most Web hosting providers will be only too happy to put together a nice little program tailored to your needs. There's also no shortage of hired guns on the Web who'll create programs to your specifications. As a starting point, check out some of the resources mentioned in the next section.

Check Out the Web's CGI Resources

If your service provider or Web hosting provider doesn't have ready-to-run CGI programs that you can use, there's no shortage of sites on the Net that are only too happy to either teach you CGI or supply you with programs. This section runs through a list of some of these sites:

Mind Your CGI Program Ps and Qs

Bear in mind that if you grab a program or two to use, you'll need to contact your service provider's administrator to get the full lowdown on how to set up the program. In most cases, the administrator will want to examine the program code to make sure it's up to snuff. If it passes muster, they'll put it in a special directory (usually called cgi-bin) and you can then refer to the program in your form.

LPAGE Internet Services Home Page   CGI tutorials, a "CGI school," example programs, and even a guest-book program that you can use simply by adding a couple of links to your page! (You have to register with LPAGE for the latter; it doesn't cost anything, but LPAGE asks that businesses sign on as sponsors for the guest book to help defray the costs.) Here's the URL of the LPAGE home page:

```
http://lpage.com/cgi/
```

Matt's Script Archive   Matt Wright has written tons of CGI scripts and graciously offers them gratis to the Web community. He has scripts for a guest book, random link generator, animation, and lots more. It's a great site and a must for would-be CGI mavens. Here's the URL:

```
http://www.worldwidemart.com/scripts/
```

NCSA - The Common Gateway Interface   This is *the* place on the Web for CGI info. NCSA (the same folks who made the original Mosaic browser) has put together a great collection of tutorials, tips, and sample programs. Here's the locale:

```
http://hoohoo.ncsa.uiuc.edu/cgi/
```

Usenet   A great spot for CGI tips and tricks, or just to hang around with fellow Web programmers, is the following Usenet newsgroup:

```
comp.infosystems.www.authoring.cgi.
```

Windows CGI 1.1 Description   Some Web servers run on Windows machines, so you can use Visual Basic to program CGI. This site was put together by Robert Denny, the fellow who invented Windows CGI. It describes Windows CGI, has example programs, and more. Here's where to find it:

```
http://www.city.net/win-httpd/httpddoc/wincgi.htm
```

Yahoo's CGI Index   A long list of CGI-related resources. Many of the links have either CGI how-to info or actual programs you can use. Here's where to go:

```
http://www.yahoo.com/Computers_and_Internet/Internet/
World_Wide_Web/CGI___Common_Gateway_Interface/
```

The Least You Need to Know

This chapter introduced you to the fabulous world of forms. Here's a fond look back at what great fun we had (!):

➤ A form is a page that's populated with dialog box-like doo-dads—such as text boxes, check boxes, and command buttons—that are used to get information from the reader.

➤ The basic form is contained in <FORM></FORM>, where the <FORM> tag includes the ACTION and METHOD attributes.

➤ To enable the user to send the form data, use a submit button:

```
<INPUT TYPE=SUBMIT VALUE="Label">
```

➤ To enable the user to clear the form data and start over, use a reset button:

```
<INPUT TYPE=RESET VALUE="Label">
```

➤ Use text boxes when you need the reader to type simple text entries:

```
<INPUT TYPE=TEXT NAME="Field Name">
```

➤ For longer or multi-line text entries, use a text area:

```
<TEXTAREA NAME="Field Name" ROWS=TotalRows COLS=TotalCols WRAP>
</TEXTAREA>
```

➤ For yes/no or true/false info, use a check box:

```
<INPUT TYPE=CHECKBOX NAME="Field Name">Type a label here
```

➤ If you want to give the reader several options, use radio buttons:

```
<INPUT TYPE=RADIO NAME="Field Name" VALUE="Value">Type a label here
```

➤ For a large number of options, use a selection list:

```
<SELECT NAME="Field Name" SIZE=Items>
<OPTION>First item text</OPTION>
<OPTION>Second item text</OPTION>
<OPTION>And so on...</OPTION>
</SELECT>
```

Chapter 13

The Elements of Web Page Style

In This Chapter

➤ Prose prescriptions for Web page writing

➤ Ideas for organizing your pages

➤ Tips on using graphics

➤ Things to keep in mind when dealing with links

➤ The do's and don'ts of world-class Webcraft

The least you can do is look respectable—Mom

Okay, that's it; the show's over. Our HTML box is now empty and all the shiny Web page baubles, bangles, and bric-a-brac have been brought out for your consideration. It's true: your HTML education is over, finito, sayonara, done like dinner. You know it all. Been there, done that.

Well, so now what? Ah, now it's time for a bit of HTML finishing school, because you may be able to dress up your Web pages, but can you take them anywhere? That is, you may have a Web page for people to read, but is it a readable Web page? Will Web wanderers take one look at your page, say "Yuck!", and click on the nearest link to get out of there, or will they stay awhile and check out what you have to say? Is your site a one-night surf, or will people add your page to their list of bookmarks?

My goal in this chapter is to show you there's a fine line between filler and killer, between "Trash it!" and "Smash hit!", and to show you how to end up on the positive side of that equation. To that end, I'll give you a few style suggestions that'll help you put your best Web page foot forward.

Content Is King: Notes About Writing

Most of the hubbub and hoopla surrounding the Web these days focuses on gorgeous graphics, fancy fonts, and other stylistic considerations. And we're just now starting to see new innovations that will make Web pages truly interactive (like being able to, say, play a game of Hangman right on the page; more about all this in Chapter 15).

But to the people who lust for flashy images and other eye candy, and to the pie-in-the-sky types who yearn for the Web's hands-on future, I have one thing to say: It's the content, stupid! For now and the foreseeable future, at least, this is the central fact of Web-page publishing, and it often gets obscured behind all the hype.

And, unless you're an artist or a musician or some other right-brain type, content means text. The vast majority of Web pages are written documents that rely on words and phrases for impact. So it makes sense, then, to put most of your page-production efforts into your writing. Sure, you'll spend lots of time fine-tuning your HTML codes to get things laid out just so, or tweaking your images, or scouring the Web for "hot links" to put on your page, but you should direct the majority of your publishing time towards polishing your prose.

That isn't to say, however, that you need to devote your pages to earth-shattering topics composed with a professional writer's savoir-faire. Many of the Web's self-styled "style gurus" complain that most pages are too trivial and amateurish. Humbug! These ivory tower, hipper-than-thou types are completely missing the point of publishing on the Web. They seem to think the Web is just a slightly different form of book and magazine publishing, where only a select few deserve to be in print. *Nothing could be further from the truth!* With the Web, anybody (that is, anybody with the patience to muddle through this HTML stuff) can get published and say what they want to the world.

In other words, the Web has opened up a whole new world of publishing opportunities, and we're in "anything goes" territory. So when I say, "Content is king," I mean you need to think carefully about what you want to say and make your page a unique experience. If you're putting up a page for a company, the page should reflect the company's philosophies, target audience, and central message. If you're putting up a personal home page, put the emphasis on the personal:

> **Write about topics that interest you.**   Heck, if *you* are not interested in what you're writing about, I guarantee your readers won't be interested, either.

Write with passion.   If the topic you're scribbling about turns your crank, let everyone know. Shout from the rooftops that you love this stuff—you think it's the greatest thing since they started putting "Mute" buttons on TV remotes.

Write in your own voice.   The best home pages act as mirrors that show visitors at least an inkling of the authors' inner workings. And the sure-fire way to make your page a reflection of yourself is to write the way you talk. If you say "gotta" in conversation, go ahead and say "gotta" in your page. If you say "I'll do such-and-such" to your friends, don't say "I will do such-and-such" to your readers. Everybody—amateurs and professional scribes alike—has a unique writing voice; find yours and use it unabashedly.

Spelling, Grammar, and Other Strangers

Having said all that, however, I'm not proposing Web anarchy. It's not enough to just slap up some text willy-nilly, or foist your stream-of-consciousness brain dumps on unsuspecting (and probably uninterested) Web surfers. You need to shoot for certain *minimum* levels of quality if you hope to hold people's attention (and get them to come back for more).

For starters, you need to take to heart the old axiom that "The essence of writing is rewriting." Few of us ever say exactly what we want, the way we want, in a first draft. Before putting a page on the Web, reread it a few times (at least once out loud, if you don't feel too silly doing it) to see if things flow the way you want. Put yourself in your reader's shoes. Will all this rambling make sense to him or her? Is this an enjoyable read, or is it drudgery?

Above all, check and recheck your spelling (better yet, run the text through a spell checker, if you have one). A botched word or two won't ruin a page but, if nothing else, the gaffes will distract your reader's attention. And, in the worst case, if your page is riddled with spelling blunders, your site will remain an eternally unpopular Web wallflower.

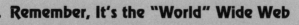

Remember, It's the "World" Wide Web

Although you should always squash all spelling bugs before a page goes public, try to maintain a charitable attitude about other people's howlers. Although the lion's share of pages are written in English, not all the authors have English as their native tongue, so you'll see some pages with spelling that's, uh, creative. If they have an e-mail link on the page, send them a gentle note pointing out their slips of the keyboard and offering up the appropriate corrections.

Grammar ranks right up there with root canals and tax audits on most people's "Top Ten Most Unpleasant Things" list. And it's no wonder: all those dangling participles, passive voices, and split infinitives. One look at that stuff and the usual reaction is "Yeah, well, split this!" Happily, you don't need to be a gung-ho grammarian to put up a successful Web page. As long as your sentences make sense and your thoughts proceed in a semi-logical order, you'll be fine. Besides, most people's speech is reasonably grammatical, so if you model your writing after your speech patterns, you'll come pretty close.

I should note, however, that this write-the-way-you-talk school of composition does have a few drawbacks. For one thing, most people get annoyed having to slog through too many words written in a "street" style; for example, writing "cuz" instead of "because," "U" instead of "you," or "dudz" instead of "dudes." Once in a while is okay, but a page full of that stuff will rile even the gentlest soul. Also, avoid "train of thought" devices such as "um," "uh," or the three-dot ellipsis thing...

More Tips for Righteous Writing

Thanks to the Web's open, inclusive nature and its grass-roots appeal, there are, overall, few prescriptions you need to follow when writing your page. Besides the ideas we've talked about so far, here are a few other stylistic admonishments to bear in mind:

Keep exclamation marks to a minimum! Although I told you earlier to write with passion, keep an eye out for extraneous exclamation marks! Yeah, you may be excited but, believe me, exclamation marks get old in a hurry! See?! They make you sound so darned perky! Stop!

DON'T SHOUT! Many Web spinners add emphasis to their epistles by using UPPERCASE LETTERS. This isn't bad in itself, but please use uppercase sparingly. An entire page written in capital letters feels like you're shouting, WHICH IS OKAY FOR A USED-CAR SALESMAN ON LATE-NIGHT TV, but it is inappropriate in the more sedate world of web-page prose. Unless you think most of your readers will be using a non-graphical browser, use italics to emphasize important words or phrases.

Avoid excessive font formatting. Speaking of italics, it's a good idea to go easy on those HTML tags that let you play around with the formatting of your text (as described in Chapter 5). **Bold**, *italics*, and `typewriter text` have their uses, but overusing them diminishes their impact and can make a page tough to read. And I said it before (back in Chapter 10, if you're keeping score), but I'll say it again: Don't use Netscape's <BLINK> tag under any circumstances.

Be good, be brief, begone. These are the "three B's" of any successful presentation. Being good means writing in clear, understandable prose that isn't marred by sloppy spelling or flagrant grammar violations. Also, if you use facts or statistics, cite the appropriate references to placate the doubting Thomases who'll want to check things for themselves. Being brief means getting right to the point without indulging in a rambling preamble. Always assume your reader is impatiently surfing through a stack of sites and has no time or patience for verbosity. State your business and then practice the third "B": Begone!

The Overall Organization of Your Web Pages

Now turn your attention to some ideas for getting (and keeping) your Web page affairs in order. You need to bear in mind, at all times, that the World Wide Web is all about navigation. Heck, half the fun comes from just surfing page to page via hypertext links. Since you've probably been having so much fun with this HTML stuff that you've created multiple pages for yourself(!), you can give the same navigational thrill to your readers. All you need to do is organize your pages appropriately and give visitors some way of getting from one page to the next.

What do I mean by organizing your pages "appropriately"? Well, there are two things to look at:

➤ How you split up the topics you talk about

➤ How many total documents you have

The One-Track Web Page: Keep Pages To a Single Topic

If there's one cardinal rule in Web-site organization, it's this: one topic, one page. Cramming a number of disparate topics into a single page is not the way to go. For one thing, it's wasteful because a reader may be interested in only one of the topics, but they still have to load the entire page. It can also be confusing to read. If you have, say, some insights into metallurgy and some fascinating ideas about Chia Pets, tossing them together in a single page is just silly. Make each of your pages stand on its own by dedicating a separate page for each topic. In the long run, your readers will be eternally thankful.

There's an exception to this one page, one topic rule for the terminally verbose: if your topic is a particularly long one, you'll end up with a correspondingly long page. Why is that a problem? Well, lengthy Web pages have lots of disadvantages:

➤ Large files can take forever to load, especially for visitors accessing the Web from a slow link. (This becomes even worse if the page is full of images.) If loading the page takes too long, most people aren't likely to wait around for the cobwebs to start forming; they're more likely to abandon you and head somewhere else.

➤ Nobody likes scrolling through endless screens of text. Pages with more than three or four screenfuls of text are hard to navigate and tend to be confusing to the reader.

Web Channel Surfers

Some studies show that many Web ramblers don't like to scroll at all! They want to see one screenful and then move on. This is extreme behavior, to be sure, and probably not all that common (for now, anyway). My guess is that many folks make a snap judgment about a page based on their initial impression. If they don't like what they see, they catch the nearest wave and keep surfin'.

➤ If you have navigation links at the top and bottom of the page (which I'll talk about later on), they won't be visible most of the time if the page is long.

To avoid these pitfalls, consider dividing large topics into smaller subtopics and assigning each one a separate page. Make sure you include links in each page that make it easy for the reader to follow the topic sequentially (more on this later).

Use Your Home Page To Tie Everything Together

Most people will begin the tour of your pages at your home page. With this in mind, you should turn your home page into a sort of electronic launch pad that gives the surfer easy access to all your stuff. Generally, that means peppering your home page with links to all your topics. For example, check out the Yahoo home page shown below. Yahoo is a giant subject catalogue of Web locations, so the home page consists mostly of links that take you to the various subject areas (Arts, Business and Economy, and so on).

Try to set up your home page so it makes sense to newcomers. Yahoo is known as a subject catalogue of sites, so the subject-related links on their home page make immediate sense. Most people's home pages aren't quite so straightforward. In this case, you'll want to include a reasonable description of each link so visitors know what to expect. For example, my home page contains just a simple introduction and then a bunch of links. As you can see below, I've included a short description beside each link that lets the reader know where the link will transport them.

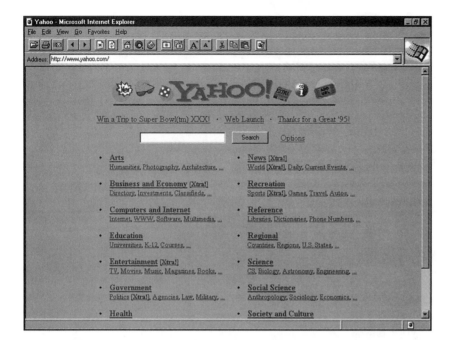

Yahoo's home page is mostly links to various subject areas.

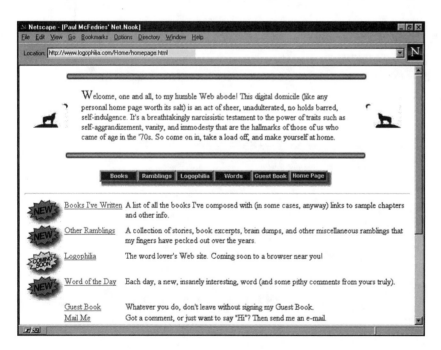

You'll usually want to include descriptions beside your home page links.

165

Use a Consistent Layout

Another thing to keep in mind when designing your pages is consistency. When folks are furiously clicking on links, they don't often know immediately where they've ended up. If you use a consistent look throughout your pages, then everyone will know that they're still on your home turf. Here are some ideas you can use to achieve a consistent look:

➤ If you have a logo or other image that identifies your site, plant a copy on each of your pages. Or, if you'd prefer to tailor your graphics to each page, at least put the image in the same place on each page.

➤ Preface your page titles with a consistent phrase. For example, "Jim Bob's Home Page: Why I Love Zima," or "Alphonse's CyberHome: The BeDazzler Page."

➤ Use the same background color or image on all your pages.

➤ If you use links to help people navigate among your pages, put the links in the same place on each page.

➤ Use consistent sizes for your headings. For example, if your home page uses an <H1> tag for the main heading and <H3> tags for subsequent headings, use these tags the same way on all your pages.

The Yahoo site provides a nice example of a consistent look and feel. For example, check out the next two figures. As you can see, the subject areas are completely different: the first figure shows Yahoo's HTML links and the second figure shows Yahoo's Karaoke links. (Karaoke-haters will note with relief that there are only three links here. This is, hopefully, a sign of Karaoke's imminent—and long overdue—demise.) However, the page layout is basically the same in both cases.

Yahoo's index of HTML links.

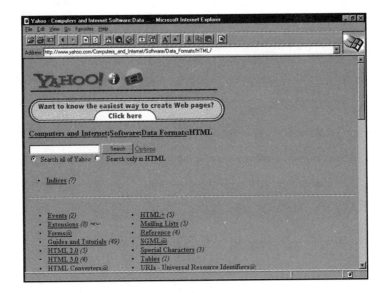

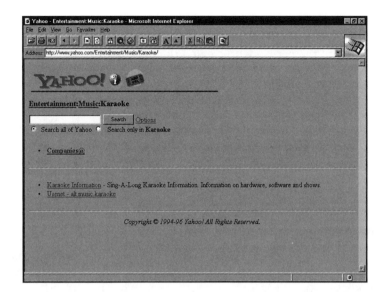

Yahoo's index of Karaoke links. Note the consistent layout between the two pages.

Organization and Layout Hints for Individual Pages

Once you get the forest of your Web pages in reasonable shape, it's time to start thinking about the trees, or the individual pages. The next few sections give you a few pointers for putting together perfect pages.

Elements To Include in Each Page

For each of your Web pages, the bulk of the content that appears will be determined by the overall subject of the page. If you're talking about Play-Doh, for example, most of your text and images will be Play-Doh related. But there are a few elements that you should include in all your pages, no matter what the subject matter:

A title A Web site without page titles is like a cocktail party without "Hi! My Name Is…" tags.

A main heading Nobody wants to scour a large chunk of a page to determine what it's all about. Instead, include a descriptive, large heading (<H1> or <H2>) at the top of the page to give your readers the instant feedback they need. In some cases, a short, introductory paragraph below the heading is also a good idea.

A "signature" If you're going on the Web, there's no point in being shy. People appreciate knowing who created a page, so you should always "sign" your work. You don't need anything fancy: just your name and your e-mail address will do. Many people also include their company name, address, phone number, and fax number.

Copyright info   If the Web pages you create are for your company, the company owns the material that appears on the page. Similarly, the contents of personal home pages belong to the person who created them. In both cases, the contents of the page are protected by copyright law, and they can't be used by anyone else without permission. To reinforce this, include a copyright notice at the bottom of the page.

The current status of the page   If your page is a preliminary draft, contains unverified data, or is just generally not ready for prime time, let your readers know so they can take that into consideration.

Check This Out...

Under Construction? Yeah, We Know!

Many Webmeisters include some kind of "Under Construction" icon on pages that aren't finished (you'll find a few examples of the species on this book's disk). This is fine, but don't overdo it. The nature of the Web is that most pages are in a state of flux and are constantly being tweaked. (This is, in fact, a sign of a good Web site.) Scattering cute construction icons everywhere will reduce their impact and annoy many of your readers.

A feedback mechanism   Always give your visitors some way to contact you so they can lavish you with compliments or report problems. The usual way to do this is to include a "mailto" link somewhere on the page (as described in Chapter 7, "Making the Jump to Hyperspace: Adding Links").

A link back to your home page   As I mentioned earlier, your home page should be the "launch pad" for your site, with links taking the reader to different areas. To make life easier for the surfers who visit, however, each page should include a link to take them back to the home page.

Most of these suggestions can appear in a separate section at the bottom of each page (this is often called a *footer*). To help differentiate this section from the rest of the page, use an <HR> (horizontal rule) tag and an <ADDRESS> tag. Depending on the browser, the <ADDRESS> tag formats text in italics and a smaller font. Here's an example footer (look for FOOTER.HTM on the disk) you can customize:

```
<HR>
<ADDRESS>
This page is Copyright & copy; 199?, your-name-here<BR>
company-name-here<BR>
company-address-here<BR>
```

```
Phone: (###) ###-####<BR>
Fax: (###) ###-####<BR>
E-mail: <A HREF="mailto:your-email-address-here">your-email-address-here</A>.
</ADDRESS>
<P>
Last revision: date-goes-here
<P>
Return to my <A HREF="home-page-URL-goes-here">home page.</A>
```

Make Your Readers' Lives Easier

When designing your Web pages, always assume your readers are in the middle of a busy surfing session, and therefore won't be in the mood to waste time. It's not that people have short attention spans. (Although I'd bet dollars to doughnuts that the percentage of Web surfers with some form of ADD—Attention Deficit Disorder—is higher than that of the general population.) It's just the old mantra of the perpetually busy: "Things to go, people to do."

So, how do you accommodate folks who are in "barely-enough-time-to-*see*-the-roses-much-less-stop-and-smell-the-darn-things" mode? Here are a few ideas:

➤ Organize your pages so people can find things quickly. This means breaking up your text into reasonably sized chunks and making judicious use of headers to identify each section.

➤ Put all your eye-catching good stuff at the top of the page where people won't be able to miss it.

➤ If you have a long document, place anchors at the beginning of each section and then include a "table of contents" at the top of the document that includes links to each section. (I explained this in more detail in Chapter 7.)

➤ Add new stuff regularly to avoid the "cobweb page" label. (A cobweb page is a page that hasn't been revised in some time.) You should also mark your new material with some sort of "New" graphic so regular visitors can easily find the recent additions.

Guidance For Using Graphics

As you saw back in Chapter 8, "A Picture Is Worth a Thousand Clicks: Working with Images," graphics are a great way to get people's attention. With images, however, there's a fine line between irresistible and irritating. To help you avoid the latter, this section presents a few ideas for using graphics responsibly.

For starters, don't become a "bandwidth hog" by including too many large images in your page. Remember that when someone accesses your Web page, all the page info—the text and graphics—is sent to that person's computer. The text isn't usually a problem (unless you're sending an entire novel, which I don't recommend), but graphic files are much slower. It's not unusual for a large image to take a minute or more to materialize if the surfer has a slow Internet connection. Clearly, your page better be *real* good if someone waits that long. Here are some ideas you can use to show mercy on visitors with slow connections:

➤ If your graphics are merely accessories, keep them small.

➤ Use the <IMAGE> tag's WIDTH and HEIGHT attributes (see Chapter 8).

➤ Avoid using graphics just to get spiffy fonts. Some authors use images only for the nice fonts available in their graphics software. This is silly and slow and should be avoided at all costs.

Understanding the Bandwidth Thing

Bandwidth is a measure of how much stuff can be crammed through a transmission medium such as a phone line or network cable. Or, to put it another way, bandwidth measures how much information can be sent between any two Internet sites. Since bandwidth is a finite commodity, many Net veterans are constantly cautioning profligate users against wasting bandwidth.

Bandwidth is measured in bits per second (bps). Here, a bit is the fundamental unit of computer information where, for example, it takes eight bits to describe a single character. So a transmission medium with a bandwidth of, say, 8 bps would send data at the pathetically slow rate of one character per second. Bandwidth is more normally measured in kilobits per second (Kbps—thousands of bits per second). So, for example, a 14.4 Kbps modem can handle 14,400 bits per second. In the high end, bandwidth is measured in megabits per second (Mbps—millions of bits per second).

Always bear in mind that a certain percentage of your readership will be viewing your pages either from a text-only browser or from a graphical browser in which they've turned off image loading. (Depending on the content of your page, the number of graphics-challenged surfers could be anywhere from 10 to 30 percent of your visitors.) If you're using an image as a link, be sure to provide a text alternative (using the <IMG> tag's ALT attribute, as described in Chapter 8). For non-link graphics, you can use ALT to describe the picture or even to display a blank. If you must use lots of images, offer people a choice of a text-only version of the page.

Finally, be careful if you decide to use a background image on your page. The Internet has lots of sites that offer various "textures" for background images. (I'll tell you about some of these sites in the next chapter.) Many of these textures are "cool," to be sure, but they're too "busy" to display text properly. For example, check out the page shown in the following figure. Now *that* is the mother of all ugly backgrounds! (Lucky for you the figure doesn't show the background in color; the actual texture incorporates various shades of sickly green.) For maximum readability, your best bet is to combine solid, light backgrounds with dark text.

Some background textures just aren't worth it!

Link Lessons: Keeping Your Links in the Pink

To finish our look at Web page style, here are a few ideas to keep in mind when using links in your pages:

➤ In your link text, don't ask the reader to "click on" something, because some of them won't have mice or other "clickable" devices. The verbs of choice are "select" and "choose."

➤ Make your link text descriptive. Link text really stands out on a page because most browsers display it underlined and in a different color. This means the reader's eye will be drawn naturally toward the link text, so you need to make the text descriptive. That way, it's easy for the reader to know exactly what they're linking to.

Always avoid the "here" syndrome, where your link text is just "here" or "click here." The snippet below shows you the right and wrong way to set up your link text. The following figure below shows how each one looks in a browser.

```
<H3>Wrong:</H3>
The Beet Poets page contains various odes celebrating our favorite
edible root,
and you can get to it by clicking <A HREF="beet-poets.html">here</A>.
<H3>Right:</H3>
The <A HREF="beet-poets.html">Beet Poets page</A> contains various odes
celebrating our favorite edible root.
```

The reader's eye gravitates toward the link text, so make sure your text is descriptive.

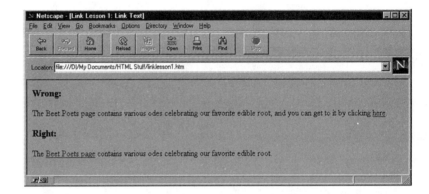

➤ If you're presenting material sequentially in multiple pages, create "navigational links" to help the reader move forward and backward through the pages. For example, each page could have a "Previous" link that takes them to the previous page, a "Next" link that takes them to the next page, and a "Top" link that returns them to the first page.

Check This Out...

The Difference Between "Previous" and "Back"

You may be wondering why the heck you'd want to bother with "Previous" and "Next" buttons when most browsers have similar buttons built in (usually called "Back" and "Forward"). Well, they're not really the same thing. For example, suppose you surf to a site and end up on a page that's in the middle of a series of pages. If you select the browser's Back button, you'll find yourself tossed back to the site you just bailed out of. If you select the page's Previous button, however, you'll head to the previous page in the series.

➤ For maximum readability, don't include spaces or punctuation marks either immediately after the <A> tag or immediately before the </A> tag.

➤ If you're planning a link to a particular page, but you haven't created that page yet, leave the link text as plain text (i.e., don't surround it with the <A> and </A> tags). Links that point to a nonexistent page (they're often called *vaporlinks*) generate an error, which can be frustrating for surfers.

➤ Try to keep all your links (both the internal and external variety) up-to-date. This means trying out each link periodically to make sure it goes where you think it's supposed to go.

➤ If you move your page to a new site, leave behind a page that includes a link to the new location (this is called a *Century 21 page).*

The Least You Need to Know

This chapter presented you with a few prescriptions for good Web page style. Here's a quick summary of a few of the do's and don'ts we covered:

Do:

➤ Write about topics that interest you, write with passion, and write in your own voice.

➤ Be brief and to the point.

➤ Keep your Web pages to a single topic.

➤ Use your home page to tie all your pages together.

➤ On each page include a title, a main heading, a "signature," and your copyright information.

➤ Include a link back to your home page.

➤ Use headers to organize your pages so readers can find things quickly.

➤ Keep your images small and use the <IMG> tag's ALT attribute to provide a text alternative to the image.

➤ Use background images judiciously; make sure any text sitting on top of the background is readable.

➤ Keep your links up-to-date.

Don't:

➤ Forget to check your spelling and grammar.

➤ Use too many exclamation marks and DON'T SHOUT.

➤ Use too much boldfacing, italics, or underlining.

➤ Use a completely different layout or color scheme on each page.

➤ Forget to give your readers a feedback mechanism (such as a *mailto* link).

➤ Use large, slow-to-load graphics if you don't need them.

➤ Use "click" or "here" links. Make your link text descriptive.

➤ Let your pages stagnate. Keep them fresh and interesting by adding new material and weeding out deadwood.

OOOOOOH...

Chapter 14

Some HTML Resources on the Web

In This Chapter

➤ Where to go to get great graphics

➤ HTML style guide sites

➤ Web page access counters without programming!

➤ HTML-related mailing lists and newsgroups

➤ A cornucopian compendium of cool HTML resources

The Internet is many things: It's a file repository, a communications medium, a shopping mall, a floor wax, a dessert topping, and a forum for all manner of kooks, crackpots, nut cases, and nincompoops. But the Internet—and the World Wide Web in particular—is mostly an information resource. Everywhere you go, some kind soul has contributed a tidbit or two about a particular subject. Now, of course, you may not be interested in, say, the mating habits of the Andorran Cow, but you can bet some surfer will be.

What you are interested in, to be sure, is HTML. Now here's the good news: There are dozens, nay hundreds—okay billions—of HTML resources scattered throughout the Internet. The bad news, though, is the usual Internet gripe: How do you find what you need quickly and easily? This is where your purchase of this book—a savvy and prudent investment on your part—really pays off. Why? Because this chapter takes you through the best of the Net's HTML resources. I'll show you great Net locales for things like graphics and style guides, HTML-related newsgroups and mailing lists, and lots more.

A Better Way to Surf This Chapter

To make surfing all these sites even easier, I've included a hypertext document on this book's disk that includes links to every site mentioned in this chapter. Look for the file named **RESOURCE.HTM**.

Graphics Goodies

The disk that comes with this book has a small collection of bullets, buttons, bars, and icons for sprucing up your Web pages. They'll do for a start, but you'll likely want to check out other images to give your page just the right touch. The next few sections show you a few of my favorite Web-based graphics stops. (Before we start, though, a caveat: Most of the graphics you'll find in these sites are free, as long as you don't use them commercially. Things change, of course, so you should always read the fine print before grabbing a graphic to use on your page.)

The Three Bs: Buttons, Bars, and Bullets

Here are some sites to check out for the little accessories that add character to a page:

Bullets by Jen   A truly massive collection of bullets, bullets, and more bullets. All Jen asks is that you let her know you're using her bullets, and then credit her on your page.

URL:

`http://mars.superlink.net/user/jen/webpages/bullets/bullets.html`

Celine's Original .GIFs   A nice collection of images created by Celine herself. If you use one of her images, she'll even put a link to your page on her graphics page.

URL:

`http://www.teleport.com/~celinec/gifs.shtml`

CSC Image Index Page   An impressive gallery of images, including lots of clip art and larger graphics.

URL:

`http://www.widomaker.com/~spalmer/`

Daniel's Icon Archive   One of the best places to go for a wide variety of quality icons, balls, bullets, and more. And, if you're feeling gung-ho, you'll also find a few graphics-related documents (GIF versus JPEG, selecting a background, and more).

URL:

http://www.jsc.nasa.gov/~mccoy/Icons/index.html

Geoff's Images Page   Lots of graphical gadgets culled from all over the Web world.

URL:

http://www.fsu.edu/~bbuchana/icons/

HTML-O-Rama   A large collection of graphics, especially the three Bs. There's also an "Images" page that has a few cool icons (see the figure below).

URL:

http://www.fau.edu/student/chemclub/dave/img1.htm

Some icons from HTML-O-Rama.

Icons and Images For Use in HTML Documents   The usual portfolio of Web page wonders, plus a few interesting variations on the standard themes.

URL:

http://www.infi.net/~rdralph/icons/

Interactive Graphics Renderer (IGR)   This site is for the do-it-yourselfers in the crowd. The IGR lets you specify what kind of bullet or ball you want (size, color, shape, and more), and then creates it for you on the spot! Loads of fun.

URL:

```
http://www.eece.ksu.edu/IGR/
```

Use the Interactive Graphics Renderer to create your own bullets and balls on the spot.   •

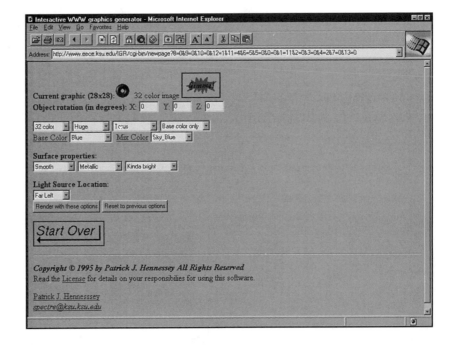

Yahoo's Icon Index   A seemingly endless list of sites that have collections of icons, bullets, and other images for Web pages.

URL:

```
http://www.yahoo.com/Computers_and_Internet/Internet/World_Wide_Web/
Programming/Icons/
```

Yet Another "B": Background Textures

I don't like background images myself, but lots of Web welders swear by them. If you'd like to give them a try, you'll find a few files at some of the sites mentioned in the last section. You'll also find lots of *textures* (as background images are often called) in the following locations:

Background Archive   Acres and acres of background textures to suit all tastes.

URL:

```
http://www.public.iastate.edu/~haley/bgnds.html
```

Background Generator   Another DIY site. This page lets you create your own backgrounds. You start with a basic texture and then "edit" it (change the colors and brightness) to get the image you want.

URL:

```
http://east.isx.com/~dprust/Bax/index.html
```

Dr. Zeus' Textures   Some truly unique and way-out images. Most of them are totally useless for displaying text, but they sure look wild!

URL:

```
http://www.best.com/~drzeus/Art/Textures/Textures.html
```

Jay's Personal Collection of Backgrounds   Lots of cool textures arranged in categories such as "Funky," "Nifty," and "Tame."

URL:

```
http://www.columbia.edu/~jll32/bg.html
```

Netscape's Background Sampler   A truckload of textures from the folks who started all this background nonsense in the first place.

URL:

```
http://www.netscape.com/assist/net_sites/bg/backgrounds.html
```

Pattern Land   "Where your pattern fantasies come to life!" I bet you didn't even know you had pattern fantasies.

URL:

```
http://www.netcreations.com/patternland/index.html
```

Yahoo's Background Index   If none of the above pages suits your fancy, Yahoo has a list of a few dozen sites that feature background images.

URL:

```
http://www.yahoo.com/Computers_and_Internet/Internet/World_Wide_Web/
Programming/Backgrounds/
```

A Guide to HTML Style Guides

Although we talked about HTML style in Chapter 12, "The Elements of Web Page Style," we didn't have room to cover everything. Fortunately, there's no shortage of Web wizards who are only too happy to give you their two-cents worth. Here's a list of some of the better ones:

Composing Good HTML   A guide by Eric Tilton that's a bit on the advanced side. It has a good section on common errors that crop up in HTML documents.

URL:

`http://www.cs.cmu.edu/~tilt/cgh/`

High Five Award Page   Although not strictly a Web style guide per se, this site presents the weekly "High Five" award to pages that exhibit "excellence in site design" (see the following figure). Checking out the winners will give you a good idea of what the top sites are doing to make themselves stand out from the Web crowd. (See also the WEB WONK page, below.)

URL:

`http://www.highfive.com/`

The High Five Award Page.

Style Guide For Online Hypertext   This is a friendly manual on good Web page design by no less an authority than Tim Berners-Lee, the fellow who invented the World Wide Web.

URL:

`http://www.w3.org/hypertext/WWW/Provider/Style/Overview.html`

Top Ten Ways To Tell If You Have a Sucky Home Page   A tongue-in-cheek (sort of) look at the ten worst things you can do in a Web page. (Number 11? Use dumb words like "sucky"!)

URL:

`http://www.winternet.com/~jmg/TopTenF.html`

What Is Good Hypertext Writing?   An excellent guide (though a bit on the pedantic side) to Web page writing and editing.

URL:

`http://www.cs.tu-berlin.de/~jutta/ht/writing-html.html`

WEB WONK   A page from David Siegel, proprietor of the High Five Award Page (see above). WEB WONK offers a few handy tips on making pages look their best.

URL:

`http://www.dsiegel.com/tips/tips_home.html`

Counter Check: Tallying Your Hits

Okay, you've labored heroically to get your pages just right, a Web server is serving them up piping hot, and you've even advertised your site shamelessly around the Internet. All that's left to do now is wait for the hordes to start beating a path to your digital door.

But how do you know if your site is attracting hordes or merely collecting dust? How do you know if you've hit the big-time, or just hit the skids? In other words, how do you know the number of people who've accessed your pages? Well, there are two ways you can go:

➤ **Ask your hosting provider.** Many companies can supply you with stats that tell you the number of "hits" your site has taken.

➤ **Include a counter in your Web page.** A counter is a little program that increments each time some surfer requests the page.

Creating a counter program is well beyond the scope of a humble book such as this (insert sigh of relief here). However, a few community-minded programmers have made counter programs available on the Web. Happily, you don't even have to copy or install these programs. All you have to do is insert a link to the program in your page, and the counter gets updated automatically whenever someone checks out the page. This section provides you with a list of some counter programs to try.

A Counter Caution

Counters are cool, and they're certainly a handy way to keep track of the amount of activity your page is generating. There are, however, three counter-related caveats you should know about:

➤ The counter program sits on another computer, so it takes time for the program to get and send its information. This means your page will load a little slower than usual.

➤ If the computer that stores the counter program goes "down for the count," the count won't appear on your page.

➤ Counters are notoriously fickle beasts that tend to reset themselves to 0 whenever they feel like it.

Internet Audit Bureau   The Internet Audit Bureau (IAB) doesn't provide you with a counter that appears on your page. Instead, the IAB maintains a registry that keeps track of the number of hits your page has generated. You can get the current hit count and other statistics by logging in to your IAB account. (The service is free, but you have to sign up with IAB before you can get your counts.)

URL:

`http://www.internet-audit.com/`

Another HTML Access Counter   This counter is very easy to use and gives you lots of options (such as the size of the counter). The figure below shows the home page for the counter. Notice how the page shows an example of the counter so you know what you're getting.

URL:

`http://www.sdsu.edu/~boyns/counter.html`

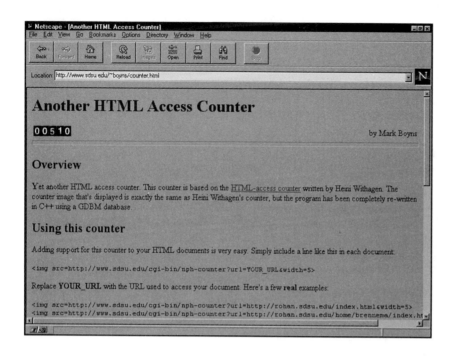

The home page for Another HTML Access Counter.

The Web-Counter A nicely implemented, no-frills counter. Note that busy sites (those getting more than 1,000 hits a day) have to pay a subscription fee to use this counter.

URL:

```
http://www.digits.com/web_counter/
```

Mailing Lists and UseNet Newsgroups

HTML is a huge topic these days, so there's no shortage of HTML-related chinwagging and confabulating on the Net. If you're stumped by something in HTML, or if you're looking for ideas, or if you just want to commune with fellow Web fiends, there are mailing lists and UseNet newsgroups that will welcome you with open arms.

Here are a few mailing lists you might want to subscribe to:

ADV-HTML A moderated mailing list for intermediate-to-advanced HTML hounds. To get subscription information, send a message to the following address:

```
LISTSERV@UA1VM.UA.EDU
```

In the message body, enter the following:

```
info ADV-HTML
```

eug_www   A mailing list devoted to Web browsing and HTML authoring. For subscription info, create a message for the following address:

```
Majordomo@efn.org
```

In the message body, enter the following:

```
info eug_www
```

HTML Authoring Mailing List   A moderated, general-purpose mailing list designed to answer queries about HTML and Web page authoring. To subscribe via e-mail, send a message to the following address:

```
listserv@netcentral.net
```

In the body of the message, enter the following (replace *Your Name* with your full name):

```
SUBSCRIBE html-list Your Name
```

You can also subscribe on the Web by pointing your browser to the following URL:

```
http://www.netcentral.net/lists/html-list.html
```

html-nonprofit   HTML and Web discussions for non-profit organizations. To find out about subscribing, send a note to this locale:

```
Majordomo@igc.apc.org
```

Enter the following text into the message body:

```
info html-nonprofit
```

UseNet also has tons of HTML and Web authoring discussions. Here's a rundown:

comp.infosystems.www.authoring.html   This busy group is chock-full of HTML tips, tricks, and instruction.

comp.infosystems.www.authoring.images   This group focuses on using images in Web pages.

comp.infosystems.www.authoring.misc   This is a catch-all group that covers everything that doesn't fit into the other two groups.

A List of HTML Lists

To finish off our look at HTML resources on the Net, this section looks at a few all-purpose, everything-but-the-kitchen-sink sites. The following pages offer one-stop shopping for links that cover all aspects of Web page production:

Creating Net Sites   A collection of HTML links and guides from your friends at Netscape.

URL:

```
http://home.netscape.com/assist/net_sites/index.html
```

D.J. Quad's Ultimate HTML Site   "Ultimate" doesn't begin to describe this site (see the figure below). It's filled to the gills with links to pages that provide you—whether you're a beginner or an expert—with the HTML know-how you need.

URL:

```
http://serv2.fwi.com/~djquad/html/index.html
```

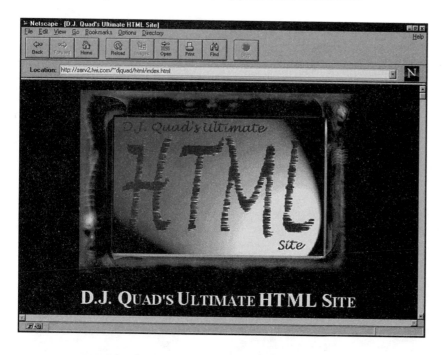

D.J. Quad's Ultimate HTML Site.

Global HTML Directory   A long list of HTML links, including tutorials and resource listings.

URL:

`http://www.cc.gatech.edu/people/home/gotz/`

HyperText Markup Language (HTML) The NCSA's list of HTML resources.

URL:

`http://union.ncsa.uiuc.edu/HyperNews/get/www/html.html`

Macmillan's HTML Workshop A nice collection of links for Websters of all skill levels. Brought to you by the same people who brought you this book!

URL:

`http://www.mcp.com/general/workshop/`

Nuthin' But Links A long list of HTML links, as well as other Internet- and computer-related links.

URL:

`http://pages.prodigy.com/FL/bombadil/home.html`

Yahoo's HTML Index An absurdly impressive (bordering on overkill) list of HTML resources from the bottomless Yahoo library.

URL:

`http://www.yahoo.com/Computers_and_Internet/Software/Data_Formats/HTML/`

The Least You Need to Know

This chapter clued you in on some of the "in" places to go on the Net for Web page resources, materials, and discussions. We looked at sites for graphics and backgrounds, HTML style guides, hit counters, mailing lists, UseNet newsgroups, and more.

Chapter 15

Hack to the Future: What's Ahead for HTML and the Web

In This Chapter

➤ Web-based programs with Java

➤ 3-D Web pages with VRML

➤ What's new in Netscape 2.0

➤ A sneak preview of Netscape Gold

➤ A far-reaching look at the shape of HTML things to come

I love watching old film reels or reading descriptions of any World's Fair from earlier in this century. There was always an "Exhibit of the Future" that—thanks to its breathless depictions of flying cars and self-cleaning homes—now provokes lots of hindsight-induced guffaws. The problem, I think, is that predicting the future is really just a fool's errand. The pace of technological change is too great and, perhaps more importantly, the direction that change takes is too unpredictable.

That, of course, is no great impediment for the world's futurologists and forecasters. These fearless prognosticators are only too happy to wax prophetic about the state of some future union, upcoming social or cultural trends, or the Spirit of Christmas Yet-to-come.

So, hey, if everybody else is doing it, why can't I? In this chapter, I'll embark upon my own complete idiot's errand and examine what's on the HTML horizon. A disclaimer, though, is in order: The World Wide Web changes so blindingly fast, it's not possible to even guess what things might be like in a couple of years. (And if you meet anyone who thinks they know, you have my permission to hit them upside the head with this book.) So, instead, I'll just focus on a few of the "bleeding edge" technologies that are emerging as this book goes to press (early 1996). (A note to those of you reading this book in 1997 or later: Try to keep the laughter down to a dull roar.)

The Java Jive: A Piping Hot Mug of Browser-Based Programs

1996 will be the year that pages move away from the simple type-it-and-send-it world of forms and start performing the Web equivalent of singing and dancing. That is, Web pages will no longer be restricted to static displays of text and graphics, but instead will become dynamic, kinetic, and, yes, truly interactive environments. Instead of mere documents to read and look at, pages will become programs that you can manipulate and play with.

The Future at Your Fingertips
I'll be mentioning quite a few sites as we work through this chapter. To give you easy access to these locations, I've included a hypertext document on this book's disk that includes links for each site. Look for the file named FUTURE.HTM.

The engine that's propelling this sea change is an amazing new technology called Java that's poised to become the biggest thing on the Web since, well, the Web itself. The idea behind Java is amazingly simple, but devilishly clever: When you access a Java Web site, your browser gets not only a page containing the usual HTML suspects, but it also receives a program. The browser (assuming it can tell a Java program from a Jackson Pollock—more on this in a sec) then runs the program right on the Web page. So if the program is, say, a game of Hangman, then you'll be able to play Hangman right on the page. Now *that's* interactive!

These Java programs (or *applets*, as they're sometimes called) are written using the Java programming language developed by Sun Microsystems. Here are a few advantages that Java programs have over traditional software:

➤ The programs are sent to your browser and are started "behind the scenes." You don't have to worry about installation, setup, or loading because your browser takes care of all that dirty work for you.

➤ The programs are designed to work on just about any system. Whether you're running Windows 95, a Mac, or a UNIX machine box, Java programs will run without complaint. (Although there are plenty of older systems—such as Windows 3.1—that Java won't work with; I talk about the Java requirements below.)

➤ Java is secure. When people hear about Java, their first concern is that some pimple-faced programmer who has succumbed to the dark side of The Force will send them a Java virus. But Java has built-in safeguards to prevent such attacks.

➤ Since you always receive the latest version of the program when you access a site, you don't need to worry about upgrades and new releases.

What You Need for Java

So what do you need to start sipping some of this Java? Well, for starters you need a computer capable of handling Java. When this book went to press, Java had been implemented for three operating systems: Windows 95, Windows NT, and SPARC Solaris (a UNIX operating system). Plans were in the cards to bring Java to Macintosh computers in early 1996. Sun has no plans to implement Java on Windows 3.1, OS/2, Amiga, NeXT, or Linux systems, but they've made the Java code available to others who might want to bring Java to these machines.

The other ingredient you need for a good cup of Java is a Web browser that knows what to do with any Java program that comes its way. Although I expect that any browser that wants to survive will become "Java-enabled" eventually, at the moment there are only two browsers that do Java:

Netscape Navigator 2.0—This is the latest release of Netscape, and it handles Java applets seamlessly. You can get a copy from the Netscape Web site:

http://home.netscape.com/

HotJava—This is a Web browser developed by Sun, the inventors of Java. You can grab it from the Java Web page:

http://java.sun.com/

Some Java Examples

Java is already the talk of the Web, but it will become huge for one simple reason: there's really no limit to the kinds of things you can do with Java programs. In these early stages of the Java revolution, many of the examples you see are simple because the programmers have just constructed quick-and-dirty programs. Animations, crude games, clocks, and calculators are the extent of the Java universe at the moment. However, it's only a matter of time before these basic applications give way to full-blown software packages: word processors, spreadsheets, real-time stock quotes and portfolio management, high-end games, and much more.

Check This Out...

Microsoft Jumps on the Java Bandwagon

At the end of 1995, Microsoft announced that it will build Java support into a future version of Internet Explorer.

Until that day comes, however, we have to content ourselves with the basic Java programs currently available. That's not to say I'm disappointed by the present crop of Java doohickeys. Far from it. This Java jazz is such a radical departure from typical Web content that interacting with even the humblest applet is a revelation. So, in that spirit, let's visit a few sites that boast some Java functionality.

The best place to start is a Web site called Gamelan, which serves as the Web's unofficial "directory and registry of Java resources." Gamelan boasts hundreds of Java programs, arranged in many different categories, including Animation, Finance, Games, and Special Effects. Here's the URL:

```
http://www.gamelan.com/
```

Our first example is a Java version of the classic arcade game Breakout. The picture below shows a game in progress. You can get to this program directly by using the following URL:

```
http://www.cee.hw.ac.uk/~calum/java/breakout.html
```

The Breakout arcade game, Java-style.

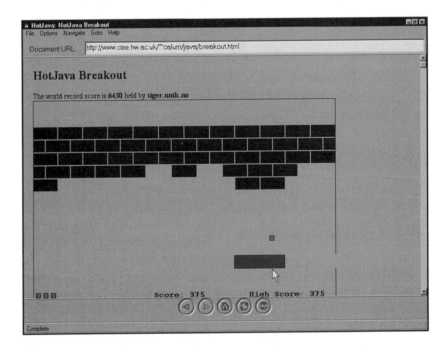

I think one of the most common Java applications you'll see is real-time updating of information, especially stock quotes, sports scores, and late-breaking news. For example, the clnet Web site features a Java program that displays a "ticker-tape" style news feed at the top of the page (see the figure below). To check it out, head to the following site:

```
http://www.cnet.com/
```

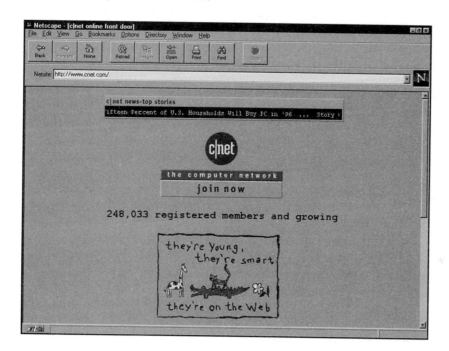

The clnet Web page uses a Java program to display a ticker-tape news feed.

There are also applets that come with the HotJava browser (including, yes, a game of Hangman), and you can find more programs at the Netscape and Java Web sites:

Netscape:

```
http://home.netscape.com/comprod/products/navigator/version_2.0/java_applets/
index.html
```

Java:

```
http://java.sun.com/applets/index.html
```

VRML: Another HTML Dimension

Java may currently be the apple of the Web's eye, but there's another technology on the horizon that promises an equally radical change in the way we approach the Web: *VRML*. VRML (which is pronounced *vermal* by the cognoscenti) stands for *Virtual Reality Modeling Language*.

Virtual Reality?! You mean I have to surf the Web wearing funny gloves and ridiculous-looking headgear?

Happily, no, that's not what VRML is all about. The VR part of VRML indicates that VRML Web sites are 3-D "worlds" that you "enter" using a VRML-enhanced browser. You can then use your mouse to "move" around this world in any direction. For example, consider a Web-based shopping mall. With a page made up of standard HTML codes, you'd probably see a few links that would take you to one store or another. If it's a shopping mall based on VRML, however, you can "walk" through the mall, examine the storefronts, and then saunter through the door of a store that looks interesting.

This sounds miraculous, and when you first try it, you can't believe you're actually doing what you're doing. But, as with Java, the underlying principle behind VRML is quite simple. Just as HTML is, in essence, a set of instructions that tells a browser how to display a document, VRML is a set of instructions that tells a browser how to create and navigate a three-dimensional world. These instructions are interpreted by a renderer, which is either a separate program or incorporated into the browser. The renderer takes the VRML instructions, uses them to build the 3-D world, and allows you to move anywhere—left and right, up and down, in and out—through this world.

VRML Browsers

To try out VRML you need to have the proper software that knows how to accept and render VRML worlds. This software comes in two flavors:

Plug-ins—These are VRML applications that fully integrate themselves with an existing browser. For example, Paper Software's WebFX "plugs in" to Netscape 2.0 and so becomes a seamless part of the browser. (See "A Look at What's New in Netscape 2.0" to learn more about plug-ins.) To learn more about WebFX and to get your mitts on a copy, head for the following URL:

```
http://www.paperinc.com/
```

Stand-alone programs—These are separate VRML programs that are also full-fledged Web browsers in their own right. An example of a stand-alone VRML program is Caligari's Fountain, which you can get from the following locale:

```
http://www.caligari.com/
```

To stay up-to-date on the latest happenings in the VRML browser world, keep an eye peeled on the VRML browsers page of Stroud's Consummate Winsock Applications site. Here's the full URL:

```
http://cwsapps.texas.net/vrml.html
```

Over, Under, Sideways, Down: Some VRML Worlds

Talking about VRML is like talking about sex: the biggest thrills don't happen until you actually get down to brass tacks and start doing it. So, now that I've piqued your interest, let's break out of boring, old 2-D cyberspace and check out some radical 3-D VRML worlds.

We'll begin our tour at the WebFX home page, which has a list of cool VRML sites at the following URL:

```
http://www.paperinc.com/wrls.html
```

There are dozens of VRML sites on this list, and any one of them is a fine way to experience the rush of VRML flying. For example, select the VRSOMA site to travel through a virtual city. Here's the URL, and the picture below shows the opening scene:

```
http://www.hyperion.com/planet9/worlds/vrsoma.wrl
```

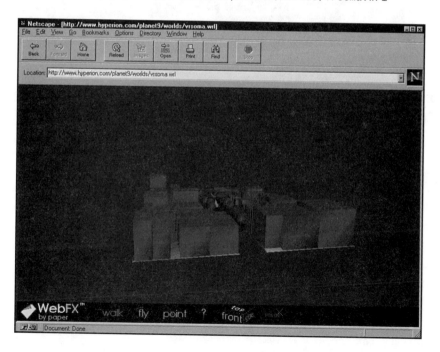

VRSOMA: a virtual city suitable for strolling.

Some VRML sites actually let you create a VRML world on the fly (so to speak). One of my favorites is the Virtual Jack-O-Lantern at the following URL:

```
http://www.chaco.com/~glenn/jack.cg:
```

You select a few options that govern the size and shape of the Jack-O-Lantern's eyes, nose, mouth, and stem, and then your Halloween pumpkin is carved up for you in a few seconds. You're then free to zoom around your creation. The picture below shows how things look from inside a Jack-O-Lantern. Scary!

The view from inside a virtual Jack-O-Lantern.

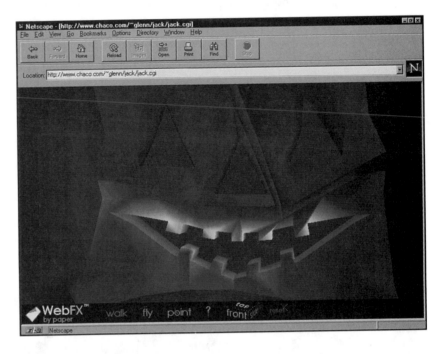

The number of VRML sites is growing rapidly, so there'll be no lack of worlds in which to do the "Sister Bertrille" thing (for you youngsters in the crowd, she was TV's Flying Nun way back when). Here are a few other general VRML sites that you can check out for the latest and greatest:

The Web Gate to VR:

```
http://Web.Actwin.Com:80/NewType/vr/vrml/index.htm
```

Protein Man's Top Ten VRML sites:

```
http://www.virtpark.com/theme/proteinman/home.wrl
```

Yahoo's VRML Index:

```
http://www.yahoo.com/Computers_and_Internet/Internet/World_Wide_Web/
Virtual_Reality_Modeling_Language__VRML_/
```

A Look at What's New in Netscape 2.0

You saw back in Chapter 10, "Fooling Around with the Netscape Extensions," that the Netscape browser leads the pack in implementing new HTML innovations. Now, with the release of version 2.0, Netscape is once again ahead of the HTML curve.

Netscape 2.0 sports all kinds of new features, including support for Java programs (as described earlier), an integrated and full-featured e-mail program, and a built-in newsreader. But there are also plenty of what-will-they-think-of-next goodies for Web weavers. The next few sections take you through the highlights.

Divide and Conquer: Frames

One of the keys to a successful Web site is to make it easy for surfers to surf your pages. This means, usually, including links at the top of the page (and sometimes at the bottom) that take the reader back to your home page or to other pages at your site. This convenience is defeated, however, if the links disappear once someone has scrolled down the page.

Wouldn't it be nice to have a "toolbar" of links that always stays visible? Well, with Netscape's new frames, you can. Frames work by dividing up a Web page into rectangular areas that contain separate chunks of text, graphics, and HTML. In other words, you can use frames to divide a single Web page into two or more separate pages. So, for example, you could have a small frame at the top of the screen that contains your navigation links, and then a second frame that displays the content. The reader can scroll through the content frame all she likes, and the navigation links remain handily in place, just like a toolbar.

Creating toolbars is only the beginning of what you can do with links. They're perfect for keeping a logo onscreen or an advertisement; you can use them for a table of contents, banners, help information, or whatever you like.

Let's check out an example: the product info page for Netscape 2.0 itself. Here's the address:

```
http://home.netscape.com/comprod/products/navigator/version_2.0/index.html
```

The following figure shows the screen you'll see. Notice how the content area is split into two sections: the bottom section shows a few navigation icons that you can click on; when you do, the results appear in the top section. For example, clicking on the Frames icon takes you to a new page that explains how frames work. As you can see below, the upper frame displays the new content while the lower frame remains the same.

A Web page with two frames.

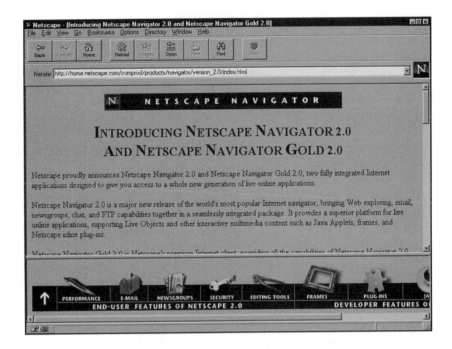

When you select the Frames icon, the upper frame displays a new page.

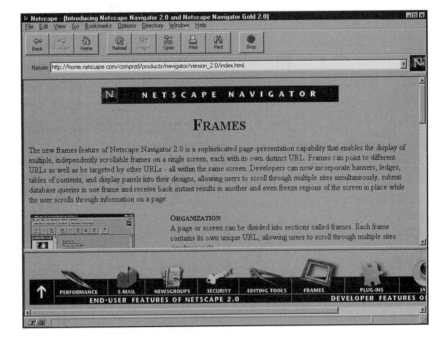

Power On Demand: Plug-Ins

Back in the old days (a couple of years ago!), Web browsers could only handle text and a few graphics. But with the multimedia boom of the past few years continuing apace, Web authors wanted to bring better bells and whistles to their creations. So while browsers weren't sophisticated enough to handle, say, sound and video files, most of them were at least smart enough to pass the buck. That is, the browser let you designate "helper applications" that would play the sound or run the video for you.

This works reasonably well, but surfers started clamoring for Swiss army knife-type browsers: programs that could handle any type of content right out of the box. That hasn't happened yet, but Netscape 2.0 takes a large leap in that direction with its new plug-in feature. A *plug-in* is a software program that fully integrates itself with Netscape. A good example is the WebFX VRML browser I mentioned in the last section. When you "plug" WebFX into Netscape, you gain the ability to view and manipulate VRML worlds. Everything happens right inside the Netscape window, so the added functionality of WebFX is completely seamless. Here's the URL of the Netscape page that discusses plug-ins:

```
http://home.netscape.com/comprod/products/navigator/version_2.0/plugins/
index.html
```

As I write this, WebFX is the only plug-in available, but there are many more in the works that should be out soon. Here's a sample:

Adobe Acrobat—This plug-in will allow Netscape to display Acrobat's PDF (Portable Document Format) files. PDF files enable you to combine fonts, colors, and graphics much more easily than you can in HTML.

Macromedia Director—This plug-in gives Netscape the ability to read and display multimedia presentations produced with the Macromedia Director software. This program lets you create documents that contain movies, animation, sound, and more.

QuickTime—This plug-in enables you to play QuickTime video files directly from the Netscape window.

Java for the Masses: JavaScript

Java is a welcome addition to the Web authoring tool chest, but its appeal is limited to hardcore programming types who live for all-night coding sessions fueled by pizza and Jolt cola. For the rest of us, Netscape has developed a scaled-down version of Java called JavaScript. Yes, it's still programming, but it's a bit more accessible to non-geeks.

JavaScript code goes right inside the Web page, just like HTML tags. When a Netscape 2.0 browser accesses the page, the JavaScript code is executed and the program does its thing. For example, the program might check the time of day and display an appropriate welcome message. Or you could embed a calculator right on the page. There's no limit to the kinds of things you can do. If you'd like to know more about it, head for the following page:

```
http://home.netscape.com/comprod/products/navigator/version_2.0/script/
index.html
```

Thar's Gold in Them Thar Pages: Netscape Gold

With the release of Navigator 2.0, Netscape is making its bid to become the all-purpose, "everything but the kitchen sink but wait until you see what we have in store for version 3," Swiss army knife of the Internet. Besides being one of the best Web browsers around, Netscape 2.0 is also stuffed with an e-mail program, a Usenet newsreader, and the ability to handle most other Net services, including FTP and Gopher. And, as you saw in the last section, you can even stick in a few extra utensils by taking advantage of plug-ins such as WebFX.

But that wasn't enough for the Web's resident greedy-guts. Oh no. They shouted "Give us more! Give us more!" so the eager-to-please souls at Netscape obliged by bringing out Netscape Navigator Gold. This version of Navigator has the same great features as the regular version, but it also includes the ability to edit HTML documents right in the browser! Cool? Way.

Unfortunately, as this book went to press Netscape Gold wasn't ready for prime-time, which means I can't discuss any of its features in any depth. But rather than simply ignoring this handy new technology, this section gives you a sneak preview of what Navigator Gold is all about and then you can try it out for yourself when the Netscape folks finally release it. (Keep your browser's eye peeled on the Netscape home page—md]http://home.netscape.com/—for announcements about the availability of Netscape Gold.)

When you load Netscape Gold, you'll see the usual Netscape screen. Hmm. No gold bars or trimmings; no gold-plated toolbar buttons; just the same ol', same ol', apparently. That's because you're looking at the *browser* part of Netscape. Recall that Netscape is now more like a Swiss army Knife, so getting to the "Gold" part means you have to "pull out" a different tool. Specifically, you have to start the Netscape Editor by pulling down the **File** menu and selecting the **Edit Document** command. Ah, that's more like it. You should now see the Netscape Editor window, with some new HTML-related toolbars and menus.

How Netscape Gold Works

When you're playing around with the Netscape Editor, bear in mind that you won't be working with HTML tags directly. Rather, you type in your document text and then use the editor's menu commands and toolbar buttons to "format" the text. This formatting is the same as adding tags, but the Netscape Editor doesn't display the HTML nuts and bolts. Instead, it just shows you what your text will look like in a browser (or, more accurately, in a Netscape browser). In other words, the Netscape Editor is a WYSIWYG display. (WYSIWYG stands for What You See Is What You Get, although some pessimistic wags prefer When You See It, Won't You Gag?) Here are the basic steps you'll follow for each document:

1. Type in your document text.

2. If you want to format some text, select the text you want to work with; if you're inserting an HTML object such as a link or an image, position the editor's cursor where you want the object to appear.

3. Choose the appropriate menu command or toolbar button.

4. Save the file from time to time.

5. Repeat steps 1–4 until you're done.

Here's a quick rundown of how the Netscape Editor handles various HTML knickknacks:

Paragraphs   Remember way back in Chapter 4, "Laying the Foundation: The Basic Structure of a Web Page," when I told you about the <P> tag? At the time, I mentioned that pressing Enter to start a new paragraph didn't work in HTML because you had to use the <P> tag, instead. Well, you can forget all that because, in the Netscape Editor, pressing Enter really does start a new paragraph. No, Netscape hasn't rewritten the HTML specifications (although, with all those darned Netscape extensions, it sometimes seems that way). Instead, pressing Enter in the Netscape Editor adds a <P> tag behind the scenes. With the WYSIWYG stuff, all you see is the result: a new paragraph.

Character Formatting   The Netscape Editor is loaded for bear with all kinds of character formatting options (most of which I droned on and on about back in Chapter 5, "From Buck-Naked to Beautiful: Dressing Up Your Page"). Again, you apply these formats just as you would with a regular word processor:

➤ If the text you want to mark already exists, highlight the text and then apply the option.

➤ If the text doesn't exist, just apply the option where the text will appear and then start typing.

199

Headings   In the Netscape Editor, headings are *styles* that you apply to a paragraph. When you apply a style for, say, an <H1> heading, the paragraph font changes to that of an <H1> heading, just like that!

Lists   If you need to add a list to your document (be it a bulleted, numbered, or definition list), the Netscape Editor can cope. (I took you through all this list lunacy back in Chapter 6, "A Fistful of List Grist for Your Web Page Mill.") The idea is that, using styles again, you first insert the list container (in the HTML world, this means <UL> and </UL> for a bulleted list; <OL> and </OL> for a numbered list; and <DL> and </DL> for a definition list), and then you format individual items as list items (the <LI> tag) in a bulleted or numbered list. If you're dealing with a definition list, you format the items as terms (the <DT> tag) and definitions (the <DD> tag)

Images   Looking to add an image or two in order to give your page some added oomph? (I gave you the big picture on images in Chapter 8, "A Picture Is Worth a Thousand Clicks: Working with Images.") In the Netscape Editor, an image is an *object* with various properties (the name of the graphics file, the alignment, the size, and so on). The Netscape Editor makes it easy to insert an image by displaying a single dialog box that lets you fill in all of these properties.

Links   Back in Chapter 7, "Making the Jump to Hyperspace: Adding Links," I showed you how to add some dynamism to your documents by inserting hypertext links. If you always have trouble remembering the proper syntax for the <A> tag, fret no more because the Netscape Editor makes it easy. In fact, there are two methods to use: you can create new links from scratch, or you can insert links from your Netscape Bookmarks. Inserting links from scratch is similar to inserting links: a dialog box appears that lays out all your choices in front of you. Just fill in things like the URL, the link text, and so on, and the link is added without any fuss. An even easier method uses your Bookmarks window. Using your mouse, you just drag a bookmark from the list and drop it on the Web page. The Netscape Editor creates the link automatically.

As you can see, Netscape Gold's editor ushers in a new era of easy-as-pie Web engineering by hiding all that HTML foofaraw. Your brain will be, I'm sure, eternally grateful.

The Least You Need to Know

In this chapter, we pulled out our crystal ball and gazed into the future of HTML. Just in case you weren't paying attention, here's a quick look at what happened:

➤ Java is a programming language that's used to create software that executes from a Web page.

➤ VRML—Virtual Reality Modeling Language—turns Web pages into three-dimensional "worlds" that you can move through.

➤ Netscape 2.0 brings three new innovations to the Web party: frames, plug-ins, and the JavaScript language.

➤ Netscape Gold eases Web-page publishing by hiding HTML tags behind a WYSIWYG display. You work with Web pages right from the browser, so you always know how your pages will look.

Part 4
Painless Page Production: Easier Ways To Do the HTML Thing

HTML certainly isn't brain surgery, or even rocket science, for that matter. You just slap up some text, toss in a few well-placed tags, and you're laughing. However, it does have a sort of primitive feel to it, as though we've taken a step backwards in electronic evolution. This is especially true for those of us who've grown accustomed to (even codependent on) the fancy-schmanciness of a graphical environment, such as Windows. We find it a little odd to be cobbling Web pages together by hand when we'd normally convince a mouse and a few menus and dialog boxes to do our bidding.

If you're looking for a more modern way to build Web pages, you've come to the right place. The chapters in this section take you through a few programs and resources that can ease the drudgery of Web page production. We'll look at a few HTML editors, which are programs that let you insert HTML tags using a civilized pull-down-menu-and-dialog-box interface. I'll also tell you about a few Net-based resources that can make it easier to create your Web masterpieces.

SHE'S AS GENTLE AS A LAMB NOW...

Chapter 16

The Best Free HTML Editor: HTML Writer

In This Chapter

➤ Getting started with HTML Writer

➤ Adjusting some HTML Writer options

➤ Using HTML Writer to add tags

➤ Lots of tips for writing HTML documents the easy way with HTML Writer

One of my goals in writing this book is to provide you with everything you need to get started in the Web page publishing profession. That's why this book's disk is filled with HTML examples, hypertext files containing links to HTML resources, graphics, an FTP program, and a graphics viewer for converting files. The final thing we need to add to this grab bag of HTML gewgaws is some HTML editing software. So I scoured the Net looking for an editor that was powerful, but also easy to use and cheap (preferably free). After auditioning plenty of pretenders to the throne, I finally settled on HTML Writer. This slick program does just about everything an editor should (except, unfortunately, edit HTML tables), and it's a snap to use. The price is right, too: HTML Writer is free, no strings attached. This chapter shows you how to use HTML Writer to create, edit, and test your hypertext documents.

Check This Out...

HTML Writer Is Free, But...

<PLEA>

HTML Writer is a free program. You can use it until you're blue in the face, or until kingdom come, and you won't have to fork out a dime. However, HTML Writer's author (Kris Nosack) calls the program *donationware*. That means he'd gladly accept donations to help defray the costs of developing the software. (The suggested donation is $10, but you can send whatever you like.) Kris, who's a graduate student, has clearly worked hard to make HTML Writer a solid program, so I encourage you to send whatever you can afford if you plan on using HTML Writer regularly.

</PLEA>

Cranking Up HTML Writer

After you install HTML Writer (see the appendix titled "The Goodies on the Disk" for instructions), the program is more or less ready for action. Your first order of business is to start HTML Writer using one of the following techniques:

➤ If you're using Windows 3.1, double-click on the HTML Writer icon in the CIG-HTML program group.

➤ If you're using Windows 95, open the Start menu, select Programs, open the CIG-HTML folder, and then select the HTML Writer item.

➤ If you don't see either the CIG-HTML program or folder, use File Manager (in Windows 3.1) or Explorer (in Windows 95) to find the directory where HTML Writer is installed, and then run the HTMLWRIT.EXE file.

Once HTML Writer loads, you'll see a screen similar to the one shown on the next page.

Getting a Document Onscreen

You can't do a whole heckuva lot with HTML Writer at first. To activate most of its options, you need to either start a fresh file, or open an existing HTML file:

➤ To start a new HTML file, select the File menu's **New** command, or press **Ctrl+N**.

➤ To open an existing HTML file, select the File menu's **Open** command (or press **Ctrl+O**), select the file from the Open dialog box, and then select **OK**.

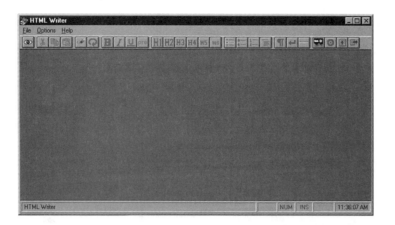

The main HTML Writer window.

HTML Writer Doesn't Do Long Filenames

If you're using HTML Writer on a Windows 95 system, note that you won't be able to save your documents with long filenames. If you already have some files with long names, they'll appear in shortened form in the Open dialog box. For example, HomeSweetHome.htm appears as homesw~1.htm, and homepage.html appears as homepa~1.htm.

Once you get a document on board, most of HTML Writer's toolbar buttons come to life, and the menu bar sprouts a few more menus. See the figure below.

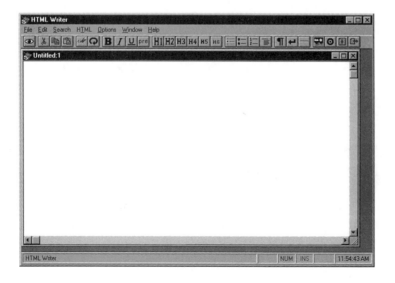

You need to start a new document (or open an existing one) to activate most of HTML Writer's options.

207

It's a Setup: Getting HTML Writer Ready to Go

Before you start working on your HTML document, there are a few setup options you should adjust so HTML Writer will work the way you do. All these options are available on the Options menu (duh), so here's a rundown of the various commands you need to check out:

Toolbar This command toggles the toolbar on and off. Unless you don't have a mouse, you should leave this option checked (i.e., activated).

Status Bar This command toggles the status bar on and off.

Button Hints When this command is checked, a short description of each toolbar button appears if you let your mouse pointer linger over a button for a second or two. (Note, as well, that the status bar also shows a description of each button.)

Word Wrap This command toggles word wrap on and off. Although this option is off by default, I'd recommend turning it on so all your text stays inside the document window.

Clock This command displays a menu of time formats, which govern the appearance of the clock that appears in HTML Writer's status bar (it's in the bottom right corner of the screen).

Templates This command displays a menu of options that let you define or select special HTML Writer files called *templates*. If you find yourself using the same basic structure for your pages, you can put that structure in a template and then reuse it for each new file. I won't cover templates in this chapter, but the Help system gives you the basics.

Uppercase Tags This command determines whether HTML Writer inserts tags either as lowercase (e.g., <b> and </b>) or as uppercase (e.g., <B> and </B>). Although it really makes no difference whether your tags are uppercase or lowercase, uppercase tags are much easier to read, so I'd recommend activating this option.

Save on Test As you'll see later on, HTML Writer lets you test your documents by loading them into a browser. If you activate this command, HTML Writer saves the document before sending it to the browser. This is a good idea, so you should activate this command.

Save as Unix Text Activating this command tells HTML Writer to save your documents using the Unix text format (which is slightly different than the format used by DOS and Windows systems). If your pages look fine on the Web, don't worry about this command; if, however, you're seeing extra garbage characters in your Web pages, activating this command might help.

Test Using   This command determines which browser you want to use for testing. In the cascade menu that appears, select either Mosaic, Cello, or Netscape. If you use another browser (such as Internet Explorer), you can ignore this command.

Screen Font   This command controls the font that HTML Writer uses to display your text and tags. (It has nothing to do with how your pages look on the Web, however.) The default font is bold italic, which is hard to read. To get something more reasonable, select this command, choose the appropriate options in the Font dialog box (such as Regular in the Font style list), and then select **OK**.

Note that you only have to adjust these options once. HTML Writer stores your preferences for you, so they'll all be set automatically the next time you load the program.

Creating an HTML Document with HTML Writer

HTML Writer is basically just a text editor that also knows how to do the HTML thing. So using HTML Writer is easy as pie: just type your regular text in the document window and then use the menu commands or toolbar buttons to insert HTML codes when you need them. Here are the basic steps you'll follow for each document:

1. Begin the document by including the HTML codes that define the structure of the document (such as <HTML>, <HEAD>, <TITLE>, and <BODY>).

2. For text not affected by any tags, just type the text into the document.

3. When you need to insert an HTML tag, position the cursor where you want the tag to appear and then choose the appropriate menu command or toolbar button. HTML Writer inserts the tag or tags. For the latter, the cursor is placed between the tags (e.g. between <I> and </I>) and then you enter your text.

> Check This Out...
>
> **Don't Forget SKELETON.HTM**
> Instead of creating the document's basic structure by hand, don't forget that this book's disk includes the file SKELETON.HTM, which includes all the tags you need. You can use the File menu's Open command to open SKELETON.HTM in HTML Writer.

4. Save the file periodically by selecting the File menu's **Save** command (or by pressing **Ctrl+S**).

5. Test the file from time to time by selecting the File menu's **Test** command (more on this later; see "Taking the Document for a Test Drive," below).

6. Repeat steps 2–5 until you're done.

The next few sections expand on step 3 by showing you how to insert the various HTML tags.

Inserting Document Tags

In HTML Writer, "document" tags are the tags that define the overall HTML structure of the file. There are four of these basic tags in all: <HTML>, <HEAD>, <TITLE>, and <BODY>. I gave you the scoop on these tags back in Chapter 4, "Laying the Foundation: The Basic Structure of a Web Page." HTML Writer also defines a fifth document tag—<ISINDEX>—that I didn't cover.

To insert one of these tags, position the cursor appropriately in the document window, pull down the HTML menu, select the **Document** command, and then select either **Html**, **Head**, **Title**, or **Body**. The following screen shows how the document looks after you select the **Html** command. Notice how HTML Writer inserts both the <HTML> and </HTML> tags and then positions the cursor in between them. (At this point, you'll probably want to press **Enter** a few times to give yourself some room for the next tags.)

A document with the <HTML> and </HTML> tags inserted.

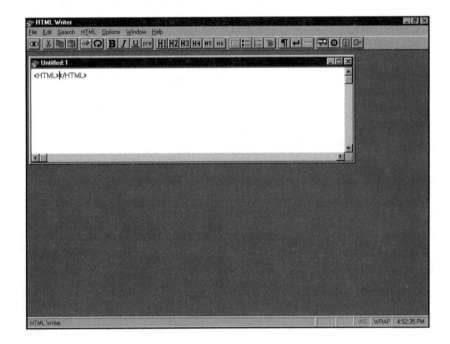

Inserting Style Tags

HTML Writer's style tags cover text formatting (such as the <I> tag for italics) and headers (such as <H1>). (If you need a refresher course on these tags, head back to Chapter 5, "From Buck-Naked to Beautiful: Dressing Up Your Page.")

210

You can apply these tags (and, indeed, many of the other tags we'll be talking about) using either of the following methods:

➤ If the text you want to mark already exists, highlight the text and then apply the tags as described later in this section. (Tip: you can highlight a single word by double-clicking on it.) In this case, HTML Writer applies the appropriate start tag (e.g., <I>) to the left of the highlighted text and the corresponding end tag (e.g., </I>) to the right of the text.

➤ If the text doesn't exist, just apply the tag where the text will appear. HTML Writer adds both the start tag and the end tag side by side (e.g., <I></I>), so you just insert your text between them.

To apply one of the text formatting style tags, first pull down the HTML menu and select the **Style** command. Then choose one of the commands listed in the following table (or you can use the toolbar buttons or keyboard shortcuts shown in the table).

Style	Tags	Command	Button	Shortcut
Bold	<B></B>	Bold	**B**	Ctrl+B
Italic	<I></I>	Italic	*I*	Ctrl+I
Underline	<U></U>	Underline	U	Ctrl+U
Typewriter	<TT></TT>	Typewriter	None	None

Check This Out...

HTML Menu Shortcut

You can display the HTML menu quickly by right-clicking on the document text. The shortcut menu that appears gives you access to all the HTML menu commands.

For the heading styles, select the HTML menu's **Style** command, then choose the **Header** command to display another cascade menu. The following table spells out which command (and toolbar button) inserts which tags.

Tags	Command	Button
<H1></H1>	1 (Top level)	**H1**
<H2></H2>	2	**H2**
<H3></H3>	3	**H3**
<H4></H4>	4	**H4**
<H5></H5>	5	**H5**
<H6></H6>	6 (Bottom level)	**H6**

Inserting Paragraph Tags

Paragraph tags? Isn't there just one paragraph tag: <P>? Well, not in the HTML Writer world where the line break (<BR>), horizontal rule (<HR>), and preformatted (<PRE> and </PRE>) tags are grouped into this category, as are a few other obscure tags that we won't worry about. (I talked about the <P> tag in Chapter 4. You'll find info on the other tags in Chapter 5.)

Hey, it's a free country, so why the heck not? You'll find the commands for these tags by pulling down the **HTML** menu and selecting the **Paragraph** command. Here's a summary of the available tags, and their corresponding menu commands, toolbar buttons, and keyboard shortcuts:

Tags	Command	Button	Shortcut
<P>	Paragraph	¶	Ctrl+P
 	Line Break	↵	Ctrl+L
<HR>	Horizontal Rule	—	Ctrl+H
<PRE></PRE>	Preformatted	pre	None

212

Inserting Image Tags

HTML Writer makes it easy to add <IMG> tags for graphics, especially tags that include options such as alternate text (ALT) and alignment (ALIGN). (This graphics stuff was explained in gory detail back in Chapter 8, "A Picture Is Worth a Thousand Clicks: Working with Images.") Here are the steps to follow to insert an <IMG> tag in your document:

1. Pull down the **HTML** menu, select the **Hyperlinks** command, and then select the **Inline Image** command. (Why is the Inline Image command stuffed inside the Hyperlinks menu? Beats me. Hey, I just write about 'em; I don't make 'em.) The Inline Image dialog box appears, as shown in the following figure.

    You can also display the Inline Image dialog box by clicking on this button in the toolbar.

Use the Inline Image dialog box to specify the options for the <IMG> tag.

2. Use the URL text box to enter the name and location of the graphics file. Note that the URL box also doubles as a drop-down list box that keeps track of the last 20 filenames you entered.

3. Use the Alternate Text box to enter a text alternative for non-graphical browsers.

4. Use the Alignment options (Bottom, Middle, Top) to choose an alignment for the image.

5. Select **OK** to insert the <IMG> tag with the options you specified.

Inserting Link Tags I: Remote Links

HTML Writer divides links into two categories: remote links that jump to a specified URL, and targets that link to a specific section of a document. (Need a link lesson? Then Chapter 7, "Making the Jump to Hyperspace: Adding Links," is the place you ought to be.) This section covers remote links; targets are covered in the next section.

Here are the steps to follow to insert a remote link in your document:

1. Enter your link text and highlight it.

2. Pull down the **HTML** menu, select the **Hyperlinks** command, and then select the **Remote** command. The Hypertext Remote Link dialog box appears, as shown in the following figure.

   You can also click on this button in the toolbar to display the Hypertext Remote Link dialog box.

3. Use the URL text box to enter the URL you want to go to when the reader selects the link.

4. Select **OK**.

HTML Writer inserts a link tag that takes the following form:

```
<A HREF="The URL you entered">Your link text</A>
```

Use this dialog box to enter the URL for the link.

Inserting Link Tags II: Targets

Recall from Chapter 7 that you can insert an "anchor" inside a hypertext document and then create a link that points to that anchor. This enables your readers to jump to specific sections of the document. HTML Writer uses the term *target* instead of anchor, but the principle is the same.

To set up the target, highlight the text, select the HTML menu's **Hyperlinks** command, and then select the **Target** command. The Hypertext Link Target dialog box appears, as shown below. In the Target Name text box, enter a name for the target (this is the name you'll use later on when you set up a link to the target) and then select **OK**. HTML Writer inserts an <A> tag of the following form:

```
<A NAME="The name you entered">Your target text</A>
```

Clicking on this button in the toolbar will also display the Hypertext Link Target dialog box.

Use the Hypertext Link Target dialog box to enter a name for the target.

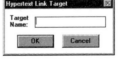

214

The next item on the agenda is to create a link that points to the target you just created. To do this, highlight the link text, select the HTML menu's **Hyperlinks** command, and then select the **Local** command. In the Hypertext Local Link dialog box that appears (see below), use the Target Name text box to enter the name of the target, and then select **OK**. HTML Writer inserts an <A> tag of the following form:

```
<A HREF="#The target name you entered">Your link text</A>
```

 Clicking on this button in the toolbar will also display the Hypertext Local Link dialog box.

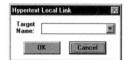

Use the Hypertext Local Link dialog box to enter the name of the target to which you want to link.

Inserting List Tags

Looking to add a list or two to your document? Whether you need a bulleted list, a numbered list, or a definition list, HTML Writer is up to the job. (I took you through lists in more detail back in Chapter 6, "A Fistful of List Grist for Your Web Page Mill.")

To insert the container tags for the list (<UL> and </UL> for a bulleted list; <OL> and </OL> for a numbered list; <DL> and </DL> for a definition list), select the HTML menu's **Lists** command, and then choose one of the commands (or toolbar buttons) shown in the following table.

Tags	Command	Button
<UL></UL>	Bulleted	
<OL></OL>	Numbered	
<DL></DL>	Definition	

To insert an <LI> tag for an item in a bulleted or numbered list, select the HTML menu's **Lists** command, and then choose **List Item** (or press **Ctrl+K**).

 You can also insert the <LI> tag by clicking on this button in the toolbar.

To insert a <DT> tag for a term in a definition list, pull down the **HTML** menu, select **Lists**, and then select **Term Item**. To insert a <DD> tag for a definition in a definition list, select the HTML menu's **Lists** command, and then select **Def. Item**.

 Clicking on this toolbar button inserts the following sequence of tags:

<DL><DT><DD></DL>.

Inserting Character Codes

If you want to insert a code for a non-standard character (i.e., those characters that don't show up on your keyboard), HTML Writer has several methods to choose from. (I went through all this character code rigmarole in Chapter 5, "From Buck-Naked to Beautiful: Dressing Up Your Page.")

To give it a whirl, pull down the **HTML** menu, select **Other**, and then choose one of the following commands:

Special Characters This command displays another cascade menu that contains a few characters, most notably the less than (<) and greater than (>) signs.

Extended Characters This command displays the Extended Characters dialog box shown below. As you can see, these are all foreign characters. Highlight the one you want and then select **OK**.

Use the Extended Characters dialog box to pick out the foreign character you want to insert.

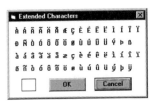

ASCII Character This command displays the ASCII Character dialog box shown in the following figure. Enter the ASCII code of the character you want and then select OK. (See the appendix titled "HTML Codes for Cool Characters" for the ASCII codes of some characters you might want to use.)

In the ASCII Character dialog box, enter the ASCII code of the character you want to insert.

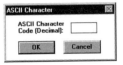

Inserting the Date

It's a good idea to include the current date and time in your page so people know when you last updated the text. You can do this in HTML Writer by selecting the Edit menu's **Time/Date** command. HTML Writer inserts both the date and the time (feel free to delete the time if you think it's overkill).

Taking the Document for a Test Drive

After you shoehorn some text and HTML tags into your document, you'll probably want to load it into a Web browser to see how things look. Normally you'd have to get out of the program you used to create the document, load the browser, and then load the document. One of HTML Writer's nicest features is that it lets you combine all these steps into a single command. Here's how it works:

1. Pull down the **File** menu and select the **Test** command.

   You can also test the document by clicking on this toolbar button.

2. If you activated the Options menu's Save on Test command and you haven't saved the document for the first time, the Save As dialog box appears. Enter a name for the document and then select **OK**.

3. If this is the first time you've run the Test command, HTML Writer will complain that it can't find your browser, as shown in the dialog box below. (By default, HTML Writer thinks you use Mosaic; don't worry, you can ignore this if you use a different browser.) Select **OK** to display the Location of Browser dialog box, where Browser is the name of your browser.

This alert appears the first time you run the Test command.

4. Use the Folders list to find the file that runs your browser (e.g. NETSCAPE.EXE), highlight it in the File name list, and then select **OK**. HTML Writer loads the browser and displays your document.

217

Keeping HTML Writer Up-to-Date

Kris Nosack, the developer of HTML Writer, comes out with new versions of the program from time to time. To keep informed of the latest developments, keep an eye peeled on the HTML Writer home page:

`http://lal.cs.byu.edu/people/nosack/`

There's also an HTML Writer mailing list you can subscribe to for technical help, questions, and to suggest improvements. If you'd like to check it out, send a subscription request to the following address:

`html-writer@byu.edu`

In the body of the message, just say you'd like to subscribe to the HTML Writer mailing list.

The Least You Need to Know

This chapter showed you how to write HTML the easy way with HTML Writer. Here's a rehash of the main events:

➤ Although HTML Writer is free, the programmer would appreciate a small donation to help cover the development costs.

➤ You start a new document by selecting the File menu's **New** command (or by pressing **Ctrl+N**). To open an existing document, select the File menu's **Open** command, or press **Ctrl+O**.

➤ Use the Options menu commands to remake HTML Writer in your own image. In particular, I'd recommend turning on **Word Wrap**, **Uppercase Tags**, and **Save on Test**. Also, use the Screen Font command to choose a more readable font.

➤ To insert a tag, highlight the affected text (if necessary) and then choose the tag you want from the HTML menu.

➤ To see how the document looks in a browser, select the File menu's **Test** command.

Chapter 17

The Best Commercial HTML Editor: HotDog

In This Chapter

➤ Downloading and installing HotDog

➤ Dealing with HotDog documents

➤ Using HotDog to add tags

➤ Previewing your documents in a browser

➤ How HotDog will make you relish (groan) creating Web pages

bandwagon \ noun, 1. A cause that attracts increasing numbers of adherents. 2. A current trend.

We've seen bandwagons come and go—hula hoops, Pet Rocks, and Barney-bashing come to mind—but the World Wide Web may turn out to be the biggest of them all. Everywhere you look, companies and individuals—elbows akimbo—are looking to carve out some sitting room on the Web bandwagon. Most of them just want to make a splash on the Web, but there's no shortage of opportunists who'd like to make a buck as well. So although the Internet has traditionally been a place where good programs could be had at a great price (i.e., free), lots of software developers are thumbing their noses at tradition and charging for their creations.

There's nothing inherently wrong with this (it's just good old-fashioned capitalism, after all), but as a consumer you want to get the biggest bang for your buck. In this chapter, we'll look at a commercial HTML editor that will give you a big-time bang and then some. It's called HotDog and it's one of the nicest HTML editors around. (Actually, the HotDog folks call their products "Web editors.") HotDog is 100 percent all-beef and packed with features that are sure to make your HTML chores easier. Although a single chapter isn't nearly enough to do justice to all of HotDog's features (that would require an entire book), I'll try to cover the most important options so you can get HotDog happening with a minimum of fuss and bother.

Getting Your Hands on HotDog

The HotDog vendor is Sausage Software, and you'll need to download a copy of the program from their Web site (see the figure below). Here's the address:

```
http://www.sausage.com/download.htm
```

You can download HotDog from this Web page.

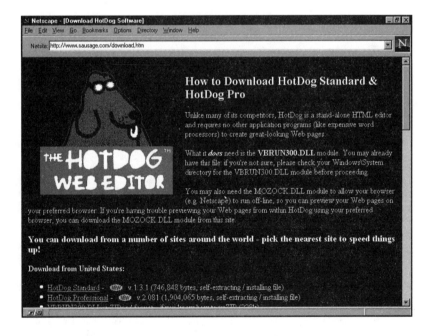

The first decision to make is which version of HotDog you want to try. HotDog Standard is a great little program that should satisfy the needs of most Web authors (it's the version I'll be talking about in this chapter). HotDog Professional is the high-end version that includes nifty features such as unlimited file size, multiple levels of Undo, a spelling checker, an HTML syntax checker, and the ability to open and save multiple documents (called a project) at once. In either case, you can use the program free for 30 days, after which it will no longer work. If you'd like to keep on using HotDog, you'll need to fork over $29.95 for HotDog Standard, or $99.95 for HotDog Professional.

Downloading the HotDog File

To download the program from the Sausage Software site, make sure you're viewing the Web page shown above, and then select either the HotDog Standard link or the HotDog Professional link. These links take you to the Sausage FTP server, which will automatically send the file to your machine. Your browser may ask you what you want to do with the file. Select the **Save to Disk** option, and then select a location on your hard drive for the file.

Installing HotDog

Here are the steps to follow in order to install HotDog on your computer:

1. In Program Manager (Windows 3.1) or Explorer (Windows 95), double-click on the HotDog file you downloaded. If you grabbed HotDog Standard, the filename is STANDARD.EXE; if your choice was HotDog Pro, the filename is HDP2INST.EXE. (Note that these filenames may change as new versions of HotDog are released.) This starts the HotDog setup program.

2. The first dialog box that appears gives you a short introduction to HotDog. (It also mentions something about needing a file named VBRUN300.DLL. If you don't have this file, the next section shows you how to get it from this book's disk.) Select **OK** to continue. The **Select Destination Directory** dialog box appears.

3. Select the drive and directory where you want HotDog installed, and then select **OK**. The setup program displays the **Make Backups?** dialog box.

4. Select **Yes** to tell the program to make backup copies of any files it replaces during the installation. Now the **Select Backup Directory** dialog box appears.

5. The default backup directory is fine, so just select **OK**. The setup program starts copying the HotDog files. When it's done, a dialog box appears asking if you want to create a program group (or a Start menu folder, if you're using Windows 95).

6. Select **Yes**. Another dialog box appears so you can select the program group or folder to use.

7. Make your choice and then select **OK**. The **Installation Complete!** dialog box appears.

8. If you're sure you have a copy of VBRUN300.DLL in your Windows SYSTEM directory, you can select **Yes** to start HotDog. If you don't have the file, select **No**, instead, and read the next section.

Installing VBRUN300.DLL

To run properly, HotDog requires a separate file called VBRUN300.DLL. You need to install this file in the Windows SYSTEM directory before starting HotDog. Why doesn't HotDog include this file? Well, lots of other programs use VBRUN300.DLL, so many people already have it installed. It's a big file (about 400K), so the HotDog folks decided to leave it out to reduce the download times. If you don't have this file in your SYSTEM directory (which is usually C:\WINDOWS\SYSTEM), follow these steps to extract it from this book's disk:

Techno Talk

What the Heck is VBRUN300.DLL, Anyway?
What's with all the fuss about VBRUN300.DLL? Well, HotDog was written in a programming language called Visual Basic (VB). VBRUN300.DLL is VB's runtime library, which allows VB programs to interact with Windows and do other low-level, behind-the-screens, technoid stuff.

1. Insert this book's disk in the appropriate floppy drive.

2. In Program Manager or File Manager, pull down the File menu and select the **Run** command. If you're using Windows 95, open the **Start** menu and select **Run**. The Run dialog box appears.

3. Type the following command:

   a:\expand vbrun300.dl_
   c:\windows\system\vbrun300.dll

   You'll need to adjust this command if the disk is in a drive other than a, or if Windows is in a directory other than c:\windows.

4. Select **OK**. VBRUN300.DLL is extracted from the disk and placed in the SYSTEM directory.

Serving Up HotDog

With HotDog now safely ensconced on your hard drive, you're ready to take your first bite. If you didn't start HotDog after the installation, you can crank it up by using one of the following techniques:

➤ If you're using Windows 3.1, double-click on the **HotDog** icon in the HotDog program group.

➤ If you're using Windows 95, open the **Start** menu, select **Programs**, open the **HotDog** folder, and then select the **HotDog** item.

The first time you run HotDog, you'll see a screen titled The Boring Legal Stuff. You can read this mumbo-jumbo if you feel brave enough, but I recommend you just select the **I Agree** button and get the heck out of there.

The second time you run HotDog (and each subsequent time during your 30-day trial period), a "nag" screen appears to let you know how many days you have left to evaluate HotDog (assuming, of course, you haven't yet forked out the hard-earned cash to register HotDog). Select **OK** to continue loading.

You'll eventually see the **Welcome to HotDog!** dialog box. You can safely ignore most of the options in this window (since you already know about HTML and I'm about to tell you how to use HotDog). If you'd rather not be bothered by this screen in the future, activate the **Don't show this screen again** check box. To get to HotDog's main screen at long last (see below), select the **Use HotDog Now** option.

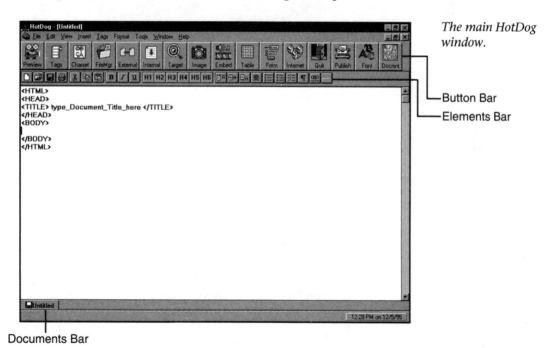

The main HotDog window.

Button Bar
Elements Bar
Documents Bar

Working with Documents

As you can see in the figure above, HotDog is kind enough not only to load a new HTML document for you at startup, but also to populate the document with the basic HTML tags. How thoughtful! (Note, however, that you'll need to replace the default title with your own invention.) Don't see a new document? Bummer. You can get one by using any of the following methods:

➤ Select the **File** menu's **New** command.

➤ Press **Ctrl+N**.

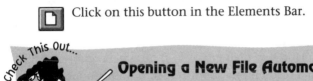 Click on this button in the Elements Bar.

Opening a New File Automatically

If HotDog doesn't automatically start a new file for you at startup, you can change that quickly enough. Pull down the **Tools** menu, select **Options**, and then select the **Saving/Starting** tab in the Options dialog box that appears. Activate the **Open New Document when HotDog starts** check box, and then select **Save Options**.

If you prefer to open an existing document, here are the methods you use to open a file:

➤ Select the **File** menu's **Open** command.

➤ Press **Ctrl+O**.

Click on this button in the Elements Bar.

In the Open File dialog box that appears, highlight the file you want to work with and then select **OK** to open it. Note that HotDog displays the name of each open file in the Documents Bar at the bottom of the screen (see the figure below). You can select a file by clicking on its name in the Document Bar, or by selecting it from the Window menu.

The Documents Bar
shows you the name
of each open file.

This document has unsaved changes.

Here are your options for saving your files:

➤ To save the active document, pull down the **File** menu and select the **Save** command, or press **Ctrl+S**.

➤ To save all the open documents, select the **File** menu's **Save All** command.

Click on this button in the Elements Bar to save the active document.

Conveniently, HotDog marks documents that have unsaved changes by placing a red "X" beside the file's name in the Documents Bar (see the figure shown earlier for an example).

Check This Out...

HotDog Doesn't Like Long Filenames

If you're using HotDog on a Windows 95 system, note that you won't be able to save your documents with long filenames. If you already have some files with long names, they'll appear in shortened form in the Open File dialog box. For example, the filename Bad Craziness.htm appears as badcra~1.htm, and homepage.html appears as homepa~1.htm.

Creating an HTML Document with HotDog

Since HotDog is really just a text editor with a whole whack of HTML bells and whistles thrown in for good measure, it's extremely easy to use. You simply type your text in the document window and then use the menu commands or toolbar buttons to insert HTML codes when you need them. Here are the basic steps you'll follow for each document:

1. Type in your document text.

2. When you need to insert an HTML tag, either highlight the text you want to affect, or position the cursor where you want the tag to appear, and then choose the appropriate menu command or toolbar button (which I'll talk about in the rest of this chapter).

3. Save the file from time to time, as described earlier.

4. Preview the file every now and then to see how things look in a browser (see "Getting a Sneak Preview of Your Document," below).

5. Repeat steps 2–4 until you've had enough.

The next few sections expand on step 2 by showing you how to insert the various HTML tags. I'll divide everything up into two separate chunks:

➤ Inserting tags directly into the document.

➤ Inserting tags by inserting "objects" such as tables and lists.

Inserting Tags Directly

The most straightforward way to toss a tag into your document is to use HotDog's **Tags** menu. The commands on this menu produce dialog boxes that give you a list of all the available tags. You select one of the items from the list, drag it into the document, and HotDog dutifully inserts the appropriate tag. For example, if you select the **Font** command in the **Tags** menu, you'll see the Tags - [Font] window shown in the following figure.

Use the Tags - [Font] window to add font-related tags to your document.

As you can see, this list includes items for all the font-related tags and attributes, including Bold (<B>) and Italic (<I>). Now you either position the cursor where you want the tags to appear, or else highlight the existing text you want to affect. From here, you can insert the tags by using any of the following three techniques:

➤ Drag an item from the list and drop it anywhere inside the document.

➤ Double-click on an item.

➤ Use the up and down arrow keys to highlight an item and then press **Enter**.

Note that the window stays on screen after you've inserted a tag, so you're free to insert tags until you're blue in the face. (You can use your mouse to adjust the position of the cursor inside the document, if necessary.) When you're done, just close the window by double-clicking on the icon in the upper-left corner, by clicking on the **Close** button (Windows 95 only), or by pressing **Alt+F4**.

Tag City

HotDog also has a Tags window that displays a monster list of all the available tags. To check it out, pull down the **View** menu and select the **Tags** command, or press **F6**.

 You can also display the Tags window by clicking on the Button Bar's Tags button.

You can also insert tags directly by using the buttons on the Elements Bar. Just position the cursor appropriately and then click merrily away. Here's a rundown of the various buttons you can use:

Tag Type	Tags Inserted	Button
Bold	<B></B>	**B**
Italic	<I></I>	*I*
<u>Underline</u>	<U></U>	U
1st-level heading	<H1></H1>	H1
2nd-level heading	<H2></H2>	H2
3rd-level heading	<H3></H3>	H3
4th-level heading	<H4></H4>	H4
5th-level heading	<H5></H5>	H5
6th-level heading	<H6></H6>	H6
Image alignment attribute	ALIGN=TOP	
Image alignment attribute	ALIGN=MIDDLE	
Image alignment attribute	ALIGN=BOTTOM	
Center text	<CENTER></CENTER>	
Numbered list	<OL><LI></OL>	
Bulleted list	<UL><LI></UL>	

continues

continued

Tag Type	Tags Inserted	Button
Definition list	<DL><DT><DD></DL>	
Paragraph	<P>	
Line break	 	
Horizontal rule	<HR>	

Font Formatting Foofaraw

By default, HotDog inserts the <STRONG> tag for bold and the <EM> (emphasis) tag for italics. If, like me, you prefer the traditional <B> and <I> tags, you can easily bend HotDog to your will. Pull down the **Tools** menu, select the **Options** command, and deactivate the **Use Strong and Emphasis, not Bold and Italics** check box. Click the **Save Options** button to put the new setting into effect.

Note that HotDog's Format menu boasts a number of commands that enable you to insert tags that format text. Most of the commands simply insert tags directly into the document. These include the commands Bold (keyboard shortcut: Ctrl+B), Italics (Ctrl+I), Underline (Ctrl+U), Blinking, and Center. If you want to insert multiple font tags at once, try the Font command (or press F2).

Inserting Objects

Inserting individual tags directly is fine for simple tags such as bold and paragraph. However, if you're working with more complex HTML constructions—such as tables and links—it can be time-consuming and it's not all that much easier than coding HTML by hand. (Except, of course, for the major bonus of not having to memorize all those tags!)

To make your Web weaving easier, HotDog offers a better way to build more sophisticated objects. The idea is that you use a dialog box to define how you want the object to appear, and then HotDog handles the dirty work of gathering up the appropriate tags and attributes and inserting them in the document. The next few sections show you how this works for images, links, tables, and lists.

Inserting an Image

As you learned back in Chapter 8, "A Picture Is Worth a Thousand Clicks: Working with Images," the <IMG> tag that inserts a graphics file has quite a few options. Toss in the Netscape extensions to the <IMG> tag (see Chapter 10), and you've got quite a load to work with. To make the <IMG> tag easier to figure out, HotDog has a dialog box that spells out the various options. To see it, select the Insert menu's **Image (Advanced)** command, or press **Ctrl+M**. The Image Properties dialog box appears, as shown below.

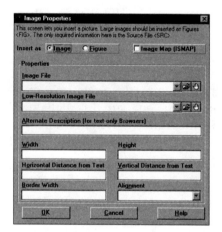

Use the Image Properties dialog box to specify the details for your <IMG> tags.

This dialog box is weighed down with all sorts of options, but there are only a few you need to worry about:

Image File   Enter the name of the graphics file.

Alternate Description   Enter a text alternative for non-graphical browsers.

Width   Enter the width, in pixels, of the image (this is a Netscape extension).

Height   Enter the height, in pixels, of the image (this is also a Netscape extension).

Alignment   Select an alignment attribute.

When you're done, select **OK** to insert the <IMG> tag with the options you specified.

To insert an image as a link, select the Insert menu's **Image** command, or click on the Image button in the Button Bar. In the Insert Image dialog box that appears, enter the image's filename in the **Image File** text box, enter the URL of the linked document in the **Document to Launch** text box, and enter a text alternative in the **Alternate Description** text box. When you're done, select **OK** to insert the link.

 The Image button from HotDog's Button Bar.

Inserting a Remote Link

HotDog enables you to insert two kinds of links: remote links that display a different document and targets that jump to another section of the current document. (A complete link lesson can be found in Chapter 7, "Making the Jump to Hyperspace: Adding Links.") This section covers remote links; targets are covered in next section.

The HotDog programmers, bless their nerdy hearts, have provided you with no less than four ways to insert a remote link in your document:

➤ **Method #1.** If you know the URL, the easiest method is to select the **Insert** menu's **Simple URL** command (or press **F4** for faster service). In the Insert URL dialog box that appears, enter the URL in the **URL** text box, enter the link text in the **Description** text box, and then select **OK**.

➤ **Method #2.** If you're just testing your links on your own system, you can insert a link to a document on your hard disk. Pull down the **Insert** menu and select the **Jump to a Document in this System** command (or press **Ctrl+J**). When the Choose File dialog box shows up, highlight the file and then select **OK**.

➤ **Method #3.** For a bit more control over the remote document's URL, try the Insert menu's **Jump to a Document on Another System** command. (You can also try slamming **Ctrl+H** on your keyboard or clicking on the External button in the Button Bar.) HotDog tosses the Build External Hypertext Link dialog box on screen, as shown in the following figure.

 The External button from HotDog's Button Bar.

Use this dialog box to build a URL for a remote link.

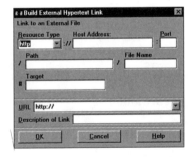

This dialog box splits the components of the URL into various controls: a Resource Type drop-down list, and text boxes for Host Address, Port (which is usually left blank), Path, File Name, and Target. (I talked about most of this stuff back in Chapter 7.) Now type your link text into the **Description of Link** text box and select **OK**. Stick a fork in it, it's done!

➤ **Method #4.** If you want your link to launch some kind of Internet service (such as e-mail or FTP), try the Insert menu's **Launch an Internet Service** command. (Keyboardists can press **Ctrl+Y** and mouse mavens can click on the Button Bar's Internet button.) HotDog displays the Create HyperText Link dialog box, shown below. Select the button that corresponds to the service you want the link to run. For example, to create a mailto (e-mail) link, you'd select the **Let the User send Mail to someone** button. Enter the appropriate data in the new dialog box that appears, and then select **OK**.

 The Internet button from HotDog's Button Bar.

Use this dialog box to select which Internet service you want the link to launch.

Inserting a Target

Recall from Chapter 7 that you can insert an "anchor" inside a hypertext document and then create a link that points to that anchor. This enables your readers to jump to specific sections of the document. HotDog uses the term *target* instead of anchor, but the principle is the same. To set up the target, highlight the text and select the **Insert** menu's **Hypertext Target** command. (Ctrl+G is the keyboard shortcut, and Target is the Button Bar button of choice.) In the **Enter Target ID** dialog box that appears, enter a name for the target and then select **OK**. HotDog inserts an <A> tag of the following form:

```
<A NAME="The name you enter">Your target text</A>
```

The Target button.

Your next task is to create a link that points to the target you just created. To do this, select the Insert menu's **Jump Within this Document** command (you can also try Ctrl+K or the Internal button). In the Select Hypertext Target dialog box (see below), highlight a name in the **Hypertext Target ID** list, enter the link text in the **Description of Link** text box, and then select **OK**. HotDog inserts an <A> tag of the following form:

```
<A HREF="#The target name you enter">Your link text</A>
```

 The Internal button.

Use the Select Hypertext Target dialog box to select the name of the target to which you want to link.

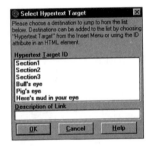

Inserting a Table

As you learned the hard way back in Chapter 11, "Table Talk: Adding Tables to Your Page," tables are complex beasts compared to most HTML tags. However, HotDog, with its usual winning way, simplifies table design and makes it almost pleasurable. Here are the steps to follow to create a table with HotDog:

1. Pull down the Insert menu and select the **Table** command. Those in a rush might want to try pressing Ctrl+T or clicking on the Button Bar's Table button, instead. HotDog heaves the Create Table dialog box onto the screen. The figure below shows a completed version of this dialog box.

    The Table button.

2. If you want to use a caption, enter it in the **Caption** text box and then choose either the TOP or BOTTOM option.

3. Enter the total number of columns in the **Columns** box, and the total number of rows in the **Rows** box.

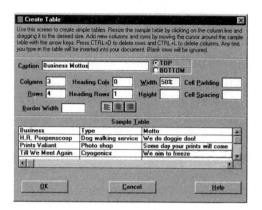

HotDog's Create Table dialog box makes it a breeze to create even the most complex tables.

4. If you want one or more columns to be headings, enter the number in the **Heading Cols** box. If you want one or more rows to be headings, enter the number in the **Heading Rows** box. (Note that these values don't affect the total number of rows or columns.)

5. If necessary, use the **Width** and **Height** text boxes to enter a width and height for the table.

6. If needed, enter a value for the **Cell Padding** and **Cell Spacing**.

7. Enter the border width you want to use in the **Border Width** text box.

8. The **Sample Table** area is a grid that shows the number of rows and columns you specified in Step 3. For each cell, select it (either by clicking on it or by using the arrow keys to move around) and enter the data that you want to appear in the cell.

9. When you're done, select **OK** to insert the table in all its glory.

Inserting a List

Looking to add a list or two to your document? Whether you need a bulleted list, a numbered list, or a definition list, HotDog is up to the task. (I took you through lists in more detail back in Chapter 6, "A Fistful of List Grist for Your Web Page Mill.")

To insert the container tags for the list (<UL> and </UL> for a bulleted list; <OL> and </OL> for a numbered list; <DL> and </DL> for a definition list), select the Insert menu's **List** command (or press Ctrl+L). In the Create List Element dialog box, choose the **List Type** (Bulleted, Numbered, or Definition List), choose the **Type** of bullets or numbers you want, and then select OK.

Inserting Character Codes

If you want to insert a code for a non-standard character (i.e., those characters that don't show up on your keyboard), HotDog has an Entity List window (see below) that lists all your choices. To display this window, select the View menu's **Special Characters** command, or press F7, or click on the Charset button in the Button Bar.

 The Charset button.

To insert a character, either double-click on the appropriate list item, or highlight the item and press **Enter**. When you're done, close the window by double-clicking on the icon in the upper-left corner, by clicking on the **Close** button (Windows 95 only), or by pressing **Alt+F4**.

Use the Entity List window to pick out the characters you want to insert.

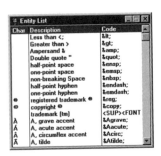

Inserting the Date

It's a good idea to include the current date and time in your page so people know when you last updated the text. You can do this in HotDog by selecting the **Insert** menu's **Special** command, and then selecting the **Date/Time** command. In the Insert Date/Time dialog box that appears, select the date format and then select **OK**.

Getting a Sneak Preview of Your Document

When you slap up some text and tags, you'll likely want to load the document into a Web browser to see if things look okay. Instead of switching to your browser and loading the document, HotDog lets you combine these steps into a single command. Here's how it works:

1. Pull down the **File** menu and select the **Preview Document** command. (You can also try pressing F5 or clicking on the Preview button.) If this is the first time you've run this command, HotDog complains that there's no default browser.

    The Preview button.

2. Select **OK** to display the Choose Browser dialog box.

3. Find and highlight the .EXE file that starts the browser program and then select **OK**. HotDog loads the browser and displays your document.

The Least You Need to Know

This chapter showed you how to cook up a tasty HTML meal using the HotDog Web editor. Here's a recap of some of the ingredients we used:

➤ To get HotDog (remember that you have to pay for HotDog if you plan on using it past the 30-day trial period), head for the following URL:

   `http://www.sausage.com/download.htm`

➤ You start a new document by selecting the File menu's **New** command (or by pressing Ctrl+N). To open an existing document, select the **File** menu's **Open** command or press Ctrl+O.

➤ To insert a tag directly, highlight the affected text (if necessary) and then choose the tag command you want from the **Tags** menu. In the dialog box that appears, double-click on the tag or drag it into the document.

➤ To insert an object such as an image, link, or table, select the appropriate **Insert** menu command and then fill in the dialog box that appears.

➤ To see how the document looks in a browser, select the **File** menu's **Preview Document** command, or press F5.

Chapter 18

The Word Wide Web: Internet Assistant for Microsoft Word

In This Chapter

➤ Downloading and Installing Internet Assistant

➤ Starting Internet Assistant

➤ Using Internet Assistant to format characters

➤ Working with styles

➤ Inserting lists, images, and links

➤ Complete coverage of all the basic HTML tags, from an Internet Assistant perspective

I think one of the reasons HTML seems so, well, *primitive*, is that most of what you're coding is stuff that even the most brain-dead word processor has been able to handle for years. Formatting characters, creating paragraphs, setting up lists, and working with heading styles are all old hat to today's crop of word processing programs. Even inline images and tables are becoming *de rigueur* in high-end word pro circles. That leaves only hypertext links as a challenge, and how hard can that be to implement?

In other words, it seems entirely logical that you should be able to chuck the old HTML-tags-in-a-text-editor model out the window and, instead, create top-notch Web pages from the friendly confines of your favorite word processor. And you know what? You can! Microsoft's Internet Assistant for Microsoft Word turns Word into a full-fledged HTML machine that lets you create Web pages as easily as you pound out memos and letters. This chapter takes you through the basics of using Internet Assistant to put together Web pages.

Grabbing Internet Assistant

Internet Assistant isn't a separate program. Instead, it extends the functionality of Word by attaching itself—Alien-like—to the program. The result, as you'll soon see, is a new collection of menu commands and toolbars that are HTML-aware. As an added bonus, you can even use Word to browse the Web. Gnarly!

So your first order of business is to grab the file that includes the Internet Assistant stuff, and a setup program. Internet Assistant comes in two flavors:

Internet Assistant for Word for Windows 95   Version 2 of Internet Assistant works with Word for Windows 95. (This is the version I'll be covering in this chapter, although I'll point out the differences between versions as we go along.) To download this version of Internet Assistant, head for the following Web page:

```
http://www.microsoft.com/msoffice/freestuf/Msword/download/ia/ia95/
default.htm
```

Internet Assistant for Word for Windows 6   Version 1 of Internet Assistant is designed for Word for Windows 6. To get this version of Internet Assistant, toddle over to the following Web page:

```
http://www.microsoft.com/msoffice/freestuf/Msword/download/ia/ia1z/
default.htm
```

In both cases, look for the section named **How to Download and Install Internet Assistant**, and click on the "download" link (the actual link text depends on which version you're downloading). This will take you to another page that gives you more info and includes a link that downloads the file. When you select this link, your browser will ask what you want to do with the file. Select the "Save to Disk" option (or whatever) and then choose an empty folder or directory for the destination. (On my system, I've set up a directory named DOWNLOAD that I use as a sort of electronic waiting room for files that I download from the Internet and computer bulletin boards.)

Check Your Word Version!

If you plan to use Internet Assistant version 1 with Word for Windows 6, you need to make sure you have the correct version of Word 6. In Word, select the Help menu's **About Microsoft Word** command. In the About Microsoft Word dialog box that appears, check out the version of Word you have. If it just says 6.0 with no letter after it, you'll need to upgrade Word to version 6.0a. You can get a "patch" from the Microsoft FTP site:

```
ftp.microsoft.com/softlib/MSLFILES/WORD60A.EXE
```

Running WORD60A.EXE extracts a few files. The file named README.TXT gives you instructions on how to proceed.

Once the file is sitting pretty on your hard drive, follow these steps to install Internet Assistant:

1. If you're using the Word 6 version of Internet Assistant, double-click on the file you downloaded. This extracts the compressed files that were crammed into the downloaded file.

2. For the Word for Windows 95 version, double-click on the file you downloaded. A dialog box then asks if you want to install Internet Assistant. Select **Yes** to continue. For the Word 6 version, run the SETUP.EXE file that was decompressed in Step 1. An introductory dialog box appears.

3. Press **Enter** to continue. After a while, the Setup program displays another dialog box with all sorts of scary-looking legal gibberish.

4. Gluttons for punishment can struggle through the mumbo-jumbo. The rest of us can just select the **Accept** button to move on. (In the Word 6 version, you need to press **Enter** a couple of times before the Accept button shows up.) Setup displays a dialog box showing the location where Internet Assistant will be installed (see the figure below).

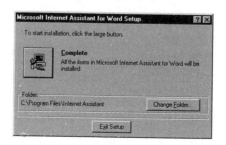

Use this dialog box to select a different location for Internet Assistant.

5. If you don't like the suggested location, select the **Change Folder** button (or the **Change Directory** button, in the Word 6 version), pick out a locale from the dialog box that appears, and then select **OK**. Otherwise, move on to the next step.

6. Select the **Complete** button in the Word for Windows 95 version, or the **Continue** button in the Word 6 version. If you're running the Word 6 Setup, a dialog box asks if you want to install the browser components. Select **Yes** or **No**. Setup starts copying the Internet Assistant files to the location you chose. When the setup program is finished, it displays a dialog box from which you can start Word.

7. Select the **Launch Word** button to crank up Word. One final dialog box shows up to let you know that the installation was completed successfully.

8. Select **OK**.

Dealing with Documents

When Word starts, you just see the regular Word screen. To get to the HTML goodies, you need to open a new document based on Internet Assistant's HTML template.

1. Pull down the **File** menu and select the **New** command. Word displays the New dialog box (the figure below shows the New dialog box from Word for Windows 95).

Selecting the File menu's New command produces the New dialog box.

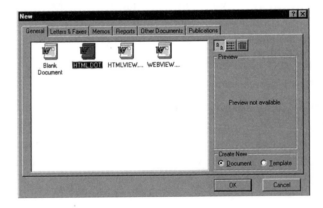

2. In the **General** tab, highlight the HTML.DOT template. (In Word 6's New dialog box, highlight the Html item in the Template list.)

3. Select **OK**. Word opens the new document.

If you'd prefer to open an existing HTML document, here are your choices:

➤ Select the **File** menu's **Open** command.

➤ Press **Ctrl+O**.

240

Click on this button in the Standard toolbar.

In the Open dialog box that appears, select **HTML Document (*.htm)** from the **Files of type** list, highlight the file you want to work with, and then select **Open**.

Later, after you've made some changes to your new HTML file, here are your options for saving it:

➤ Pull down the **File** menu and select the **Save** command.

➤ Press **Ctrl+S**.

 Click on this button in the Standard toolbar.

What Happens to Word

Opening an HTML document changes Word's menus and, as you can see in the figure below, the toolbars get a facelift as well. The idea behind these changes is twofold:

➤ To give you access only to those commands and features that produce legal HTML tags.

➤ To extend Word so it can handle things like links and document titles (i.e., the <TITLE> tag).

Formatting toolbar   Standard toolbar

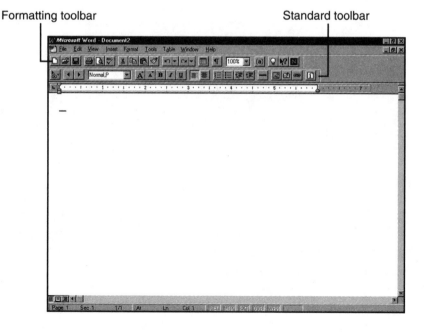

Word's toolbars and menus change when you open an HTML document.

Internet Assistant: WYSIWYG Web Weaving

Internet Assistant, like the Netscape Gold editor I covered back in Chapter 15, doesn't show HTML tags on screen. You use a combination of formatting commands (such as boldfacing), styles (such as headings), and objects (such as links and tables) to produce your Web page. All this produces a document with the correct HTML knickknacks, but you don't see any of it. Instead, Internet Assistant just shows you what your text will look like in a browser. That is, Internet Assistant is a WYSIWYG display. (WYSIWYG stands for What You See Is What You Get, although some wags prefer Why Your Screen Will Inadvertently Yield Garbage.) Here are the basic steps you'll follow for each document:

1. Type in your document text.

2. If you want to format some text or apply a style, select the text you want to work with. If you're inserting an HTML object such as a link or an image, position the editor's cursor where you want the object to appear.

3. Choose the appropriate menu command or toolbar button (I'll go through the available commands and buttons in the rest of this chapter).

4. Save the file from time to time, as described earlier.

5. Repeat steps 1 through 4 until you're done.

The next few sections expand on step 3 by showing you how to work with Internet Assistant's menus and toolbars.

Got a Hankering for HTML?

If you find you miss the HTML tags, it's easy enough to see them if you're using version 2 of Internet Assistant. Save the document and then select the **View menu's HTML Source** command. Feel free to edit the tags as necessary, and then select the **Close** button on the HTML toolbar to return to the regular view.

Adjusting the Title

When you start a new document, Internet Assistant tosses in all the basic tags that define the skeleton of the page: <HTML> and </HTML>, <HEAD> and </HEAD>, <BODY> and </BODY>, and <TITLE>. The default title (in version 2 only) is **HTML document for the World Wide Web**, which is probably a bit too vague for most folks' needs (!). To change this title, either select the **File** menu's **HTML Document Info** command, or click on the **Title** button in the Formatting toolbar. In the HTML Document Head Information dialog box that appears (see below), use the Title field to change the title and then select **OK**.

 The Title button.

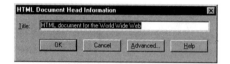

Use this dialog box to adjust the title of your Web page.

Need a New Paragraph? Just Press Enter

Back in Chapter 4, "Laying the Foundation: The Basic Structure of a Web Page," I mentioned that pressing Enter to start a new paragraph didn't work in HTML because you had to use the <P> tag, instead. Internet Assistant changes all that because pressing Enter really does start a new paragraph. In reality, pressing Enter in Internet Assistant adds a <P> tag behind the scenes. With WYSIWYG, all you see is the result: a new paragraph.

Formatting Characters

Thanks to the word processing ground upon which it sits, Internet Assistant has no shortage of options for formatting characters. (See Chapter 5, "From Buck-Naked to Beautiful: Dressing Up Your Page.") You can work with these options using either of the following methods:

➤ If the text you want to mark already exists, highlight the text and then apply the option. (Here are some text selection shortcuts that may come in handy: double-click on a word to select it; hold down **Ctrl** and click on a sentence to select it; triple-click on a paragraph to select it.)

➤ If the text doesn't exist, just apply the option where the text will appear and then start typing.

The basic formatting options—bold, italic, and underline—are available only from the Formatting toolbar or via keyboard shortcuts. The following table shows you the buttons and keys associated with each option.

Style	Button	Shortcut
Bold	**B**	Ctrl+B
Italic	*I*	Ctrl+I
<u>Underline</u>	<u>U</u>	Ctrl+U

For other kinds of formatting, you have the following choices:

➤ To set the font (Internet Explorer recognizes different fonts), font size, color, or superscripts and subscripts (version 2 only), select the Format menu's **Font** command (or press **Ctrl+Shift+F**). In the Font dialog box that appears (see below), enter your options and then select **OK**.

Use this dialog box to set some character formatting options.

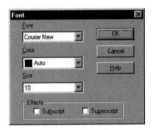

➤ To increase the font size relative to the base font (see Chapter 10 for more info on the base font; this is available in version 2 only), select the Format menu's **Increase Font Size** command, press **Ctrl+>**, or click on the **Increase Font Size** button in the Formatting toolbar.

 The Increase Font Size button.

➤ To decrease the font size relative to the base font (version 2 only), select the format menu's **Decrease Font Size** command, press **Ctrl+<**, or click on the **Decrease Font Size** button in the Formatting toolbar.

 The Decrease Font Size button.

➤ Select one of the character styles from the Style list (see the next section for details). The Style list has entries for monospaced text (the <TT> tag; use the *Typewriter,TT* style), preformatted text (the <PRE> tag; use the *Preformatted,<PRE>* style), and more.

244

Working with Styles

Much of HTML involves applying a particular style to a section of text or an entire paragraph. For example, a heading is a style that consists of bold text in a particular font size with an extra blank line before it. So it makes sense, then, that Internet Assistant uses a large collection of defined styles to insert HTML tags.

Internet Assistant gives you two ways to see a list of the available styles:

➤ Open the Formatting toolbar's Style drop-down list.

 The Style list.

➤ Pull down the **Format** menu and select the **Style** command to display the Style dialog box shown in the following figure.

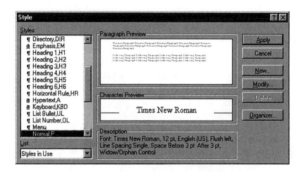

Much of Internet Assistant's HTML is produced using styles.

In the Style dialog box, styles preceded by a paragraph symbol ( ) are paragraph styles: they apply to the entire current paragraph. Styles with the underlined letter *a* beside them are text styles: they apply to the currently selected text.

For example, if you wanted to format a paragraph as a top-level heading (the <H1> tag), you'd place the cursor inside the paragraph and then apply the Heading 1,H1 style.

Working with Numbered Lists

Inserting a numbered list in your HTML document is no different than doing it in a regular Word document. To start the list, use either of the following techniques:

➤ Select the Format menu's **Numbering** command.

➤ Click on the **Numbered List** button in the Formatting toolbar.

 The Numbered List button.

245

Internet Assistant inserts the numbered list container (the <OL> and </OL> tags), adds the first item, and formats it with the List Number,OL style. (This style name is a bit confusing. The item is actually preceded by the <LI> tag, so a better name would be List Number,LI. Oh well.) Enter the item text and then press **Enter** to generate the second item automatically.

Working with Bulleted Lists

As with numbered lists, creating a bulleted HTML list is just the same as creating a bulleted list in a regular Word document. To begin, use either of the following techniques:

➤ Select the Format menu's **Bullets** command.

➤ Click on the Bulleted List button in the Formatting toolbar.

 The Bulleted List button.

Internet Assistant inserts the bulleted list container (the <UL> and </UL> tags), adds the first item, and formats it with the List Bullet,UL style. Again, enter the item text and then press **Enter** to generate the next bullet automatically.

Check This Out...

Customizing Numbered and Bulleted Lists

Internet Assistant gives you a few options for customizing your lists. For example, if you'd like to use a different numbering scheme or a different bullet style, select the Format menu's **Multilevel Numbering** command. The Bullets and Numbering dialog box lists all the available choices.

Working with Definition Lists

Definition lists operate a bit differently. Since there is no equivalent in regular Word documents, you have to use styles to build the list. Here's how it's done:

➤ To insert the definition list container (the <DL> and </DL> tags), apply the Definition List,DL style.

➤ To format an item as a term (the <DT> tag), apply the Definition Term,DT style.

➤ To format an item as a definition (the <DD> tag), press Tab after the term (there's no separate style for the definition).

246

Inserting an Image

Do you feel like snazzing up your page with a nice graphic or two? (I explained graphics in gory detail back in Chapter 8, "A Picture Is Worth a Thousand Clicks: Working with Images.") Here's how it's done in Internet Assistant:

1. Position the cursor where you want the image to appear.

2. Pull down the **Insert** menu and select the **Picture** command, or click on the Picture button in the Formatting toolbar. The Picture dialog box appears, as shown in the following figure. (Version 1 uses a different dialog box.)

 The Picture button.

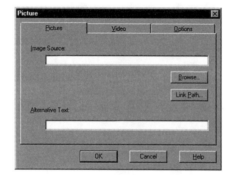

Use the Picture dialog box to construct the <IMG> tag for the graphic you want to insert.

3. Enter the name of the graphics file in the Image Source text box.

4. Use the Alternative Text field to enter the text that will be displayed in non-graphical browsers.

5. (Optional; version 2 only) Activate the **Options** tab and enter values for the Height and Width. If you want a border, activate the **Display Border** check box and enter a value for the Border Size. You can also use the Alignment with Text list to select an alignment option.

6. When you're done, select **OK** to insert the image.

Inserting Hypertext Links I: Remote Links

Internet Assistant divides links into two categories: remote links that jump to a specified URL, and bookmarks that link to a specific section of a document. (For the complete link lowdown, jump to Chapter 7, "Making the Jump to Hyperspace: Adding Links.") This section covers remote links, and bookmarks are covered in next section.

Here are the steps to follow to insert a remote link in your document:

1. Place the cursor where you want the link text to appear.

2. Pull down the **Insert** menu and select the **HyperLink** command, or click on the Hyperlink button in the Formatting toolbar. The HyperlinkInsert dialog box appears, as shown in the following figure. (Version 1 uses a different dialog box.)

 The Hyperlink button.

Use this dialog box to set up the <A> tag for the link.

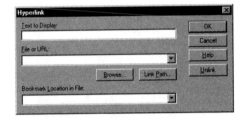

3. Enter the link text in the Text to Display field.

4. Use the File or URL text box to enter the URL you want to display when the reader selects the link.

5. Select **OK**.

Internet Assistant inserts a link tag that takes the following form:

```
<A HREF="The URL you entered">Your link text</A>
```

Inserting Hypertext Links II: Bookmarks

Recall from Chapter 7 that you can insert an "anchor" inside a hypertext document and then create a link that points to that anchor. This enables your readers to jump to specific sections of the document. Internet Assistant uses the term *bookmark* instead of anchor, but the principle is the same.

To set up the bookmark, highlight the text and select the Edit menu's **Bookmark** command, or click on the Bookmark button in the Formatting toolbar. In the Bookmark dialog box that appears (see below), enter the name you want to use and then select the Add button. Internet Assistant inserts an <A> tag of the following form:

```
<A NAME="The name you entered">Your bookmark text</A>
```

 The Bookmark button.

248

Use the Bookmark dialog box to enter a name for the bookmark.

Now you need to create a link that points to the bookmark you just created. This is almost identical to creating a remote link:

1. Place the cursor where you want the link text to appear.

2. Display the Hyperlink dialog box by pulling down the **Insert** menu and selecting the **HyperLink** command, or by clicking on the Hyperlink button in the Formatting toolbar.

3. Enter the link text in the **Text to Display** field.

4. Select the bookmark from the **Bookmark Location in File** list.

5. Select **OK**.

Internet Assistant inserts an <A> tag of the following form:

```
<A HREF="#The bookmark name you selected">Your link text</A>
```

Constructing Tables

Microsoft Word has been table-aware for a few years now, and the latest versions make it a breeze to set up and format tables in your documents. Happily for us HTML types, Internet Assistant version 2 leverages all this table know-how, so you can create HTML tables just as easily as you can regular Word tables. (I talked about HTML tables ad nauseum in Chapter 11, "Table Talk: Adding Tables to Your Page." Note that Internet Assistant version 1 doesn't do the table thing.) Not only that, but Internet Assistant teaches Word a table trick or two, so that you can adjust things like the table borders, the cell width and spacing, and more.

Internet Assistant gives you two methods for creating a table:

Creating a Table—Method #1 First, position the cursor where you want the table to appear. Now pull down the **Table** menu and select the **Insert Table** command. Word displays the Insert Table dialog box, shown in the following figure. Define the layout of your table by entering values in the **Number of Columns** spinner and the **Number of Rows** spinner. Select **OK** and Word inserts the table.

249

Use the Insert Table dialog box to define your table.

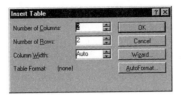

Creating a Table—Method #2 Position the cursor where you want the table to appear, then click on the Insert Table button in the Standard toolbar. A table grid appears. Hold down the left mouse button and drag the pointer through the number of rows and columns you want. Release the mouse button to insert the table.

 The Insert Table button.

The **Table** menu boasts all kinds of commands for fine-tuning your HTML table. Place the cursor inside the table and then choose from the following commands:

Borders This command displays the Borders dialog box, from which you can turn borders on and off and select the border thickness and color.

Cell Width and Spacing This command lets you adjust the width of individual columns as well as specify the amount of space between each cell.

Cell Type With the cursor inside a cell, use this command to designate the cell as a header (the <TH> tag) or as data (the <TD> tag).

Align This command displays the Align dialog box, which enables you to choose the overall alignment of the table as well as the alignment for text within the cells.

Caption Use this command to enter a caption for the table and to choose whether the caption appears above or below the table.

Background Color This command lets you specify a background color for either the entire table or just the current cell. (This is an extension used by Internet Explorer.)

A Few Odds and Ends

To round out our look at what Internet Assistant can do, this section presents a few HTML odds and ends, including horizontal rules, character codes, background colors, and more:

➤ To add a horizontal rule (the <HR> tag), either select the Insert menu's **Horizontal Rule** command, or click on the Horizontal Rule button in the Formatting toolbar.

The Horizontal Rule button.

➤ To insert a character code, pull down the Insert menu and select the **Symbol** command. In the Symbol dialog box that appears, select (normal text) from the Font list, highlight the character you want, and then select **Insert**.

➤ If you'd like to insert the current date, select the Insert menu's **Date and Time** command. In the Date and Time dialog box that appears, choose the format you want to use from the **Available Formats** list and activate the **Update Automatically (Insert as Field)** check box. Activating this option tells Word to update the date each time you open the file. Select **OK** to insert the date.

➤ To center some text (the <CENTER> tag), select the Format menu's **Center Align** command (version 2 only), press **Ctrl+E**, or click on the **Center** button in the Formatting toolbar.

 The Center button.

➤ To paint the background with a color or image, select the Format menu's **Background and Links** command. Word displays the Background and Links dialog box. If you want to use an image, enter its filename in the **Image** text box. If you'd prefer to use a color, select it from the **Color** drop-down list. Note, too, that you can use this dialog box to specify colors for the body text, new (unvisited) links, and old (visited) links.

The Least You Need to Know

This chapter showed you how to use Microsoft's Internet Assistant to wield the full power and splendor of a high-end word processor—Word for Windows to create Web pages. Time for a nostalgic look back:

➤ If you have Word for Windows 95, you need version 2 of Internet Assistant, which can be downloaded from the following Web site:

```
http://www.microsoft.com/msoffice/freestuf/Msword/download/ia/ia95/
default.htm
```

If you have Word for Windows 6 (version 6.0a or later), you need version 1 of Internet Assistant. Use the following page to download it:

```
http://www.microsoft.com/msoffice/freestuf/Msword/download/ia/ia1z/
default.htm
```

Chapter 19

Getting Your Web Words Online with America Online

America Online (AOL) is the largest of the big-time online services and they achieved this exalted status the old-fashioned way: They earned it. How? Well, for starters, they sent out copies of the AOL software to, it seems, every person on the planet. If you've got a pulse, you've probably received an AOL disk in the mail. Maybe even twice. Toss in all those freebie copies of the software that appear in computer magazines and we're all drowning in AOL disks. "Okay, okay, I'll join! Just stop sending me disks!" (This aggressive marketing approach does have its drawbacks however: *disk dancers*. These are (usually) kids who install the AOL software, use up the free time, and then move on to another disk.)

Another reason AOL has been so successful is its unabashed embrace of all things on the Internet. AOL members can e-mail Internet types without having to jump through a bunch of hoops; they can read Usenet newsgroups, tunnel to Gopher sites, FTP files, and, of course, surf the Web. That's pretty impressive, but the AOL brain trust isn't content to rest on these Net laurels. They continue to push the online envelope by offering not one, but two choices for publishing pages on the Web. This chapter gives you the details on both choices.

America Online's Web Page Publishing Possibilities

AOL Web wannabes have two ways to create their own pages and get them on the Web: My Home Page and My Place. Although you can always switch from one service to another down the road, you'll save yourself some time if you decide now which of the two you want to use.

My Home Page is a simple, step-by-step method for creating a page. It's definitely a no-frills approach, but it just may be the easiest way to get a home page up and surfing. Here's what you get with My Home Page:

➤ A single Web page

➤ You create the page while you're hooked up to AOL.

➤ The page includes the info from your AOL member profile.

➤ You can add text, links, graphics, and sounds to the page.

➤ You don't need to know a stitch of HTML to create the page.

The second Web page service is called My Place. This is a more full-featured service for people whose Web plans are more ambitious than a single page. Here's the deal with My Place:

➤ You get a whopping 2 MB of disk space on AOL's FTP site.

➤ You can include as many Web pages as you like.

➤ You create the pages off-line and then use AOL's FTP service to upload the files to My Place.

➤ You can include whatever you like in the pages.

So which one should you choose? Well, if all you want to do is slap up a quick home page, then My Home Page should do the job. However, since you bought this book (thanks!), I assume you don't mind wrestling with a bit of HTML in order to gain more control over your pages. In that case, the My Place service is probably more up your alley.

Working with My Home Page

Let's check out the My Home Page service and see how you can use it to crank out a quick home page for yourself. Sign in to America Online and then head for the keyword **MyHomePage**. (That is, you pull down the **Go To** menu, select the **Keyword** command, enter **MyHomePage** in the Keyword dialog box, and then select the **Go** button.) AOL displays the Personal Publisher window, as shown in the following figure.

The Personal Publisher window is your jumping-off point for creating and editing My Home Page.

To get started, slam the **Create/Edit My Home Page** button. AOL gathers info from your member profile and then displays it in the Create/Edit My Home Page window, shown on the next page. (In case you're wondering, the **Searchable by** section tells AOL who can view your page; I'll talk more about it later, in the section called "Editing My Home Page.")

Check This Out...

Improving Your Profile

My Home Page uses the vital statistics from your AOL member profile to populate your page. To make sure this info is up-to-date and ready for public consumption, pull down the Members menu and select **Edit Your Online Profile**. You can also change your profile while you're working in the My Home Page area. See "Editing My Home Page" later in this chapter.

My Home Page begins with your member profile data.

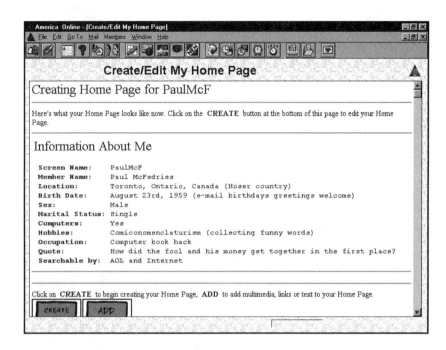

Adding Text, Links, and Graphics

Your member profile is a good start, but even the raciest profile makes for dull reading. To crank things up a notch on the old variety-is-the-spice-of-life meter, throw in a few extras, such as graphics and hypertext links. To try this, select the **Add** button at the bottom of the window. The new window that appears (see next page) lets you jazz up your page by adding text, links, graphics, and sounds.

Plan Your Page!

Keep in mind that the order you add your text, links, graphics, and sounds is the order they appear in the page. There's not a whole lot you can do to change this order, either, so you might want to take a minute or two before diving in and plan out where you want everything to appear.

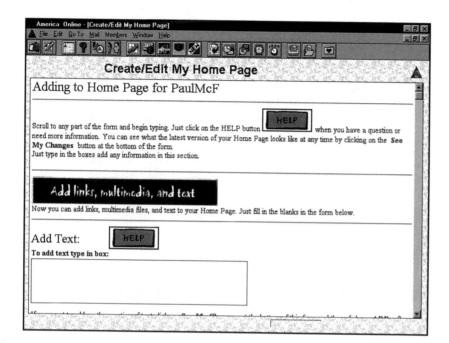

Use this window to add some extra toppings to your home page.

Tossing in Some Text

If you want to include an introductory message, or some jokes, or a first draft of your latest short story, you can use the Add Text section (see the previous figure) to add a chunk of prose to the page. Just enter the text in the **To add text type in box** area. You can be as verbose as you like, and you can start new paragraphs by pressing **Enter**. This text appears below your member profile.

Inserting a Link

If you scroll down the page a bit, you'll stumble upon the Add Link section (see the figure on the next page). You use this area to insert a hypertext link into your page. (The link will appear below the text you entered in the last section.) To set up the link, you fill in the following three options:

> **Select the type of link you want to add** Use this drop-down list to specify the type of link you're inserting. You have three choices: Web URL, Inline Image URL,

257

Creating a mailto Link

Would you like to include an e-mail link so folks can send a missive to your AOL account right from your home page? No sweat. Choose Web URL as the type of link and then enter the URL as follows:

`mailto:ScreenName@aol.com`

Here, *ScreenName* is your AOL screen name.

and AOL Keyword. (Note that, for the latter, only folks surfing your site using the AOL browser will be able to link to the AOL site given by the keyword.)

Type in Web URL or keyword in box   Use this text box to enter a Web URL, the name of a graphics file (this is, usually, the name of a file you've uploaded to AOL; see the next section), or an AOL keyword.

Type a description about this place on the Web or AOL in box   Use this text box to enter the link text.

Use the Add Link section to insert a link in your page.

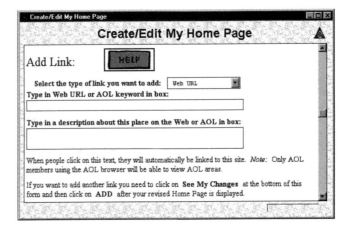

Sending a Multimedia File to AOL

If you'd like to brighten your Web page with a well-chosen graphic image, you first need to send the file to AOL. That's what the Upload Multimedia File section (shown in the following figure) is all about. (*Upload* means to send a file from your computer to another computer; as you might expect, it's the opposite of download.) You use it to send a graphics file (GIF or JPEG; see Chapter 8) or even a sound file (which is why it's called the Upload *Multimedia* File section) to your AOL storage area. You can then insert this image or sound in your Web page (which I'll show you how to do in the next section).

Use the Upload Multimedia File section to send an image or sound file to AOL.

Here are the steps to follow to send a multimedia file to AOL:

1. Enter the name of the file in the **Type in the name of the file to uploaded** (*sic*) text box. Technically, the name you enter is the name the file will have once it's been shipped to the AOL FTP site.

2. Select the **Upload Multimedia File** button. A new Uploading File "*filename*" window appears, where *filename* is the name of the file you entered (see below).

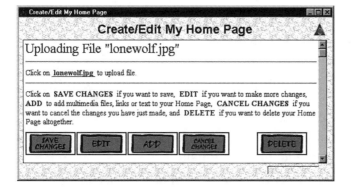

A window like this one appears when you select the Upload Multimedia File button.

3. Click on the filename. AOL displays the Upload File dialog box.

4. Choose the **Select File** button, highlight the file in the Attach File dialog box that appears, and then select **OK**.

5. Select the **Send** button. AOL grabs the file and then displays the File Transfer dialog box when it's done.

6. Select **OK**.

Adding a Multimedia File to Your Page

After you transport an image or sound file to AOL, you can insert it into your page. Here's how it's done:

1. At the bottom of the Create/Edit My Home Page window, select the **Add** button to return to the adding window.

2. Scroll down to the Add Multimedia File section (shown in the figure below).

Use the Add Multimedia File section to insert an image or sound file in your page.

3. If you uploaded multiple files, highlight the one you want from the **Select a multimedia file (sound or graphic) to add** list.

4. Use the **Type in description of this file in box** area to enter a description of the file. This description appears below the image on your page.

5. Use the **Select position of this file on your page** drop-down list to select the position of the file on the page (After Personal Information or Before Personal Information).

6. Use the **Select how this file is displayed on your page** list to select how the file will be displayed (On Your Page or As A Link).

Seeing the Changes to Your Page

When you're done, select the **See My Changes** button (it's at the bottom of the screen) to eyeball your updated page. To continue from here, the bottom of your home page gives you the following buttons:

Save Changes   Saves the changes you've made in this session.

Edit   Allows you to make changes to the page (see the next section).

Add   Allows you to continue adding text, links, and multimedia files.

Cancel Changes   Wipes out the changes you've made since the last time you saved the page.

Delete   Deletes the home page off the face of the earth.

Editing My Home Page

If you make a mistake or just want to update the info on your page, AOL makes it easy to edit every aspect of your page. To see how, select the **Edit** button at the bottom of the Create/Edit My Home Page window. The new window that appears (see the figure below) presents the following sections for adjusting your page:

Information About Me   This is your member profile info and you adjust it by adding to or editing what's in the text boxes. In particular, look for an option named **You can choose who can view your Home Page** at the bottom of the section. (The option you select appears in the **Searchable by** section of My Home Page.) If you want to give both AOLers and Internet types access to your home page, activate the **AOL and Internet** option; to mark your page as "AOL-only," activate the **AOL members** option; if you only want to see the page yourself, activate the **myself only** option.

Edit Text   One of these sections appears for each chunk of text you added. Select the **delete** option if you want to get rid of the text; otherwise, select **update** and edit the text shown in the box.

Edit Link   One of these sections appears for each link you added. Again, activate **delete** to blow away the link, or activate **update** and make your changes to the link info.

Edit Multimedia File One of these sections appears—you guessed it—for each multimedia file you inserted in the page. Choose the delete option to expunge the file from your page; otherwise, select update and adjust any of the following options: **To edit your file description type changes in box, Select position of this file on your page,** and **Select how this file is displayed on your page.**

When you're done, select the **See My Changes** button to, well, see your changes. If you'd rather not update the page, select the **Undo Changes** button instead.

Use this window to edit My Home Page.

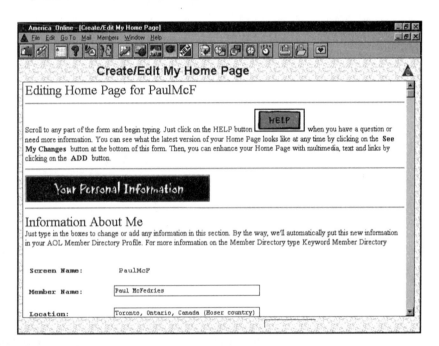

What's Your My Home Page URL?

If you want to surf over to your new page (or if you want to tell others how to get there), here's the general form for the My Home Page URL:

```
http://home.aol.com/ScreenName
```

Here, *ScreenName* is your AOL screen name. For example, my screen name is PaulMcF, so my URL is the following:

```
http://home.aol.com/PaulMcF
```

Making My Place Your Web Home

My Home Page is certainly the easiest method for creating a home page that we've seen so far. You have a nice variety of content (profile, text, links, images, and sounds) and it's all done without an HTML code in sight. It's certainly not perfect, though. In particular, My Home Page suffers from three glaring problems:

➤ You can't expel the profile data from the page. Oh sure, you can leave the fields blank if you don't want any Nosy Parkers to find out if you're single (or whatever), but the blank fields still show up on the page.

➤ You have very little control over the appearance of your page. For example, you can't boldface or italicize words or phrases, you can't use headings, and you can't include link text as part of a larger sentence or paragraph.

➤ You get only one page to show off your wealth of knowledge and extol your virtues as a human being.

The solution to all these problems is to ignore My Home Page altogether and move into My Place, instead. My Place is for full-fledged Web engineers who don't mind getting their hands dirty with HTML (or who have their own HTML editing software that they use to construct pages). My Place is really just a storage location for your Web documents. You create everything on your own and then send it off to My Place.

Assuming you have some HTML stuff you want to put online, let's see how you go about sending it to AOL. I'll divide the process into two steps: accessing your FTP directory from AOL and uploading files.

Accessing Your AOL FTP Directory

For each member, AOL sets aside 2 MB of disk space on its FTP site (this is called the member's *FTPspace*). My Place is, essentially, any and all Web-related files (HTML documents, graphics files, and so on.) that exist in your FTP directory. Here are the steps to follow to upload files from your computer to the AOL FTP site:

1. Sign in to AOL, if you haven't done so already.

2. Pull down the Go To menu, select **Keyword**, enter **FTP** in the Keyword dialog box, and then select **OK**. AOL displays the File Transfer Protocol (FTP) window.

3. Select the **Go To FTP** button. The Anonymous FTP window appears, as shown on the next page.

Use this window to select an FTP site.

4. Select the **Other Site** button.

5. In the **Site Address** text box, enter **members.aol.com/** followed by your screen name (e.g., members.aol.com/PaulMcF).

6. Select **Connect**. AOL displays the Connected dialog box.

7. Select **OK**. A new window appears, showing your AOL FTP directory (see the following figure).

My FTP directory.

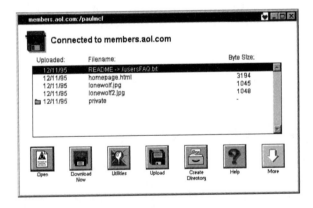

A Faster Way to Get Here from There

That's a lot of steps just to log in to an FTP site! To save wear and tear on your typing fingers, you can set up your FTP directory as one of your Favorite Places. With your FTP directory window on screen, all you do is select the Window menu's Add to Favorite Places command. Then, the next time you want to log in, open the Favorite Places window (by selecting the Go To menu's Favorite Places command), highlight the FTP directory, and then select the **Connect** button.

Uploading Files to Your FTP Directory

Now that you've arrived safely in your FTP directory, your next step is to furnish My Place with some HTML files. Here's how it's done:

1. In the FTP directory window, select the **Upload** button. AOL displays the members.aol.com dialog box.

2. In the **Remote Filename** text box, enter the name you want to use for the file (that is, this will be the name of the file as it appears in the AOL FTP directory).

3. If you're sending a plain text file (such as an HTML document), activate the **ASCII (text document)** option. For all other files, make sure the **Binary (programs and graphics)** option is selected.

4. Select the **Continue** button. The Upload File dialog box appears.

5. Choose the **Select File** button to display the Attach File dialog box.

6. Highlight the file you want to send and then select **OK**. AOL returns you to the Upload File dialog box.

7. Select the **Send** button. AOL displays a dialog box when the transfer is complete.

8. Select **OK**.

9. Repeat Steps 2–8 to upload more files.

10. When you're done, select **Cancel** in the members.aol.com dialog box. The files you sent now appear in your FTP directory.

11. Close the FTP window.

What's Your My Place URL?

My Place uses a different URL than My Home Page:

```
http://members.aol.com/ScreenName/filename
```

Here, *ScreenName* is your AOL screen name, and *filename* is the name of your home page. For example:

```
http://members.aol.com/PaulMcF/homepage.html
```

The Least You Need to Know

This chapter showed you how to use America Online's My Home Page and My Place services to get your Web work online. Here's a look at what the heck happened:

➤ My Home Page lets you create a Web page without resorting to any HTML shenanigans. For more serious Web sites, you'll want to use the My Place service instead.

➤ To get started with My Home Page, jump to the keyword **MyHomePage**.

➤ To create your My Home Page (or edit your existing My Home Page), select the Create/Edit My Home Page button in the Personal Publisher window.

➤ In the Create/Edit My Home Page window, select the Add button to add text, links, and multimedia files to your page.

➤ To access your AOL FTP directory, jump to the keyword FTP.

Chapter 20

Assorted Other Ways to Create HTML Documents

In This Chapter

➤ Quick looks at a few more HTML editors

➤ Pilfering HTML from existing Web pages

➤ How to create Web pages on the Web

➤ Converting existing documents into HTML format

➤ A veritable cornucopia of handy-dandy HTML tools

The last few chapters concentrated on individual HTML programs: Netscape Gold, HTML Writer, HotDog, Internet Assistant, and America Online's My Home Page. You can think of these chapters as single-course meals: nourishing enough, but lacking in variety. This chapter, however, takes more of a smorgasbord approach. I'll be plying you with various Web page–production snacks, including a savory selection of HTML editors (the best of the rest), some tasty techniques for slicing HTML codes from existing pages, some mouth-watering Web-based page-creation engines, and some scrumptious software for convert-ing existing files into HTML format. Hope you brought your appetite!

Rapid Reviews of a Few More HTML Editors

Chapters 15 through 18 covered the HTML editors that are, in my semi-humble opinion, the best in the five main categories of Web authoring tools. (Those categories are: browser-based editors, such as Netscape Gold; free editors, such as HTML Writer; commercial editors, such as HotDog; word processor templates, such as Internet Assistant; and online page creation engines, such as My Home Page.) But the Web is such a gigantic phenomenon that it seems everybody and his sibling is coming out with a new program for editing HTML. Even though all of the programs we've looked at are excellent tools, they may not be just right for your needs as a budding Web welder. So, to give you a taste of what else is available, this section introduces a few more HTML editing programs and tells you where to go to pick them up.

Getting the WebEdit Page Editor

When I was evaluating commercial HTML editors for this book, I had a tough time trying to decide which one was best. Although I eventually settled on HotDog, I came *this* close to going with Kenn Nesbitt's excellent WebEdit program. It has an intuitive interface and support for just about every HTML tag on the planet, and it's really fast (way faster than HotDog, which runs like a dachshund through cheese dip). In the end, though, I chose HotDog because it was geared more towards beginning and less-experienced Web authors; WebEdit is, hands down, the editor of choice for experienced HTML hounds. Here are some of WebEdit's features:

- ➤ A clean, easy-to-figure-out interface.

- ➤ A Home Page Wizard that lets you create a Web page step-by-step.

- ➤ A spell checker.

- ➤ Support for HTML 3.0 tags, including a WYSIWYG table builder.

- ➤ Support for Netscape's extensions.

- ➤ The ability to convert certain spreadsheet and database files to HTML format.

WebEdit costs US$79.95 for corporate and government types. Home users, schools, and other nonprofiteers only have to shell out US$39.95. There's also a demo version that you can try out for 30 days. To download the demo version of WebEdit, first head for the WebEdit home page at the following URL:

```
http://www.nesbitt.com/
```

Surfing This Chapter on Easy Street

This chapter is chock full of links to Web pages and FTP sites. Rather than typing in these links yourself, you can take a load off your fingers by loading up the file named ASSORTED.HTM from this book's disk. This file contains links to all the sites mentioned in this chapter.

The WebEdit Download Page that appears has links to several Net locations from around the world that will serve up a copy of the WebEdit file. Click on any link that's nearby or strikes your fancy and save the file to your hard disk. The file you get (it's called WEBEDIT.ZIP, but that name may change as new versions are released) is compressed in ZIP format, so you need to use the WinZIP program (available on this book's disk; see the appendix named "The Goodies on the Disk" for instructions) to decompress it.

Once the decompression is complete, you should have a program named SETUP.EXE on your hard disk. Running this file starts the WebEdit installation program. Follow the instructions on the screen to install WebEdit on your system. When the installation is done, double-click the WebEdit icon (it should be in a program group named Nesbitt Software) to fire up WebEdit. The screen below shows the main WebEdit window.

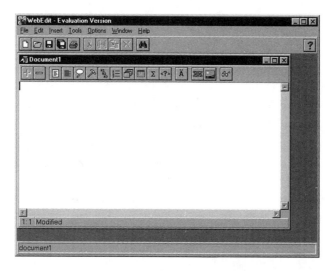

The main WebEdit window.

Professional HTML Editing with HTMLed Pro

HTMLed Pro is a powerful program that can tackle any HTML project, large or small. It has some outstanding features, including the following:

➤ Support for HTML 3.0 and Netscape extensions.

➤ HTML Page Builder—a tool that leads you step-by-step through the creation of a page.

➤ Table Designer—a visual tool that lets you create tables quickly.

➤ The ability to import files in RTF (Rich Text Format) and convert them to HTML.

➤ Page text shown in different colors: regular text is black, HTML tags are blue, character entities are red, and so on.

➤ The ability to save files to your Web server right from HTMLed Pro without using any kind of FTP middleman.

HTMLed Pro costs US$99.95, or US$69.95 for educational institutions. You can also download a time-limited demonstration version (good for about one month) to check out HTMLed Pro before forking over any cash. To get your mitts on HTMLed Pro, surf to the following Web page:

```
http://www.ist.ca/htmledpro/
```

Follow the instructions on the screen to download HTMLed Pro to your computer. I'd recommend creating a new directory for HTMLed Pro (called, say, HTMLED) and saving the file into that directory. The file is compressed in ZIP format, so you need to use the WinZIP program (available on this book's disk; see the appendix named "The Goodies on the Disk" for instructions) to decompress it.

If you downloaded the demo version, you can get started right away by running the HTMLEDPR.EXE file. If you have the full version, run the installation program and then crank up HTMLEDPR.EXE. The screen below shows the HTMLed Pro window, which demonstrates this program's Achilles' heel: its interface. As you can see, thanks to all those buttons HTMLed Pro's screen is cluttered and uninviting. It's certainly as powerful and full-featured as anything on the HTML editor market (all those darn buttons have gotta do something!), but I'd like to see a facelift before I'd use this program full-time.

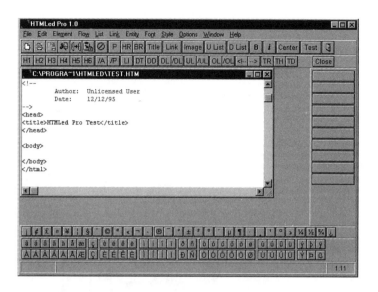

HTMLed Pro's window: an exercise in yucky interface design.

Stop the Web Presses: It's NaviPress!

In the last chapter, you learned how to create pages using America Online's My Home Page service. I also showed you how to use the My Place service to host multiple Web pages. But AOL's commitment to Web authoring goes deeper than that and it applies to non-AOL subscribers as well. AOL has come out with a new program called NaviService that aims to be "a one-stop solution for building and maintaining your web site." NaviService is actually two separate products: a browser/HTML combo called NaviPress (which I'll talk about here) and a collection of Web hosting services designed for different users (personal, corporate, and so on).

NaviPress takes a Web browser and a WYSIWYG HTML editor, ties them up in a bow, and presents them as a seamless, unified package. In other words, like Netscape Gold (see chapter 15), as you're creating a Web page, you can see exactly how it will look on the Web because you're building the page right in the browser. It's nice technology and it's a truly civilized way to construct a Web page. Here are a few other features of NaviPress:

➤ Dialog boxes for constructing elements such as links and images

➤ Extensive commands for creating and formatting tables

➤ Support many of Netscape extensions and HTML 3.0 tags

➤ Large number of configuration options, including a customizable toolbar

➤ MiniWebs that show a collection of pages, their connections, and all related files (such as images)

On the down side, NaviPress is very slow, so you'll need a good supply of patience. If you'd like to give NaviPress a go, here's the URL of the NaviService home page:

```
http://www.naviservice.com/
```

Here you'll find a link for downloading NaviPress. Follow the link, and then follow the instructions for saving the version you need (NaviPress comes in Windows, Macintosh, and Unix flavors) to your hard drive. When that's done (it's a large file, so the download may take a while), decompress the file (in Windows, you just need to run the NAVIPRES.EXE file) and then run the Setup program.

When Setup is complete, double-click the NaviPress icon to get the show on the road. The figure below shows the NaviPress screen.

The NaviPress screen combines a browser and an HTML editor.

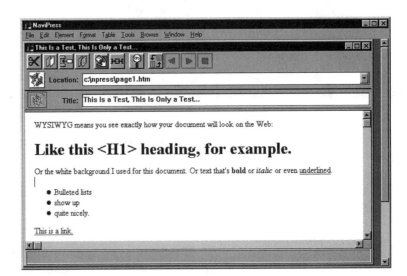

The Step-by-Step Web: WEB Wizard

If you've used any of Microsoft's Office products—Word, Excel, PowerPoint, and Access—you've probably come across a Wizard or two in your travels. Wizards are helpful tools that take you through complex tasks one step at a time. At each step, the Wizard presents a dialog box that asks you questions and gives you controls (such as text boxes and option buttons) for entering data and setting options.

WEB Wizard is a software program that takes the Wizard concept and applies it to creating Web pages. During a WEB Wizard "interview" (as it's called), a series of dialog boxes take you step-by-step through the creation of a simple page. You begin by specifying the page title, then subsequent dialogs prompt you for the background, images, text, lists, links (including a mailto link), and a filename.

WEB Wizard is perfect for folks who are scared to death of HTML and just want to put a page together as painlessly as possible. Even if you know how to use HTML, WEB Wizard is still a handy tool. You can use it to throw together your page basics, then you can load the file into a text editor (or an HTML editor) to fine-tune things.

To grab yourself a copy of WEB Wizard, get your browser to conjure up the following URL:

```
http://www.halcyon.com/artamedia/webwizard/
```

WEB Wizard comes in two Windows versions (a Mac version may be available by the time you read this): 16-bit (for Windows 3.1 and Windows for Workgroups) and 32-bit (for Windows 95 and Windows NT). Click on the appropriate link in the WEB Wizard home page, and then follow the instructions in the new page that's displayed. The downloaded file is compressed in ZIP format, so you need to use the WinZIP program (available on this book's disk; see the appendix named "The Goodies on the Disk" for instructions) to decompress it.

To start WEB Wizard, run the decompressed EXE file (WEBWIZ16.EXE or WEBWIZ32.EXE, depending on the version you downloaded). WEB Wizard will lead you through a series of dialog boxes in which you fill out various options and enter the page info. For example, you use the dialog box shown below to enter the title of the page and an optional subheading.

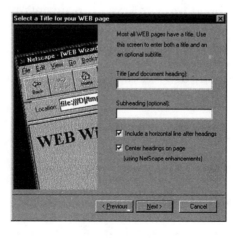

WEB Wizard leads you step-by-step through the page creation process.

Faded Glory: HoTMetaL

Back in the old days of the Web (say, about a year ago!), HTML editors were as rare as hens' teeth. In fact, about the only editor game in town was a program called HoTMetaL, which therefore held a virtual monopoly, both in mind and market share. As other editors quickly entered the fray, HoTMetaL held its own for a while, but it just couldn't keep up with the upstarts.

That's not to say that HoTMetaL is a bad program; far from it. (It wouldn't appear in this chapter if it were.) In fact, HoTMetal PRO 2.0 has even won some awards (such as *PC Magazine's* Editor's Choice Award). To my mind, though, it's just not quite as slick and easy to use as the other editors we've looked at. However, HoTMetaL is still worth considering because it packs a lot of features. In the free version, for example, you get the following:

➤ Supports HTML 3.0 (including a WYSIWYG table builder) and Netscape extensions.

➤ Checks your documents for HTML no-nos.

➤ Context-sensitive search-and-replace.

➤ The ability to view inline images while working in HoTMetaL.

➤ A preview feature that loads the document into a Web browser.

If you move up to HoTMetaL PRO (which will set you back big bucks: US$195), you get these extra features:

➤ A spell checker and thesaurus.

➤ The ability to import word-processing documents and convert them to HTML automatically.

➤ MetalWorks, an add-on graphics package.

➤ Easy updates for any new Netscape and HTML tags that come down the pike.

➤ User-definable keyboard macros.

If you'd like to try out HoTMetaL for yourself, the free version is available at the following Web address:

```
http://www.sq.com/
```

Find the link that takes you to the HoTMetaL Free page, click on the Download HoTMetaL Free link, and save the file to your hard disk (saving it to an empty directory is best). When the download is complete, double-click on the file to extract the HoTMetaL setup files. Now run SETUP.EXE and follow the instructions on-screen to install HoTMetaL. The figure below shows the basic HoTMetaL screen.

The HoTMetaL window.

HTML Editors for the Mac

Most of the editors we've looked at so far have been Windows-based. Mac mavens in the crowd shouldn't feel slighted, however, because there's no shortage of editors available for the Mac. Besides the Mac versions of NaviPress, WEB Wizard, and HoTMetaL mentioned earlier, you might want to check out the following programs:

HTML Grinder HTML Grinder isn't an HTML editor, per se. Instead, it's a powerful set of tools for automating repetitive tasks, such as finding and replacing text in multiple documents, date-stamping pages automatically, appending text to multiple documents, adding Next Page and Previous Page links, and lots more. To check it out, head for the following address:

```
http://www.matterform.com/grinder/htmlgrinder.html
```

Page Mill From Adobe—the PageMaker people—this program lets you create pages in a simple-to-use, word-processing layout. All HTML tags are hidden, and the screen gives you a WYSIWYG look at how your page will appear on the Web. Here's the address of the Page Mill home page:

```
http://www.adobe.com/Apps/PageMill/
```

World Wide Web Weaver This is a powerful text editor that makes it easy to insert HTML tags. To find out more, check out the Web Weaver home page:

```
http://www.northnet.org/best/Web.Weaver/WWWW.html
```

More Mac HTML Editor Info

Of the six HTML editors I mentioned here (well, five if you don't count HTML Grinder), you're bound to find one you like. Don't despair, however, if nothing turns your crank. You can get info and reviews on lots more editors at the following site:

```
http://www.comvista.com/net/www/editor.html
```

Grabbing HTML from an Existing Page

Have you ever come across a particularly striking Web page and wondered just how the heck the author pulled it off? Or have you been struggling to duplicate the layout of a favorite page, only to be thwarted by the intricacies of some obscure HTML tags? Well, I have good news for you: most Web browsers have a feature that lets you peek under the hood, so to speak, and eyeball the page's underlying HTML tags. Not only that, but it's also possible in most cases to make a copy of either the entire page or of a chunk of HTML that suits your needs. You can then incorporate this purloined code into your own pages.

Is this ethical? That depends. Obviously, if you just copy another author's page verbatim and reprint it on your own site, it's not only unethical but it's illegal. The key here is the page text, which is protected by copyright law. The HTML tags, however, have no such protection, so there's nothing wrong with using them wholesale. After all, life's too short to be constantly reinventing HTML wheels. As long as you change the text between the tags, you'll be okay.

Here's how you grab a page's underlying HTML using Netscape, NCSA Mosaic, and Internet Explorer:

Netscape   To copy the entire page, pull down the **File** menu, select the **Save As** command, and then use the Save As dialog box to save the file to your hard disk. To grab just a piece of the page, select the **View** menu's **Document Source** command and then copy the tags you need from the window that appears (just highlight them and press Ctrl+C).

NSCA Mosaic   To make a copy of the whole page, lock, stock, and barrel, select the **File** menu's **Save As** command, and then use the Save As dialog box to save the file to your hard disk. To pocket just a piece of the page, select the **File** menu's **Document Source** command and then copy the tags you need from the window that appears.

Internet Explorer   To copy the document as a whole, pull down the **File** menu, select the **Save As** command, and then use the Save As dialog box to save the file to disk. If you only need part of the document, pull down the **View** menu and select the **Source** command. Internet Explorer loads the text and tags into Notepad (see the figure below), from which you can copy whatever HTML hunks you need.

In Internet Explorer, selecting the View menu's Source command loads the document's HTML into Notepad.

Web Pages That Create Web Pages

The WEB Wizard program we looked at earlier (see "The Step-by-Step Web: WEB Wizard") enables you to create a simple home page just by filling in a few dialog boxes. The Web equivalent of dialog boxes are, of course, forms (which I talked about back in Chapter 14, "Hack to the Future: What's Ahead for HTML and the Web"). So it makes sense that some intrepid soul would take the WEB Wizard concept, apply it to the Web itself, and come up with Web pages that help you create Web pages.

And, by golly, someone has actually done it! Actually, quite a few Webmeisters have done it, so you have a choice of Web-based page-creation engines. Here's a rundown of some of the better ones:

Automatic Home Page Generator   This is a simple form that lets you specify, among other things, inline images, a background image, text (or *comments*, as they're called), your current interests and projects, and hypertext links. Once you've filled in the blanks, select the Submit button at the bottom of the page to see how things look. You can then copy the page to your computer (as described in the last section) for use on your Web site. Here's the URL:

```
http://ugweb.cs.ualberta.ca/~ritter/cgi-bin/hpg.html
```

Create a Homepage   This is a well-designed form with a few extra bells and whistles (see the following figure). For example, there are fields for specifying the background image (with lots of examples), the color of the regular text and the link text, the title, headings, body text (you can even enter HTML tags for things like boldfacing and italics, if you like), sections (such as a sports section), and lots more. When you're done, select the Create your homepage! button and a compressed file containing your page will be e-mailed to you. Here's the address of Create a Homepage:

```
http://the-inter.net/www/future21/create1.html
```

Create a Homepage has a few extra options not found in other page-creation forms.

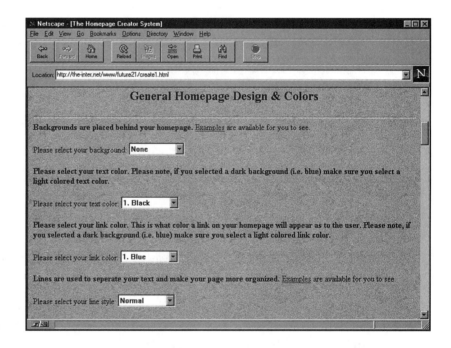

Make Your Own Home Page   This is a form that lets you include an opening image, text, your own HTML, and links. For the latter, the page has dozens of suggested links to choose from. You can also select whether you want the results e-mailed to you or displayed on-screen (which you can then copy to your computer, as described in the last section). When you've completed the form, select the **Make me a home page** button to finish the job. You can find Make Your Own Home Page at the following address:

```
http://www.goliath.org/makepage/
```

WWW Newbies Web Page Creator This form gives you lots of options for the background color, text color, and link color. You can also enter headings, several paragraphs of text, and up to five links. Select the Send my home page button at the bottom of the form and the page will be e-mailed to you. You can find this form at the following URL:

```
http://www.soos.com/homepage/homepage.html
```

Converting Existing Documents to HTML

Throughout this book I've concentrated on creating HTML documents from scratch. But what do you do if you have an existing non-HTML document—such as a spreadsheet, database, or word-processing file—and you'd like to publish it on the Web? In some cases, you may be able to tack on the appropriate HTML bric-a-brac by hand, but that can be time-consuming. A better approach is to find a program that will automatically convert the document into its Web-ready, HTML equivalent. This section runs through a few conversion programs for popular file formats.

Converters Galore

This collection of converters is by no means exhaustive. If you don't see the converter you need, or if you don't like any of my suggestions, here are a couple of sites that boast more extensive converter listings:

```
http://union.ncsa.uiuc.edu/HyperNews/get/www/html/converters.html
```

```
http://www.yahoo.com/Computers_and_Internet/Internet/World_Wide_Web/
HTML_Converters/
```

For starters, you should know that some HTML editors have conversion features built right in. For example, WebEdit (see "Getting the WebEdit Page Editor," earlier in this chapter) can convert some spreadsheet and database formats to HTML. Also, HTMLed Pro (see "Professional HTML Editing with HTMLed Pro") can convert RTF documents into HTML. (RTF is a document format developed by Microsoft. Many word processors—including Word and WordPerfect—can read and write RTF documents.) Otherwise, you might want to check out any of the following conversion programs:

The Ant Converts Word for Windows and Word for Mac documents to HTML (and vice-versa).

```
http://mcia.com/ant/
```

BeyondPress   Converts QuarkXPress files to HTML.

`http://www.astrobyte.com/Astrobyte/BeyondPressInfo.html`

CyberLeaf   Converts word-processing files (including Word, WordPerfect, and FrameMaker) to HTML.

`http://www.ileaf.com/ip.html`

dbf2html   Converts dBASE files to HTML.

`http://users.aol.com/hoskinsora/windows/dbf2html.zip`

Excel to HTML Table Converter   Converts Excel worksheet data into an HTML table. Works with Excel 5.0 for Windows and the Mac, as well as Excel 7 for Windows 95.

`http://rs712b.gsfc.nasa.gov/704/dgd/xl2html.html`

Excel (Mac) to HTML Conversion Utility   Converts Excel 5 for the Macintosh worksheet files into HTML tables.

`http://www.rhodes.edu/software/readme.html`

rtftohtml   Converts documents in Rich Text Format (RTF) to HTML.

`ftp://ftp.cray.com/src/WWWstuff/RTF/rtftohtml_overview.html`

WPTOHTML (for WordPerfect 5.1)   Converts WordPerfect 5.1 for DOS documents to HTML format.

`ftp://oak.oakland.edu/SimTel/msdos/wordperf/wpt51d10.zip`

WPTOHTML (for WordPerfect 6.0)   Converts WordPerfect 6.0 for DOS documents to HTML format.

`ftp://oak.oakland.edu/SimTel/msdos/wordperf/wpt60d10.zip`

The Least You Need to Know

This chapter closed out our look at painless page production by examining miscellaneous methods for creating Web documents. I reviewed a few more HTML editors, showed you how to scoop out HTML from existing Web pages, examined some sites that let you create Web pages right on the Web, and listed some programs that enable you to convert documents in other formats to HTML.

Speak Like a Geek: The Complete Archive

access counter   A small program inserted in a Web page that tracks the page's hit count (how many times it's been accessed).

access provider   See *service provider*.

anchor   A word or phrase in a Web page that's used as a target for a link. When the user selects the link, the browser jumps to the anchor, which may exist in the same document or in a different document.

anonymous FTP   An FTP session where you log in using "anonymous" as your user ID, and you enter your e-mail address as the password. Most modern Web browsers support anonymous FTP and will handle the logging in part for you automatically. 99 and 44/100 this of all your FTP sessions will use anonymous FTP.

applet   A Java program.

arachnerd   A person that spends way too much time either surfing the Web or fussing with their home page.

archie   An Internet service that searches a database of FTP sites for a file. Named after, but not to be confused with, the comic strip character of the same name.

bandwidth   A measure of how much stuff can be stuffed through a transmission medium such as a phone line or network cable. There's only so much bandwidth to go around at any given time, so you'll see lots of Net paranoia about "wasting bandwidth." Bandwidth is measured in baud or bits per second.

Barney page   A page whose sole purpose in life is to capitalize on a trendy topic. The name comes from the spate of pages bashing poor Barney the Dinosaur that were all the rage a while back. Recent Barney pages have been dedicated to O.J. and the Pentium chip fiasco.

baud   This is a measure of how much bandwidth a transmission medium has. Its technical definition is "level transitions per second," but nobody knows what that means. Most people prefer to use bits per second to describe bandwidth because it's easier to understand.

bit   The fundamental unit of computer information (it's a blend of the words "binary" and "digit"). Computers do all their dirty work by manipulating a series of high and low electrical currents. A high current is represented by the digit 1 and a low current by the digit 0. These 1's and 0's—or bits—are used to represent absolutely everything that goes down inside your machine. Weird, huh?

bit-spit   Any form of digital correspondence.

bits per second (bps)   Another, more common, measure of bandwidth. Since it takes eight bits to describe a single character, a transmission medium with a bandwidth of, say, 8 bps would send data at the pathetically slow rate of one character per second. Bandwidth is more normally measured in kilobits per second (Kbps—thousands of bits per second). So, for example, a 14.4 Kbps modem can handle 14,400 bits per second. In the high end, bandwidth is measured in megabits per second (Mbps—millions of bits per second).

body   The section of the Web document where you enter your text and tags. See also *head*.

bookmarks   In a Web browser, a list of your favorite Web pages, which you can set while you are surfing. To return to a page, just select it from the list. In the Internet Assistant HTML editor (see Chapter 18), *bookmark* is another name for an anchor.

bps   See *bits per second*.

browser   The software you use to display and interact with a Web page. When cobbling together your own pages, you'll need to bear in mind that there are two kinds of browsers: those that display only text and those that support graphics and other fun elements.

byte   Eight bits, or a single character.

byte-bonding   When computer users discuss things that nearby noncomputer users don't understand. See also *geeking out*.

Century-21 site   A Web site that has moved to a new location and now contains only a link to the new address.

character reference   Sounds like something you'd put on your résumé, but it's really an HTML code that lets you insert special characters in your Web pages (such as é). See also *entity name*.

clickstream   The "path" a person takes as they navigate through the World Wide Web.

cracker   A programmer who breaks into computer systems either to trash them or just for the sheer thrill of doing it (and, of course, to brag about it later). A hacker who has succumbed to the dark side of The Force.

cyberspace   The place you "go to" when you reach out beyond your own computer (usually via modem) and interact with information or people on other computer systems.

cybersurfer   A person who surfs cyberspace.

digerati   The beautiful people of the online world; the Internet intelligentsia. It's a blend of the phrase "digital literati."

dirt road   A frustratingly slow connection to a Web site. "Geez, that GIF still hasn't loaded yet? The Web server must be on a dirt road." See also *JPIG* and *spinner*.

domain name   The part of your e-mail address to the right of the @ sign. The domain name identifies a particular site on the Internet.

emoticon   See *smiley*.

entity name   An HTML code that lets you insert special characters in your Web pages (such as © and ö). Entity names are easier to use than character references, but they aren't supported by all browsers.

external image   A Web page image that the browser can't handle, so it passes the buck to a graphics program that displays the image in a separate window. See also *inline image*.

FAQ   The aficionado's short form for a Frequently Asked Question. The correct pronunciation is *fack*.

flooded   A page rendered unreadable because of a poorly chosen background image. "I had to bail out of that page because the background was flooded with some butt-ugly tartan." See also *wrackground image*.

foo, **bar**, and **foobar**   These words are used as placeholders in descriptions and instructions. For example, someone might say "To change to the /foo directory on a UNIX system, use the command cd /foo." Here, "foo" acts as a generic placeholder for a directory name. If two placeholders are needed, then both "foo" and "bar" are used, like so: "To FTP two files named foo and bar, use the mget command: mget foo bar." "Foobar" is often used as a single place-holder. It's derived from the military acronym FUBAR (sanitized version: Fouled Up Beyond All Recognition).

form   A Web document used for gathering information from the reader. Most forms have at least one text field where you can enter text data (such as your name or the keywords for a search). More sophisticated forms also include check boxes (for toggling a value on or off), radio buttons (for selecting one of several options), and push buttons (for performing an action such as submitting the form).

283

frames   In Netscape 2.0, rectangular Web page areas that contain separate chunks of text, graphics, and HTML. In other words, you can use frames to divide a single Web page into two or more separate pages.

Frequently Asked Questions list   A list of questions that, over the history of a newsgroup or Web site, have come up most often. If you want to send a question to a newsgroup or to a Web site's administrator, it's proper netiquette to read the group's FAQ list to see if you can find the answer there first.

FTP   File Transfer Protocol. This is the usual method for retrieving a file from another Internet computer and copying it to your own. Note that it's okay to use FTP as both a noun (a method for transferring files) and a verb ("Hey bozo, before posting to this group you should FTP the FAQ file and give it a good look"). See also *anonymous FTP*.

geek   Someone who knows a lot about computers and very little about anything else. See also *nerd*.

geeking out   When geeks who are byte-bonding start playing with a computer during a noncomputer-related social event.

GIF   Graphics Interchange Format. The most commonly used graphics format on the Web.

Gopher   A system that displays Internet documents and services as menu options. You just select a menu choice and the Gopher will either display a document or transfer you to a different gopher system. Gophers get their name from the mascot of the University of Minnesota, where the first Gopher system was born.

greenlink   To use the Web for monetary gain.

hacker   Someone who enjoys exploring the nuts and bolts of computer systems (both from the hardware side and, more often, from the software side), stretching these systems to their limits and beyond, and programming for the sheer pleasure of it. Not to be confused with *cracker*.

head   This is like an introduction to a Web page. Web browsers use the head to glean various types of information about the page (such as the title). See also *body*.

hit   A single access of a Web page. A hit is recorded for a particular Web page each time a browser displays the page.

hit-and-run page   A Web page that gets a huge number of hits and then disappears a week later. Most hit-and-run pages contain pornographic material and they get shut down when the Web site's system administrators figure out why their network has slowed to a crawl. See also *slag*.

hit count   The number of hits a particular page has had. Many pages have installed access counters to track (and display) the number of hits they've had.

home page   The first Web document displayed when you follow a link to a Web server.

horizontal rule   A straight line that runs across a Web page. Useful for separating sections of the page.

host   See *Web server*.

hosting provider   A company that provides you with storage space (usually at a fee) for your Web pages. The company runs a Web server that enables other Internauts to view your pages.

hot potato   A shortcut pronunciation of http://. See also *triple dub*. For example, instead of spelling out http://www.yahoo.com, you could say "hot potato triple dub dot yahoo dot com."

hotlist   A collection of links to cool or interesting sites that you check out regularly.

HTML   HyperText Markup Language. The collection of tags used to specify how you want your Web page to appear.

HTML editor   A program that makes it easier to mark up a document by using menu commands and toolbar buttons to insert tags.

hypertext link   See *link*.

Image map   A "clickable" inline image that takes you to a different link, depending on which part of the image you click on.

inline image   An image that gets displayed within a Web page. See also *external image*.

Internaut   An Internet traveler; a cyberspace surfer.

Internet   A worldwide collection of interconnected networks. A breeding ground for geeks, nerds, hackers, and crackers.

jargonaut   A person who deliberately creates and disseminates Internet jargon; someone interested in Net jargon.

Java   A programming language designed to create software that runs inside a Web page.

JPEG   A common Web graphics format developed by the Joint Photographic Experts Group. See also *GIF*.

JPIG   A Web page that takes forever to load because it's either jammed to the hilt with graphics, or because it contains one or two really large images. See also *dirt road* and *spinner*.

Kbps   Kilobits per second (thousands of bits per second).

link   A word or phrase that, when selected, sends the reader to a different page or to an anchor.

luser   A blend of "loser" and "user." Someone who doesn't have the faintest idea what they're doing and, more importantly, this individual refuses to do anything about it.

Mbps   Megabits per second (millions of bits per second).

mouse potato   The computer equivalent of a couch potato.

multimediocrities   CD-ROM discs that are jam-packed with second-rate pictures, sounds, and programs. Also applies to some lame Web sites.

nerd   An idiot totally lacking in personal hygiene and social skills.

Net   The hip, short term for the Internet.

netiquette   An informal set of rules and guidelines designed to smooth Internet interactions. Netiquette breaches often result in the offender being flamed (sent a nasty e-mail message).

network   A collection of two or more computers (usually dozens or hundreds) connected via special cables so they can share resources such as files and printers. The Internet is, in its most prosaic guise, a worldwide collection of networks.

newbie   A person who is (or acts like they are) new to the Internet. Since this term is almost always used insultingly, most Net neophytes try to behave as non-newbie-like as possible. The best way to avoid this label is to bone up on netiquette.

notwork   A downed network.

nymrod   A person who insists on converting every multiword computer term into an acronym.

one-link wonder   A Web page that contains only a single useful link.

plug-in   A program that attaches itself to a Web browser. The functionality of the program then becomes an integral part of the browser. An example is WebFX, a VRML plug-in for Netscape.

publish   To make a Web page available to the World Wide Web community at large.

roadblock   A Web page that serves no other purpose other than to let you know that there is nothing available at this URL, but that something will be coming soon.

Serial Line Interface Protocol   A method of Internet access that enables your computer to dial up a service provider and exchange info reliably.

server   A computer that sends out stuff. Check out *Web server* for an example.

service provider   A business that sells Internet connections to individuals and small companies. Also called an *access provider*.

slag   To bring a network to its knees because of extremely high traffic. "That Babe of the Week page has totally slagged the network." See also *notwork*.

SLIP   See *Serial Line Interface Protocol*.

smiley A combination of symbols designed to indicate the true intent or emotional state of the author. The classic smiley is the sideways happy face :-). Smileys are fine in moderation, but overusing them not only indicates that your writing isn't as clear as it could be, but it also brands you as a newbie.

spinner An extremely slow link. The name comes from Mosaic's globe icon, which spins while the program tries to access a site. If the site is particularly slow, the only sign you have that anything is actually happening is the spinning globe. See also *dirt road* and *JPIG*.

sundowner A person who changes his or her daily sleep schedule to coincide with being awake when Web traffic is lowest (i.e., late at night).

surf To leap giddily from one Web page to another by furiously clicking on any link in sight; to travel through cyberspace.

tags The HTML commands, in the form of letter combinations or words surrounded by angle brackets (<>). They tell a browser how to display a Web page.

target See *anchor*.

Telnet A program that lets you log onto another computer on the Internet and use its resources as though they existed on your machine. The most common use for Telnet is to use software (such as an e-mail program) on another computer.

title A short description of a Web page that appears at the top of the screen.

triple dub A shortcut pronunciation of WWW. See also *hot potato*.

ubiquilink A link found on almost everyone's hotlist. "Yahoo must be on every hotlist on the planet. It's a total ubiquilink."

Uniform Resource Locator See *URL*.

URL A Web addressing scheme that spells out the exact location of a Net resource. For example, Yahoo's URL is http://www.yahoo.com/. See Chapter 7, "Making the Jump to Hyperspace: Adding Links," for an almost-comprehensible explanation of how URLs work.

Usenet A system that distributes a collection of newsgroups throughout the Internet.

vanity plate An annoyingly large Web page graphic that serves no useful purpose. See also *JPIG*.

vaporlink A link that points to a nonexistent Web page.

VRML Virtual Reality Modeling Language. Used to create Web sites that are 3-D "worlds" that you "enter" using a VRML-enhanced browser. You can then use your mouse to "move" around this world in any direction.

Web See *World Wide Web*.

Web browser   See *browser.*

Web host   See *Web server.*

Web server   A computer that stores your Web pages and hands them out to anyone with a browser that comes calling. Also known as a *Web host.*

World Wide Web   A system of documents containing text, graphics, and other multimedia goodies. Each Web document serves two purposes: It contains information that is useful in and of itself, and it contains specially marked words or phrases that serve as "links" to other Web documents. If you select the link, the Web loads the other document automatically.

wrackground image   A background image that ruins a page by making the text unreadable. See also *flooded.*

WWW   See *World Wide Web* and *triple dub.*

YOYOW   You own your own words. This refers to the copyright you have on the text in your Web pages.

HTML Codes for Cool Characters

This appendix presents a few useful signs, symbols, and foreign characters that you can insert into your Web pages. None of these hieroglyphics are available from your keyboard, so you need to use either the symbol's character code or its entity name. (I explained all this in more detail way back in Chapter 5, "From Buck-Naked to Beautiful: Dressing Up Your Page.")

Symbol	Character Code	Entity Name
Nonbreaking space		
¡	&#161;	&iexcl;
¢	&#162;	&cent;
£	&#163;	&pound;
¤	&#164;	&curren;
¥	&#165;	&yen;
¦	&#166;	&brvbar;
§	&#167;	&sect;
¨	&#168;	&uml;
©	&#169;	&copy;
ª	&#170;	&ordf;

continues

continued

Symbol	Character Code	Entity Name
«	«	«
¬	¬	¬
–	­	­
®	®	®
¯	¯	¯
°	°	°
±	±	±
²	²	²
³	³	³
´	´	´
µ	µ	µ
¶	¶	¶
·	·	·
¸	¸	¸
¹	¹	¹
º	º	º
»	»	»
¼	¼	¼
½	½	½
¾	¾	¾
¿	¿	¿
À	À	À
Á	Á	Á
Â	Â	Â
Ã	Ã	Ã
Ä	Ä	Ä
Å	Å	Å
Æ	Æ	Æ
Ç	Ç	Ç

Symbol	Character Code	Entity Name
È	È	È
É	É	É
Ê	Ê	Ê
Ë	Ë	Ë
Ì	Ì	Ì
Í	Í	Í
Î	Î	Î
Ï	Ï	Ï
Ð	Ð	Ð
Ñ	Ñ	Ñ
Ò	Ò	Ò
Ó	Ó	Ó
Ô	Ô	Ô
Õ	Õ	Õ
Ö	Ö	Ö
×	×	×
Ø	Ø	Ø
Ù	Ù	Ù
Ú	Ú	Ú
Û	Û	Û
Ü	Ü	Ü
Y	Ý	Ý
Þ	Þ	Þ
ß	ß	ß
à	à	à
á	á	á
â	â	â
ã	ã	ã
ä	ä	ä

continues

continued

Symbol	Character Code	Entity Name
å	å	å
æ	&#230	æ
ç	ç	ç
è	è	è
é	é	é
ê	ê	ê
ë	ë	ë
ì	ì	ì
í	í	&iacute
î	î	î
ï	ï	ï
ð	ð	ð
ñ	ñ	ñ
ò	ò	ò
ó	ó	ó
ô	ô	ô
õ	õ	õ
ö	ö	ö
÷	÷	÷
ø	ø	ø
ù	ù	ù
ú	ú	ú
û	û	û
ü	ü	ü
ý	ý	ý
þ	þ	þ
ÿ	ÿ	ÿ

HEEEY!!

The Goodies on the Disk

As I've mentioned before, this book's whole purpose is to be a one-stop shop for budding Websmiths. To that end, the text is geared towards getting you up to speed with this HTML rigmarole without a lot of fuss and flapdoodle. But fine words butter no parsnips, as they say, so you'll also find a disk full of useful stuff pasted into the back of the book. This disk is jammed to the hilt with handy files and software that should get your Web authorship off to a rousing start.

Just so you know what to expect, here's a rundown of the various goodies you'll find on the disk:

The HTML examples from the book   Many of this book's chapters (especially those in Part 2) contained examples showing HTML tags in action. If you'd like to incorporate some of these examples into your own Web work, don't bother typing your poor fingers to the bone. Instead, all the example files are sitting on the disk, ready for you to use.

Sample graphics   Back in Chapter 8, "A Picture Is Worth a Thousand Clicks: Working with Images," you saw how a graphic or two can add a nice touch to an otherwise drab Web page. Then, in Chapter 13, "Some HTML Resources on the Web," I mentioned a few spots on the Web where you can find images to suit any occasion. But before you go traipsing off to one of these sites, you might want to check out what's on the disk. I've included a few dozen files that give you everything from simple bullets and lines to useful icons and pictures.

Where to Find 'Em Once you install the examples and the graphics files, they'll be sitting in the EXAMPLES subdirectory of whatever directory you used for the installation. For example, if you used the default C:\CIG-HTML directory, you'll find the examples and graphics in the C:\CIG-HTML\EXAMPLES directory.

HTML Writer This is the freebie HTML editor we looked at in Chapter 16, "The Best Free HTML Editor: HTML Writer." Just install the program from the disk and it's ready to go!

WEB Wizard If you'd rather avoid HTML altogether (or if you know someone who would), may I suggest WEB Wizard. As you learned back in Chapter 20, "Assorted Other Ways to Create HTML Documents," WEB Wizard creates simple pages just by asking you a few questions. Again, just install the program from the disk and then crank it up. (Although you can use WEB Wizard for free, you should probably register the program if you find you use it regularly. It'll only set you back 10 measly bucks, and the developer will be able to use these proceeds to improve the program.)

WS_FTP This is a nice program for doing FTP file transfers. You'll find you use it a lot for downloading HTML-related programs and other tools. Once it's installed from the disk, WS_FTP is ready to go.

Lview This is the graphics conversion program that we discussed in Chapter 8, "A Picture Is Worth a Thousand Clicks: Working with Images." You can use it to convert images from non-standard Web formats (such as Windows' BMP format) into GIF or JPEG files.

PKUNZIP This program decompresses (or unzips) files that have been squashed in the common ZIP format. For easy access, the installation program copies PKUNZIP.EXE to your Windows directory.

How to Use PKUNZIP to Unzip Files

To use PKUNZIP, pull down Program Manager's File menu and select the **Run** command; if you have Windows 95, select the Start menu's **Run** command, instead. In the Run dialog box, type **pkunzip** followed by the drive, directory, and name of the file you want to decompress. For example, if the file is C:\DOWNLOAD\WEBEDIT.ZIP, you'd enter the following:

```
pkunzip c:\download\webedit.zip
```

Select **OK** and PKUNZIP will go to work.

The disk comes with its own installation program (called Setup) that lets you choose which programs and files you want to install. Here are the steps to follow to install the disk:

1. Place the disk in drive A or drive B (wherever it fits).

2. In Program Manager, select the File menu's **Run** command; if you're running Windows 95, open the **Start** menu and select **Run**, instead. In either case, the Run dialog box appears.

3. Type **a:setup** or **b:setup** (depending on which drive the disk is in), and then select **OK**.

4. Setup takes a few seconds to pull itself up by its own bootstraps, and then it displays the Setup dialog box shown in the figure below.

Use the Setup dialog box to choose where you want the files installed.

5. If you want the files copied to a drive or directory other than C:\CIG-HTML, make your changes in the Install To text box.

6. Select **Continue** to proceed with the installation. The Setup Options dialog box appears, as shown in the following figure.

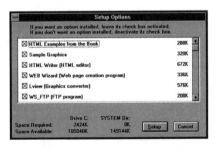

Use the Setup Options dialog box to select which files you want to install.

7. In the list of options, deactivate the check boxes for those files you don't want, and leave the check boxes activated for those you do.

8. Select the **Setup** button. Setup copies the selected files, creates a program group named CIG-HTML, and inserts icons for the programs you selected.

Okay, you're all set. If you installed any of the software (except PKUNZIP), icons for each program will appear in the CIG-HTML program group. Just double-click on an icon to crank up the program. Have fun!

Legal Stuff

By opening this package, you are agreeing to be bound by the following agreement:

This software product is copyrighted, and all rights are reserved by the publisher and author. You are licensed to use this software on a single computer. You may copy and/or modify the software as needed to facilitate your use of it on a single computer. Making copies of the software for any other purpose is a violation of the United States copyright laws.

This software is sold *as is* without warranty of any kind, either express or implied, including but not limited to the implied warranties of merchantability and fitness for a particular purpose. Neither the publisher nor its dealers or distributors assumes any liability for any alleged or actual damages arising from the use of this program. (Some states do not allow for the exclusion of implied warranties, so the exclusion may not apply to you.)

Index

Symbols

O

P

Q-R-S

307

309

311

Y